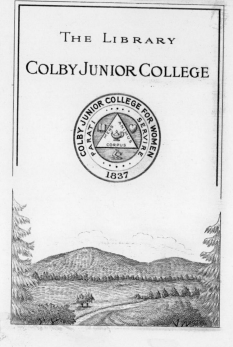

WORKS ON THE STAGE

BY THE SAME WRITER

LIFE OF GARRICK
LIVES OF THE KEMBLES
LIVES OF THE SHERIDANS
LIFE OF SIR HENRY IRVING
LIFE OF WATTS PHILLIPS
LIFE OF ALEXANDRE DUMAS
THEATRICAL ANECDOTES
NEW HISTORY OF THE ENGLISH STAGE
ROMANCE OF THE ENGLISH STAGE
ART OF THE STAGE: A LECTURE AT THE
  ROYAL INSTITUTION
CHARLES LAMB ON THE STAGE
PRINCIPLES OF COMEDY & DRAMATIC
  EFFECT
PROVERBS AND COMEDIETTAS
VANDERDECKEN: A DRAMA
THE WORLD BEHIND THE SCENES
SHAKESPEAREAN REPRESENTATION:
  ITS LAWS AND LIMITS
SAMUEL FOOTE: A BIOGRAPHY

SAMUEL FOOTE

Samuel Foote.

after the painting by Sir Joshua Reynolds.

SAMUEL FOOTE

A BIOGRAPHY

By

PERCY FITZGERALD, M.A.

"HE WAS A FINE FELLOW IN HIS WAY; AND THE WORLD IS
REALLY IMPOVERISHED BY HIS SINKING GLORIES: I WOULD REALLY
HAVE HIS LIFE WRITTEN WITH DILIGENCE."   DR. JOHNSON

LONDON: CHATTO & WINDUS
MCMX

CONTENTS

CHAPTER   PAGE

I. THE FAMILY—SCHOOL-DAYS—LIFE AT COLLEGE - 1

II. THE GOODERE MURDER—FOOTE ON TOWN - - 20

III. UPON THE STAGE - - - - - 33

IV. MIMICRY - - - - - - 45

V. "THE DIVERSIONS OF THE MORNING" - - 57

VI. FOOTE'S FIRST COMEDY, "THE KNIGHTS"—ELOPE-
MENT TO FRANCE - - - - 70

VII. FOOTE, GARRICK, AND JOHNSON - - - 80

VIII. TATE WILKINSON - - - - - 112

IX. DRURY LANE CONFUSION - - - - 127

X. "THE AUTHOR"—VISITS TO SCOTLAND - - 145

XI. DUBLIN BROILS - - - - - 166

XII. "THE MINOR" - - - - - 176

XIII. "THE MINOR"—continued - - - 183

XIV. FOOTE, WIT AND HUMORIST - - - 197

XV. "THE MAYOR OF GARRATT"—GEORGE FAULKNER - 225

XVI. A SERIOUS ACCIDENT—HAYMARKET PATENT 245

XVII. THE HAYMARKET THEATRE - - - 251

XVIII. FOOTE'S COMEDIES - - - - - 264

XIX. FOOTE'S COMEDIES—continued - - - 286

XX. THE STRATFORD JUBILEE—"THE MAID OF BATH" - 301

XXI. PUPPET-SHOWS - - - - - 318

XXII. THE "TRIP TO CALAIS" - - - - 335

XXIII. FINALE - - - - - - 359

INDEX - - - - - - 375

SAMUEL FOOTE

CHAPTER I

1720—1740

THE FAMILY—SCHOOL-DAYS—LIFE AT COLLEGE

It might, perhaps, seem an exaggeration or a surprise were I to say that I am about to introduce to the reader the most remarkable and one of the most gifted persons that ever figured on the English stage. It would indeed be difficult to decide whether he was more remarkable on the stage or off it. No actor has been so successful as dramatist, no actor such a wit or humorist, and, finally, no actor has had so stirring and adventurous a course. He was a gentleman by birth and breeding, yet grew up and was trained in taverns and pothouses. He spent his life mimicking respectable people, making them odious and ridiculous, and thus secured a handsome living—yet was never challenged or chastised. He was said to have run through three large fortunes. There is no story, therefore, more likely to be full of interest and excitement. A restless, energetic personage—perpetually moving to and fro—now in this kingdom, now in that. A strange parti-coloured life indeed, full of contrasts—he was now flourishing, now in straits

1

—but always contrived to come to the surface. People are very partial to such adventurous careers; we must ever follow with the most intense interest the most vivacious and "incompressible" being of his time—a professed and ever-ready wit, a brilliant writer, an excellent actor, though chiefly in his own pieces. In fact, his play and himself were inseparable.

It is odd that, while everybody with a life worth writing has had his life written, this remarkable and attractive man should have been passed by. My old friend John Forster indeed devoted a *Quarterly Review* paper to a complete account of him and his works, expounded in that rather impressive magisterial tone which is found in most of his writings. But though he was an admirable critic, well schooled, far beyond any that we can boast at the present time, and full of knowledge of the period, one is surprised at the too partial and too indulgent tone in which he deals with Foote's character and proceedings. One would think he was dealing with one of the respected, well-established, irreproachable personages of that era, such as Garrick or Goldsmith. He overlooks always the turbulent and dramatic— if utterly irresponsible—character of Foote's course, which seemed to be directed by no principle but the wanton humours of the moment.*

It is certain that the popular estimate of Foote will have to be revised. He is usually assumed to have been merely a rough jester, a clever dramatist and indifferent actor; he passes across Bozzy's pleasant stage one in a long procession of performers. It is clear now that he was a great force in the society which he

---

* The account, much enlarged, was later included in his agreeable volume of collected essays.

ruled and intimidated for nearly the whole of his career, and that he attracted all eyes. What Mr. Foote said or did or would do was a matter of importance, and he did pretty much as he liked without anyone daring to interfere. This alone was an extraordinary performance and quite unique. Like Johnson, he ruled in every degree of society. He must really be classed, therefore, with the great leading group—with Johnson, Garrick, Goldsmith, Boswell; indeed, one might put him with Garrick and Johnson for his power and directing influence on society. I fancy no one will rise from the perusal of these pages without assenting to this conclusion.

Foote's father was a man of some importance in the town of Truro, and is described as " a very useful magistrate." He was Member of Parliament for Tiverton, Commissioner of the Prize Office, and Receiver of Fines for the Duchy. He died at his country-house on March 12, 1754, when seventy-six years of age, and was buried at St. Clement, Truro. He thus witnessed much of his erratic son's course. The family had another residence at Lambesco, where their ancestors had lived at the time of Charles II. His marriage with Eleanor, only daughter of Sir Edward Goodere, was to further strengthen its importance, and shows that Mr. Foote was an ambitious and pushful man. This lady lived to be eighty-four, and seems to have had but a distressful, chequered life. Her famous son, who was certainly accountable for many of her troubles, was christened at St. Mary's Church, Truro, in January 1720.

Samuel is commonly stated to have been born at the Red Lion in Boscawen Street, at one time the residence of Henry Foote, his relative. But he first

saw the light at Johnson Vivian's house, close by the
inn. The owner was twice Mayor of Truro—in 1741
and in 1754. The house has been pulled down.
The letters J. F. are still to be read over the inn
door, or were some years ago.*

We find a Samuel Foote who was born in 1761,
and who claimed to be connected with the greater
Samuel. It is known that the actor left two illegitimate sons, one of whom would most likely have been
named after him. This Samuel went into the army,
but speedily left it and became manager at Plymouth,
where his daughter, afterwards the celebrated singer,
was born. It is not at all unlikely that their theatrical
complexion was due to a connection with the great
jester. I have often thought also that Jesse Foot—
without the final *e*—may have been connected with
the actor, as he was intimate with Murphy and wrote
his life. Polwhele, in his reminiscences, seems to
make allusion to Foote's wife, " a near relative of my
mother's and a bosom friend of Sam Foote's wife, of

* In the libellous letter which the pseudo-Duchess of Kingston
wrote to Samuel Foote during the disastrous conflict that destroyed
him, we find this passage :

" Mr. Foote is said to be descended in the female line from one
Harnass (Harness?), a merry-andrew who exhibited at Totnes
in Devonshire, and afterwards figured in the character of a mountebank at Plymouth. This same merry-andrew's daughter married
a Justice Foote of Truro, Cornwall. There is a man now living
who has often been more delighted with the nimble feats of this
active merry-andrew than with all the grimace of features it is
in the power of our modern Aristophanes to assume." I recall with
pleasure a truly interesting evening I spent seated beside the
Rev. Mr. Harness, who was of this family. It was at the send-off
dinner, on the eve of Dickens's second visit to America. All the
time I was thinking, Could this hale and hearty old person have
actually been at school with Byron?

St. Clement's, who had possibly pretensions to beauty. But she was as arrant a fool as our comedian's ' pretty simpleton.' "

Samuel Foote was indeed to shed an heraldic lustre over the guild of wits and dramatists, for few could boast better pedigree or connections—at least, on his mother's side. His mother, Eleanor Goodere, was daughter of a Baronet, Sir Edward Goodere, of Hereford. She had two brothers—John and Samuel —each of whom succeeded to the baronetcy in an unusual and unexpected way, both dying violent deaths within a few weeks. Samuel left five children, the eldest of whom, Sir Edward, became a lunatic. Amid such strange and gloomy associations was the obstreperous and jovial wit to start on his course. But such recollections never disturbed him for a moment.

To a strain of insanity, inherited or developed, might be traced something of Foote's erratic course. His forbears on the mother's side were certainly thus tainted. His two uncles must have been thus partially afflicted. There was a third uncle, Sir John Dinely, whose eccentricities and oddities were familiar to the public. Mrs. Foote, his mother, though a well-born lady, was at least *singular* in her manners. As to Foote himself, he was so disorderly and incon-stant, so reckless in his habits, so devoted to pleasures and revelling, that he can hardly be considered to have been directed by ordinary common - sense or restraint.

This alliance with the Gooderes was to bring to the Foote family an inheritance of tragic horrors. Sir Walter Scott might have wrought them into a tale as gloomy as that of Lammermoor. Strange that one whose life was a perpetual jest should have come of such sad forbears !

The third son of Sir Edward Goodere, of Burhope in Herefordshire, was Edward; his mother a sister of Lord Rockingham's. The Goodere estate was slender, worth not more than a thousand or so a year. The young man fell in love with the only daughter of Sir John Dinely, a great heiress, as she was considered, having about £3,000 a year. She encouraged his addresses, which were prosecuted with great secrecy; but the matter was discovered, and her family showed much hostility. The young lady, however, had her way, and the pair were married. On her father's death she inherited the whole of his estate, which brought a substantial addition to the fortunes of the Goodere family. All was settled on the eldest son, who was to take the name of Dinely. There were three sons and one daughter; the second and third sons were to be heroes of the tragical episode. The eldest was brought up to great expectations, to be the Squire and inheritor of the estate; the other two were sent to sea. The heir went to Ireland, and was there killed in a duel. Dying, Lady Goodere left her whole fortune to her second son, excluding her husband from any share—to his deep resentment; but later on he "married a fortune." Here was the first stage or beginning of the series of vendettas and animosities which were to rage in this ill-starred family. The now elder brother, Sir John Dinely Goodere, nourished an unreasoning hatred and dislike of the younger, who was a good officer and much esteemed by his friends. Sir John had been unfortunate in his second marriage, and was believed to have treated his wife with cruelty. The younger brother took her

part, and tried to protect her. Sir John determined
to cut off the entail as soon as his son grew up, so as
to exclude the brother from any chance of succeeding.
The son, however, died, and the whole property was
then settled on the daughter, who, we are told, "was
married to *one Mr. Fote*, a gentleman belonging to
the law"; after her on her son, Edward; and eventually on the celebrated wit and player. When Sir
Edward Goodere died, he had left his own estate of
Burhope to his eldest son, Sir John, but for his life
only; after which it was to pass to the Captain.

The new Baronet was furious at this disposition,
grudging his brother even this small and rather remote
solatium. It was even said that Sir John denied his
father a decent funeral, giving him merely a pauper's
burial, which the other tried in his own way to protest
against. This further inflamed the enmity between
the brothers.

Sir John's matrimonial trouble now took a strange,
disastrous turn. He presently brought an action for
crim. con. against a Sir R. Jason, and gained £500
damages; though there was a story that one of the
witnesses confessed on her death-bed to having been
suborned to give false testimony. Next we hear of
this extraordinary Baronet indicting his wife for a
conspiracy to take his life, the lady being found
guilty and ordered to be imprisoned and pay a fine.
The Captain brother lent her the money. What
unseen strife must have been raging all the time
beneath the surface!

Sir Edward died insane about 1761, and was succeeded by his brother John, a spendthrift. What
little of the family estate remained the latter soon
wasted; and about 1770 he was obliged to sell the

family place—Burhope—to Sir James Peachey, and
he was speedily reduced to a state of destitution.
The legend, therefore, of some two or three fortunes
coming to Foote through his mother seems improb-
able enough. Such estate as there was passed to
John Foote, his elder brother. But it has been stated
over and over again that she became a wealthy
heiress, owing to the unlucky fate of her brothers.

Reduced to penury, the last Baronet, Sir John,
obtained, through the interest of Lord North and
other friends, a nomination as a Knight of Windsor.
He dropped the title of Goodere, and was henceforth
known as Sir John Dinely. He, too, was certainly
an oddity, his eccentricities verging on lunacy.
Charles Lamb has left a quaint and sympathetic
account of his oddities, very minutely etched. His
costumes were grotesque, in spite of which he always
obtruded himself into crowds. His aim was to dispose of his title in marriage, and on profitable terms.
He had a sort of form of proposal drawn up and
printed, which he distributed among "likely" ladies.

To William Cooke, known as "Conversation"
Cooke—who has not been much considered in literary
annals—we owe a great deal, owing to his acquaintance with two distinguished personages of his era,
namely, Goldsmith, his fellow-countryman, and Foote,
with whom he was most intimate. Had we been
without his recollections of "Goldy," we should have
lost one of the most valuable and "characteristical
portions" of his life. For the two Irishmen, so alike
in their careless lack of responsibility, cast their lot
together and opened their hearts to each other.
Cooke *understood* "Goldy" better than most of his
friends. He seems to "have hung loose" upon

society, especially in connection with what might be called " the *rowdier* element," and in this way became intimate with Foote.*   He was, moreover, a man of solid gifts, had been called to the Bar, and was the author of a legal work that has passed through several editions.   He survived until 1824, at which time he must have met and helped Mr. Croker in his great work.

This legal training and legal practice—for he followed the circuit—must have lent a certain exactness to what he reported of Foote.   His information is very full, and there are few mistakes.   He seems to have been on confidential terms with the wit, to have been his companion at suppers and other jovialities, and, above all, to have displayed a sympathy and intelligence which proves that he understood his hero's character.   The style, however, is bald and commonplace, though his dramatic criticisms are fairly intelligent.   Without him it would have been impossible, early or late, to draw up any memoirs of this remarkable man—hence our deep obligation to him.

Cooke gives this account of the boy and his early education :

"The school to which he was sent [Worcester Grammar-School] was at that time under the care of Dr. Miles, a particular friend of his father's, and a man of great eminence in the discharge of his duties. Many stories are told of his freaks while he resided at this school, such as his being the leader and contriver of a 'barring-out,' of blacking his master's face while asleep, forming artificial earthquakes under his

---

* He wrote a poem called "The Art of Living in London," which by a strange error Boswell has attributed to Johnson : " His *Ofellus,* or the Art of Living," etc.

master's chair, etc. ; all of which, however, did not impede his progress in learning, as he went through his school exercises with at least as much credit as some of the first scholars in his class.

" Though these frolics marked the general eccentricity of his mind, the following circumstance first unfolded those peculiar talents for mimicry which afterwards so much distinguished him among all classes of society.

" Being at his father's house during the Christmas recess, a man in the parish had been charged with a bastard child ; and this business being to be heard the next day before the bench of justices, the family were conversing about it after dinner, and making various observations. Samuel, then a boy between eleven and twelve years of age, was silent for some time ; at last he dryly observed, ' Well, I foresee how this business will end, as well as what the justices will say upon it.' — ' Ay,' said his father (rather surprised at the boy's observation) ; ' well, Sam, let us hear it.' Upon this the young mimic, dressing up his face in a strong caricature likeness of Justice D——, thus proceeded :

" ' Hem ! hem ! here's a fine job of work broke out indeed ! a *feller* begetting bastards under our very noses (and let me tell you, good people, a common labouring rascal, too), when our taxes are so great and our poor-rates so high ; why, 'tis an abomination . . . therefore, I say, let him be fined for his pranks very severely ; and if the rascal has not money (as, indeed, how should he have it ?), or can't find security (as, indeed, how should such a *feller* find security ?), let him be clapped up in prison till he pays it.'

" ' Justice A—— will be milder, and say, " Well,

well, brother, this is not a new case . . . therefore, though the man has committed a crime—and indeed, I must say, a crime that holds out a very bad example to a neighbourhood like this—yet let us not ruin the poor fellow for this one fault : he may do better another time, and mend his life ; therefore, as the man is poor, let him be obliged to provide for the child according to the best of his abilities, giving two honest neighbours as security for the payment."'

" He mimicked these two justices with so much humour and discrimination of character as ' to set the table in a roar ' ; and among the rest his father, who demanded why *he* was left out, as he also was one of the Quorum. Samuel for some time hesitated ; but his father and the rest of the company earnestly requesting it, he began :

" ' Why, upon my word, in respect to this here business, to be sure it is rather an awkward affair ; and to be sure it ought not to be—that is to say, the justices of the peace should not suffer such things to be done with impunity : however, on the whole, I am rather of my brother A——'s opinion, which is, that the man should pay according to his circumstances, and be admonished—I say *admonished**—not to commit so flagrant an offence for the future.' "

That worthy and industrious scholar, Dr. Nash of Worcestershire, tells us that the boy Foote's turn for mimicry was perfectly natural—*i.e.*, it came to him

---

* " This word ' admonished ' was a favourite word of his father's on the bench, which, with his plain, matter-of-fact manner of pronouncing it, and twirling his thumbs at the same time, drew so correct a picture of the justice as met the warmest approbation of the whole company, and even of his father, who, so far from being offended, rewarded him for his good humour and pleasantry."

by nature. " When a boy of ten years old, he excelled
in it, and being acquainted with and related to many
of the principal families at Worcester, where I went
to school with him, he was frequently invited to their
houses on Sundays and holidays. The next day the
whole school was made idle by attending to Foote's
taking off and ridiculing all the parties he had seen
the preceding day."

On his completing his course at the grammar-
school, a happy chance suggested his being sent to a
University. It fell out that Worcester College, after
several changes of fortune, and after bearing the name
of St. John Baptist's Hall, was refounded as it
were by Sir Thomas Cookes, who was a second cousin
of our hero. The young Samuel Foote had thus a
claim to be received on the foundation, and on application was duly elected scholar, Dr. Gower being
Provost, of whom an account is found in Dr. King's
" Anecdotes."

Here is the college record, extracted from the
books :

EXTRACT FROM MINUTES OF WORCESTER COLLEGE

Under date June 8, 1737.

At the Election of Scholars, Samuel Foote at Worcester School
put in his claim as relation to the Founder, upon which the Provost
and Mr. Tottie, Electors, thought it expedient to have recourse to
some civilian. Dr. Brookes, Professor of Law, was consulted, and
gave his opinion in favour of the claim.

Mr. Foote was accordingly elected.

June 29, 1737.

Scholars Admitted.

Samuel Foote.
Samuel Neale.

Pedigree submitted to Dr. Brookes, who reported upon it that
Samuel Foote was Founder's kin—consanguineous and cognatus:

Sir Edward Dinely⸗Founder's mother

Sir Edw. Goodyer⸗daughter

Mr. Foote⸗daughter

Samuel Foote.

(Our Founder was Sir Thomas Cookes, Bart.)

His course seems to have been a lawless and
tumultuous one, and, strange to say, was tolerated by
the authorities, just as in his later life he all but compelled the public to endure his excesses. During
his residence he paid a visit to Bath to enjoy its
gaieties; when returning to Oxford he astonished the
Dons with a sort of triumphant entry. He was
seated on a coach, a disreputable companion by his
side, two footmen behind, and all his clothes laced
over. For this he was duly reprehended, and Mr.
Forster says he quitted the college in consequence of
this freak, "but without any public censure." This,
it will be seen, is a mistake. The tradition, however,
among his intimates was that he in some sort attended
to his studies, that he was well read in the belles-lettres,
and showed genuine taste for Latin and Greek, which
he never lost. This is proved by the many allusions
in his dramas, which could have been furnished only
by a well-educated man. He had always, indeed, a
pride in his classical gifts.

Long after, when his master, Dr. Miles, went to
see him, the pupil gave him a handsome piece of plate
from his sideboard. The old man admired his fine
things, and asked what they might have cost. " I

know not what they cost," said Foote, "but I shall soon know what they will fetch."

Cooke must have had from Foote himself these reminiscences :

" Gower was a man of considerable learning, but rather of a grave, pedantic turn of mind ; and pedantry was to Foote an irresistible bait for every kind of wit and humour. . . .

" One of the first tricks he played upon the doctor was the following : The church belonging to the college fronted the side of a lane where cattle were sometimes turned out to graze during the night, and from the steeple hung the bell-rope, very low in the middle of the outside porch. Foote saw in this an object likely to produce some fun, and immediately set about to accomplish his purpose. He accordingly one night slily tied a wisp of hay to the rope, as a bait for the cows in their peregrination to the grazing-ground. The scheme succeeded to his wish. One of the cows soon after smelling the hay, as she passed by the church door, instantly seized on it, and, by tugging at the rope, made the bell ring, to the astonishment of the sexton and the whole parish. . . .

" An event of this kind was to be explored, for the honour of philosophy as well as for the quiet of the parish. Accordingly the doctor and the sexton agreed to sit up one night, and, on the first alarm, to run out and drag the culprit to condign punishment. Their plan being arranged, they waited with the utmost impatience for the appointed signal : at last the bell began to sound its usual alarm, and they both sallied out in the dark, determined on making a discovery.

" The sexton was the first in the attack. He

seized the cow by the tail, and cried out 'it was a gentleman commoner, as he had him by the tail of his gown'; while the doctor, who had caught the cow by the horns at the same time, immediately replied, 'No, no, you blockhead! 'tis the postman, and here I have hold of the rascal by his blowing-horn.' Lights, however, were immediately brought, when the character of the real offender was discovered, and the laugh of the whole town was turned upon the doctor.

"At another time, when Foote was enjoined to learn certain tasks in consequence of his idleness, he used to come forward with a large folio dictionary under his arm, and present himself before the doctor with great seeming gravity and submission. 'Well, sir, what do you want?'—'Sir, I am come to do away the imposition laid upon me.'—'What do you mean by *imposition*? I would have you know, sir, I impose upon nobody.'—'I am sure then, sir, if you did not *impose* this duty upon me, I should never have taken a natural fancy to it.'

" Here the doctor usually growled, and desired him to go on, which the other generally did with a degree of talent and perspicuity that often confounded his examiner. After this the doctor would read his pupil a lecture on idleness, and on the great danger of following the ebullitions of fancy in preference to the dictates of sober judgment; describing also the figure he might make in the world if he took the proper course, and, on the contrary, the contempt and misery which must follow a life of inattention and dissipation.

" The doctor, in delivering this lecture to his pupil, did it in a sour, dogmatical, pedantic manner, accom-

panied with a number of hard words and quaint
phrases ; the other, being prepared for these, immediately interrupted him, and after begging pardon, with
great formality, would take his dictionary from under
his arm, and, pretending to find the meaning of the
word, would say, 'Very well, sir ; now please to
go on.' "

It is strange that so exuberant an alumnus should
not have been recalled by his contemporaries.   But
we search the innumerable memoirs without finding
any mention of this lively scholar.

Dr. Nash, who was his school-fellow, has some
anecdotes of his eccentric doings, which forecast
vividly enough all the special traits of the later
Foote.   Thus, the boy ridiculing the families whom
he had amused with his mimicries, for his own enjoyment, was truly the later Foote when at full growth.
It was what he called a favourite trick of his.   He
was likely also to entertain his college with the
same arts.

Nash mentions a little college incident which
throws much light on Foote's position and status.
He was called upon to repeat in Hall some classical
extracts.   He selected Horace's "Ibam forte viâ
sacrâ," which he recited with such infinite dramatic
humour that the whole college, even the gravest of
them, could not refrain from loud laughter.   This
shows that he was respected and tolerated for his
cleverness ; and this idea of interpreting the satire
after a theatrical fashion was original in a mere youth.
No doubt he was encouraged ; they were, perhaps,
rather proud of him, and inclined to shut their eyes
to his licence.

In spite of many pranks and irregularities, young

Foote contrived to remain at the college for over three years. His behaviour, however, gave serious displeasure to the authorities. But at last matters came to a crisis. He began to find all restraint intolerable, and finally took the course of leaving the college for days at a time. This could not be endured, and was at last dealt with in summary fashion. An extract from the college minutes very graphically sets out his fate. Thus early do we find the real Sam Foote exactly what he was always to be—reckless, impudent, careless of his own interests. The mystery is, how he contrived to remain so long and keep up the necessary attendance at schools, lectures, etc. Long after, he actually appealed to his " University education " as a claim for respect.

In January, 1740, his friends and relatives were to learn that he had mysteriously disappeared—having " taken French leave "—and I am indebted to the kindness of the present Master of Worcester College for the following pithy extracts from the books, which tell the tale :

January 28, 1740.

Samuel Foote, after a course of many irregularitys and lying out of the College, upon the 30th of December was imposed by the Provost, which he neglected to bring, but lay out of College again on the 16th day of January, and went the next day out of town without leave, for which reasons a citation was ordered to be put up as this day in the following form :

Whereas Samuel Foote, Scholar of the College, has, in defiance of the Statutes and the authority of the College, presumptuously and insolently absented himself without leave asked of the Provost, this is to require the said Foote to return to the College within twenty days after the date of this present, and to answer to such things as shall be alledged

2

against him, or to be deprived of his Scholarship and of all privileges and advantages belonging to it.

February 25.

The said Foote not appearing to the citation, his Scholarship was declared void this day.

It will be seen that nearly a month's grace was allowed him for his return. This short and business-like record was the finale or " curtain" of the first portion of Foote's career. His fate, however, was different from that of Shelley and others who have been expelled or " drummed out." He is fairly entitled to claim that he had not been compelled to leave. *He* had quitted the college, and, as a penalty, forfeited his office and its emoluments. Though he did not choose to return, we do not find that his name was removed from the books. Long after, Foote used to boast of his University training, which he would hardly have done had he been disgraced.* That he was well grounded in the classics Mr. Forster has shown by testimony—" well known in living memory at Eton " (that is, at the date of his writing)—of a venerable Mr. Knapp. This gentleman used to be invited to dinner with Foote by Dr. Barnard, the Provost, and distinctly recalled Foote reciting long passages from Aristophanes in the

---

* His friend Dr. Johnson also had been obliged to quit his college, but from default of funds, after three years' stay, and without a degree. We can scarcely accept Mr. Croker's and Dr. Birkbeck Hill's theory, that Johnson only remained about a year at Oxford. He would never have assumed the airs of a University man on so slender a foundation. Boswell, who questioned him closely on many occasions as to his University life, states positively that he was there for over three years.

original Greek. In fact, all through he displayed an unostentatious familiarity with " the classics," and the spirit of the classics, that seems unusual. The college authorities must have been satisfied with their pupil, and, but for his disorderly life, he might have taken a good degree—which, like his admirer Johnson, he had to forego.*

* I have been able to find only one representative of the family, Mr. Thomas Foote, of Trenwheal, Godolphin, in Cornwall. He is the grandson of one of Foote's sons, and he has been good enough to supply me with some particulars. When I was a boy there was a "high toast" snuff in fashion, known as Lundy Foot. I well remember his shop in Dublin, at the corner of Great Brunswick Street, and always had a suspicion that this merchant belonged to the Foote family. It seems that Jeffrey Foote (born in 1704) had married a daughter of one Lundy. They had a son, Lundy Foote, who died in 1805, and was, no doubt, the snuff-manufacturer. My speculation that Miss Foote the singer was also a connection is confirmed by Mr. Thomas Foote. He tells me that she was a daughter of his father's cousin. Lundy Foote's son was a sea-captain, and was drowned in the Tamar River.

CHAPTER II

1741

THE GOODERE MURDER—FOOTE ON TOWN

ONLY a week or two after this flight the whole kingdom was busy with a crime of an appalling character, which became the "sensation of the hour." This was the murder of Foote's uncle, Sir Edward Goodere, by his brother, under circumstances of atrocious violence and cruelty. The incidents are found in an account of the trial, which took place on March 25, 1741, and which it were best to give in full : *

The trial was on March 25, 1741. Smith, an attorney, related how, on "the Sunday before this murder was committed, the deceased, by my invitation, was to dine at my house the Sunday following ; of which the prisoner being apprised, came into the neighbourhood, and having sent for me, earnestly entreated me to admit him, the prisoner, into the

---

* The strange character of this "murder most foul," and the unusual recklessness, with indifference to consequences, of the murderer, suggests another more modern case of the same violence, viz., Thurtell's murder of Weare at Elstree, dictated by the same unleavened motive of pure hatred. Thurtell had much the same determined purpose. Both showed the same hardened coolness and indifference after the deed. Late in life Foote had a cottage at Elstree, which might have been Thurtell's.

company of his brother, the deceased, under pretence
(as the prisoner said) of accommodating their differ-
ences in an amicable manner.   He was at the College
Green coffee-house.   I went to him ; and was so
pleased with the proposal of the prisoner, and the
hopes of their accommodation, that without the least
hesitation I immediately introduced the prisoner into
the company of his brother, the deceased ; and in
such a manner did the prisoner behave, that, seemingly, the deceased and he were as good friends as
ever.   After dinner I withdrew, and left them by
themselves for the space of an hour, till I was called
in ; and after we had smoked a pipe together, Mr.
Goodere took his leave of Sir John in the most
friendly and affectionate manner possible.   I believe
it might be near six o'clock in the evening."

Next is the testimony of one of the gang of mur-
derers, Charles Bryant: " I was one of the six men
hired by Captain Goodere, the prisoner at the bar, to
seize the deceased, and forcibly to run him aboard
the *Ruby* man-of-war, then lying in King's Road.
We met by the prisoner's directions at the White
Hart, on College Green, where we had a handsome
dinner ; and were placed in the balcony, that we
might be ready to receive the signal, and obey the
word of command, without giving the least suspicion
to the people of the house. . . . About six o'clock in
the evening the signal was given ; when we left the
White Hart, and overtook the deceased just before
he came to College Green coffee-house ; where I and
five others seized him at the word and command of
Goodere.   We then immediately rushed on the deceased, and dragged him along towards the Rope
Walk, where was a gang of twelve more, who were

ready to assist us according to the prisoner's instructions. We then hurried the deceased along towards
the Hot Wells, where a boat waited purposely to
receive him."

As to what took place on board, Jones, cooper of
the *Ruby*, swore : "On Sunday, January the 18th,
about seven at night, the Captain brought his brother,
Sir John, on board, and conveyed him down to the
Purser's cabin by force. When he was down, the
Captain asked 'whether the cabin was clear' (for
the Thursday before the murder the Captain had
ordered me to get the Purser's cabin ready for a
gentleman who was coming on board). I answered,
'Yes, sir.' Then he opened the door, and the people
of the ship forced Sir John in, he groaning all the
while.

"When he was in, the Captain called for his
steward, and told him to bring a bottle of rum and a
glass. The Captain then asked Sir John how he
did. Sir John complained of pains, especially in his
thigh. The Captain asked him 'if he would drink a
dram.' Sir John said 'he had drunk nothing but
water for two years.' The Captain then asked him 'if
he would have any rum to bathe his thigh.' Sir John
answered, 'No.' Then the Captain ordered a dram
for Mahony and Elisha Cole (the person first designed
to commit the murder, but was too drunk for the
purpose), and after they had a dram they all came
out of the cabin.

"Shortly after this, the Captain called one of the
carpenters to put two strong bolts on the Purser's
cabin door, which was accordingly done, when Sir
John asked 'if he could speak with any of the officers
on board.' The carpenter made answer, and said, 'I

am the carpenter.' Sir John asked 'if he could speak
a word with him.' He replied, 'an hundred if he
pleased.' Then the carpenter opening the door in
order to clench the staples, Sir John asked him
'what his brother Sam was going to do with him.
—What! is he going to murder me?' The carpenter
replied, 'No, he is willing to have your company, sir;
he does it for your good.' 'But,' said Sir John,
'what will become of all my servants and estate all
this time?' On this the carpenter retired. . . .

"I then went to bed, when about two or three in
the morning my wife waked me, and I heard a vast
struggling at first, and the old gentleman crying out,
'Twenty guineas—take it—take it—oh! must I die?
must I die?' when very soon after all was quiet.
Then a candle was handed into the cabin, and I saw,
through the crevice of the partition, Mahony hold the
candle in his hand, and White plunder Sir John's
pockets, turning his body in order to come at them,
and then take out his watch and money; but White
not getting the watch out of Sir John's pocket easily,
Mahony said to him, 'Damn it! lay hold of the
chain,' by which they got the watch out. In about
a minute after this, I saw a *white hand* on the throat
of the deceased, which I took to be the Captain's,
when presently all went out of the cabin and left the
deceased alone.

"Then I went to the Doctor's mate and sentry, and
by their opinion they took the old gentleman to be
dead; from thence I went to the Lieutenant, and
told him what I had heard and seen, and that
Mahony and White had murdered the gentleman,
and that I believed the Captain was concerned. The
Lieutenant was very dubious about this matter at

first, telling me 'he did not think the Captain would
be guilty of any such thing'; but in giving him such
plain demonstrations of the fact he began to think
there was something in it.   While they were talking,
a midshipman came to acquaint the Lieutenant that
the Captain had ordered White and Mahony ashore,
but he swore they should not go ashore, for that they
were the two persons who killed the gentleman; but
the midshipman returning to the Captain, he ordered
'that they should be put ashore immediately,' and
accordingly they were.

   " About nine or ten in the morning, the Lieutenant
and gunner contrived a method how they should
secure the Captain, which was, that I should go in
and complain that I had lost six guineas out of my
chest.   Accordingly, going in with this complaint, I
seized him as he was walking with his hands behind
his back, and the rest immediately rushed in and
secured him.   Upon the Captain's being thus seized,
he cried out, 'Hey dey! what have I done? what
have I done?'—I replied, 'Sir, you are my prisoner;
you was the cause of your brother's death last night.'
—The Captain replied, 'If there is murder done in
the ship, I know nothing of it.'   Accordingly he was
secured, and the barge ordered out for four of the
crew to pursue White and Mahony. . . .

   " The Captain being called upon for his defence,
pleaded the utmost innocence, alleging, 'how it
could be thought he could be guilty of the murder
of his brother Sir John, whereas by his death he lost
at least *forty thousand pounds*—that the sickness and
disorder of the house he was confined in debarred
him of his lawyers and friends conversing with
him. . . .

" In vindication of his causing Sir John to be seized
in the manner he was, he urged that he was a lunatic,
and therefore he did it in order to take better care of
him; that his being taken in the daytime on board
was plain there was no secret design, or that he was
to have any harm come to him; and that even at
Mr. Smith's he behaved in a very mad manner, and
took no leave; that the people on board knew of his
coming a week before, therefore, he said, he must be
very silly to bring a person before three hundred evidences to commit so vile an act, where nothing can
be a secret above four hours. The prisoner then
called two young women to prove Sir John a lunatic;
one of whom believed him to be a lunatic or mad,
because he would get up in the middle of the night
and disturb the family; and the other, because he
would sometimes busy himself in *hanging on the pot*,
and other such menial offices. A gentleman was called
to prove that Sir John had made his will several
months before; but being asked concerning the disposition of Sir John, he replied 'that he was a good
friend, a loving neighbour, and a kind landlord; and
that he was so far from being a lunatic, as to be fully
competent to negotiate all his own affairs with his
tenants, etc.'

" Another gentleman was called by the prisoner to
his character: when being asked whether he knew
Sir John to be anyways mad, or the like, he declared 'that he thought him so far from it, that
he had more sense than all the whole family put
together.' Mr. Smith also proved Sir John to be in
his perfect senses when he left his house on Sunday,
the 18th of January.—The trial lasted nine hours;
when the evidence appeared so full and satisfactory

to the jury, that in less than fifteen minutes they returned a verdict of *guilty* against the Captain and Mahony.

"Charles White was tried the next day for the said murder, and for robbing Sir John of eight guineas and a gold watch; who was found guilty on both indictments. The day after, they all three received sentence of death, and in a few days afterwards suffered the public execution of the law."

Such was the dreadful tale. And who would not conceive that the young lad Foote—for such he was —just escaped from college, would be overwhelmed and crushed by the terrible and disgraceful catastrophe?—he would fly from the town to some obscure corner in the country, go abroad or anywhere to hide his head. But nothing of the kind occurred.

There was a vein of eccentricity, coupled with a lack of feeling, always to be displayed in his character; and on this occasion he "carried it off" with a certain coolness and indifference that approached effrontery. It did not affect him in the least. He even suffered himself to be introduced by his friend Cooke in a mixed company as "*the young gentleman whose uncle had been hanged for the murder of his brother*," a presentation which, no doubt, had great success, and caused much amusement. This was quite in character with his reckless temperament.

It will, indeed, be found, as we go on, that almost everything in Foote is to be a surprise. The unexpected is always certain to happen. This was owing to the reckless caprice of his character. But who could have expected that a young fellow of good connections and fashion—for he was now being launched in society—should have set his name to a

sort of "catchpenny" or Newgate Calendar pamphlet*
that set out a popular account of the tragedy, including even the "last dying speech of the male-
factor"? It seems incredible!

The vulgar form of the hawker's broadsheet is
adopted. Here is a young fellow of twenty, fond of
pleasure, wasteful, busy about town, a gentleman,
and yet he writes and publishes "a full and true"
account of his two uncles' disgrace, in phrases
borrowed from the Calendar! What could he
mean? Mr. Forster, charitable to him always,
thinks that it was to earn a few pounds—ten, it was
said—which he needed much. But this does not
account for his lack of propriety. I am inclined,
however, to fancy that an explanation can be found
less discreditable to Foote's character. There were
quite a number of these pamphlets issued, all
describing the incidents of this "brutal and bloody"
murder, and the execution, "last words," etc. But
in one of them, which is before me, there is a vindication of the murderer, or at least an extenuation of
his acts. This could only have been written by a
relation, who shows himself well acquainted with the
family history. Foote's name is not to this pamphlet.

The murdered Baronet had left a widow, who
married again. She, too, had her eccentric chapter.

* "The Genuine Memoirs of Sir John Dinely Goodere, Bart.,
who was murdered by the Contrivance of his Own Brother on Board
the *Ruby* Man of War in King's Road, near Bristol, Jan. 17, 1740.
Together with the Life History and *Last Dying Words* of his Brother,
Captain Samuel Goodere, who was executed at Bristol on the 15th
day of April, 1741, for *the Horrid Murder* of the said Sir J. D.
Goodere. Dedicated to the Rt. Worshipful H. Combe, Mayor of
Bristol. *By S. Foote, of Worcester College, Oxford, etc., and nephew
to the late Sir John D. Goodere.* Price 6d."

There was a sort of adventurer named William
Rayner, a printer in Whitefriars, who in 1730 published "an infamous libel," for which he was brought
before the Court of King's Bench and imprisoned. He
had been appointed guardian to a family of the name
of Spendelows, but through some chicanery contrived
to secure his ward's property. He then married the
widow, through whom the property of Charlton,
which was her dower, came into his hands; this he
speedily disposed of. Thus even the connections of
this ill-fated family were to have this sort of doubtful
cast.

Owing to the catastrophe in the Goodere family,
the estate of the murdered man seems to have passed
to the murderer brother for but a brief tenure, and
from him to Mrs. Foote, of Truro. This sudden
accession of wealth did not, of course, benefit "Sam,"
as he was only the third son, the eldest being a
clergyman, the second John. The eldest seems to
have inherited no cash, and as he was a feeble sort of
creature, and actually dependent on his brother Sam,
it must be that the estates passed to his brother
John, who assumed the name of Dinely.

Mrs. Foote, as we have seen, had become an heiress. Her son fancied that he was likely to become
wealthy, and accordingly we find him recklessly
embarking on a course of extravagance and folly.
He has always been supposed to have entered at the
Temple, but his name is not to be found in the
books, so that he must simply have had rooms there,
living as a sort of *fashionable* Templar.

His friend Cooke tells us that "he was seen at the
Temple *pro formâ*, in handsome chambers, surrounded by a well-furnished library. He is remem-

bered by a few now living, in that situation ; and they report him to have been one of the greatest beaux (even in those days of general dress) as well as one of the most distinguished wits who frequented the Grecian and the Bedford.

" These coffee-houses at that period (now full sixty years ago) were frequented principally by dramatic wits and young Templars. The Grecian had held its charter for wit and taste ever since the beginning of the last century. Here the Templars opened their morning rounds in their elegant *robes de chambre* and morocco slippers, and from this place many of the papers of Addison in the *Spectator* are dated.

" The Bedford principally laid claim to dramatic criticism, when that science bore a much prouder name in the annals of literature than it does at present. Here the wits generally supped after the play, and passed judgment freely on the several authors, actors, and managers."

At the coffee-houses " Foote appeared in the flush of youth, wit, and fortune. Dr. Barrowby, no mean judge in everything which respected elegant knowledge, was present at his first exhibition at the Bedford, and he always spoke of him as a young man of most extraordinary talents. ' He came into the room,' said he, ' dressed out in a frock suit of green and silver lace, bag-wig, sword, bouquet, and point ruffles, and immediately joined the critical circle of the upper end of the room. Nobody knew him. He, however, soon boldly entered into conversation, and by the brilliancy of his wit, the justness of his remarks, and the unembarrassed freedom of his manners, attracted the general notice. The buzz of the room went round, " Who is he ? Whence comes

he ?" etc., which nobody could answer ; until, a handsome carriage stopping at the door to take him to the
assembly of a lady of fashion, they learned from the
servants that his name was Foote, that he was a
young gentleman of family and fortune, and a student
of the Inner Temple.' . . .

"But he was incapable of the ordinary restraints of
life. He dashed into all the prevailing dissipations
of the time, and what the extravagance of dress,
living, etc., had not done, the gaming-table finally
accomplished. He struggled with embarrassments
for some time, but . . . soon found himself at a stand ;
his creditors grew obstinate and impatient; his friends,
as is usual in such cases, deserted him, and he found
that something must necessarily be done to provide
the means of subsistence." Thus reduced to actual
poverty, he suffered severe privations, and was hardly
sure of a dinner. But his boisterous, irrepressible
spirit carried him through. Once, finding his stockings in holes, he purchased a pair and threw away the
old ones, intending to put the new ones on at some
retired corner. He was, however, captured and
carried away to dine by some jovial friends, who
presently " smoked "—according to their slang—his
boots, and hailed the discovery. But the ready
Foote was prepared for them. " In the summer," he
explained, " I never wear stockings until I dress for
the evening. You see I have them here, quite
ready ;" and he pulled out his pair. So it passed as
one of his frolics.

This coffee-house and tavern life, so followed by
gentlemen of condition, seems strange. Nothing is
more singular than the contrast between the common
social life in London of those times and that of our

own day. Conviviality and pleasant company was
the prevailing note ; much time was devoted to the
coffee-house and club life, where people sat and
drank and talked for half the night. There was,
apparently, not much to do except to " live pleasantly."
Joking, too, and frolics of various kinds were in
demand. A genuine humorist had a reputation,
and became a conspicuous public character. Nowadays such gifts bring no actual profit, save among the
humorist's own intimates. Conviviality of the uproarious, enjoyable kind is not in vogue, perhaps
because there is no one now possessed of such entertaining gifts as to make his company sought for. The
meeting for talk, discussion, pleasantry, has disappeared. It is no libel on our society to say that nowadays nobody knows how to talk, and few care to listen.
How wonderful it seems, to think of people going to
a coffee-house or tavern, of set purpose, to sit there
till the small-hours, discussing interesting topics,
making merry and saying witty things, as Johnson
and his Bozzy used to do, and as some years later Coleridge and Lamb did at the old Salutation Tavern.
The Literary Club—who could conceive of it now as
it was in its prime days, when the members met at
the tavern to talk !*

It is strange, however, that in most capitals, save
that of England, this sort of coffee-house intercourse

* Many years ago I was the founder of a society called the Boz
Club, in memory of Dickens, which originally counted not more
than thirty members or so. We met for a social dinner, when those
who had known Dickens told, one after the other, their experiences.
We had discussions, too. But by-and-by the spirit of the day
prevailed. The club was re-formed, enlarged to 150 members, and
a single annual dinner at the Savoy Hotel was established. Thus
it had to fall into line with the others.

still continues.   Nothing so much astonishes the un-
sophisticated tourist as the brilliant scene of an evening on the Paris boulevards, where the huge spaces in
front of the cafés are black with vast crowds of talkers
and drinkers ; and the same is witnessed in almost
every leading town.   It is so, too, in Germany and
Belgium.*

So lately as the time of the last French Empire
this coffee-house life still obtained, and there were
vast numbers of witty writers who spent their nights
at cafés famous for their choice living.   There is a
curious record called " Les Soupeurs de mon Temps,"
which describes the jovial doings of these places—the
rare dishes, the drinks, and, above all, the wit and
practical jokes.   If we read the life of Vivier, the
horn-player, we shall become acquainted with, perhaps,
the best practical jokers that ever lived.   These men
were ever ready with repartee or bon-mot, and were
lineal descendants of our Foote.   But all, almost
without exception, ended disastrously, dying of
apoplexy, paralysis, idiocy, and other miseries, and,
of course, steeped in debt as well as in wine.

* Lately, arriving in Brussels at night-time, I found the huge
Place in front of the Nord Station almost filled with seated crowds,
all busy chattering—a most animated and dramatic scene.

CHAPTER III

1744

UPON THE STAGE

To return to our hero. The University had been tried and given up; the law had been attempted and given up; society and the coffee-houses had failed him. What was he to turn to next?

It seems extraordinary that a young gentleman of good family and connections, after having tried his hand at the Bar, should ever have thought of the stage. He was conscious that he had a gift of mimicry, but he cannot have hoped to live on this unsubstantial prop. It is not unlikely that he thought of the success of his friend Garrick, a gentleman who had also tried mimicry, and had gone on the stage; and why should not another gentleman of talent do just as well?—for Foote did not lack a good conceit of himself, and even then may have felt the envy, jealousy, and dislike always to be found in his relations with the actor. Though he had learnt nothing of the law, yet from his satirical parodies, his knowledge of the terms, processes, and absurdities, it is clear that he was well skilled in its devices. He was devoted to a gay life; he could tell a story, make a humorous joke, and, above all, *take off* with any man! He knew all the players, and went behind the scenes.

How natural, then, that he should think of the stage ! In no profession are assurance, confidence in oneself, disregard or contempt of others, with the knack of persuading others, such valuable assets as upon the stage. In our experience, how often have we seen men with small gifts thus compelling the public to accept them, and their own fellows to believe in them ! If they are rough-tongued in addition, the terror of being able to punish is added. Foote, young as he was, took his place at once. He questioned the authority of old stagers, and laid down the law with the best. His convivial mimicries were applauded. He was an extraordinary amateur. There have been a number of "gentlemen" on the stage, some even managing, but some still amateurs, and amateurs they will be to the end.*   At the same time, where real ability is present, it breaks down all the barriers of caste, lack of apprenticeship, etc. Foote was of good lineage—of "gentle blood" on both sides. When at the full tide of success, he and Garrick might be said to "top" or dominate the stage; the spectacle was presented of two "gentlemen born" holding the very first position, each with his own theatre and company. It might be said that the mark of the amateur is practically *indelible ;* for the difference between such and the true professional is marked, because the amateur has never been disciplined. His social position gives him an introduction ; he is spared, or spares himself, training and discipline. But the discipline of the true actor is, or should be,

* A curious illustration of this truth could be found in a comparison of George Grossmith and Corney Grain, the latter an amateur *pur sang.* He was amusing and entertaining ; but there was a solidity and certainty about "Gee-Gee," due to training, which made him superior.

more moral than technical—a training to be patient, bear privation and delays, study hard, hope for the best, and wait promotion. Modesty and obedience also must be there. Only long years of service will teach these things. Now that the country stock companies are gone, there can be none of this education. Actors are now trained by the run of a single play, which is no training at all, whereas under the old system an actor has been known to play two or three hundred characters within a year.

It should be borne in mind that native force of character and an ardent ambition go almost as far upon the stage as talent; and so does personality. These qualities, as in Foote's case, are as good as talent, and are not to be resisted. Garrick also, besides his store of ability, had a strange charm in private life that drew admiration. He was a man of genuine ability in all directions. The pair, both gentlemen and amateurs, were thus able to dispense with the proper schooling or education, though Garrick—and this is not generally known—had much practice with a sort of travelling company. He certainly played in London under an assumed name before his first appearance at Goodman Fields; and at Ipswich, where he is supposed to have had merely one trial performance, I find he acted regularly with the company.

There was about town at this time a very remarkable, rather eccentric man and actor, Charles Macklin, well noted for his violent ways, who was ever in revolt or conflict, but who generally carried his purpose by a power of tongue and action. He was an admirable performer, and in his view of stage propriety far in advance of his time; an excellent dramatist, with wonderful observation of character and human nature; a cultivated man, able to set forth his views in lectures. He has always been presumed to have been a centenarian, but, as the date of his birth cannot be ascertained, this must be a matter of speculation. He, however, lived very nearly for the full term of a hundred years, in a strange series of embroilments. He actually killed a fellow-actor in a brawl. His hard, grinding voice and bitter tongue were the subject both of fear and ridicule. His correct reading of Shylock as an ordinary human being, and not as a grotesque buffooning Jew, or as the late Henry Irving's "gentlemanly Jew," won for him the praise of Pope. His face was all gnarled and scored—"cordage" some- one called the lines; so that Quin declared: "If the Almighty writes a legible hand, that fellow is a villain!"* It is curious to note how much violence, assault, and quarrelling in his time prevailed on the stage. Violence was his regular method of protest.

What an amazing, unreasoning, violent, and gifted group was that of the four actor Irishmen—Macklin, Mossop, Sheridan, Murphy — all tumultuous, all inviting someone to "tread on the tail of their coat"; while three of the four were fine, conspicuous players. It might be said that most actors from that country have had this characteristically impetuous nature.†

* Macklin had three pauses: the first moderate, the second longer, the last—or "my grand pause," as he termed it—so long sustained that the prompter thought his memory had failed, and loudly gave him his cue several times over, so that the audience heard. The actor was so infuriated that he rushed from the stage and knocked his unhappy prompter down. "The fellow interrupted me in my grand pause!" This has a suggestion of Macready.

† The extraordinary and inexplicable contribution of Ireland to the English stage is something marvellous. The list includes every

Macklin's course shows clearly that the actor of the time had not merely to win his position on the stage, but had also to fight his way in the common social life of the day.   There were *factions* to which prominent players belonged ; each having his party and partisans.   This led to the formation of marked combative characters, with endless jealousies, hatreds, and even serious battles.   As actor he was remarkable ; as writer of comedies he was really at the top. One cannot say too much in praise of his admirably-conceived character of Sir Pertinax in his great comedy.*   It is difficult to account for the sort of "hooligan" or disorderly element, as it might be termed, then rife among the players of the period.   It was due, I think, to the unrecognized conditions under which the profession was then followed.   Perhaps "profession" is almost too respectable a word for the time. Up to the passing of the Licensing Act, which was but half a dozen years before Foote came on the scene, there were droves of persons who went about

---

chief performer : Quin, Delane, Clive, Woffington, FitzHenry, O'Neill, Macready, Moody, Charles Kean, Mrs. Glover, Boucicault, the Farrens, Barry, Miss Smith (the admired of Paris and Berlioz), Abington, Mossop, Sheridan, Macklin, Murphy, Barry Sullivan, Gustavus Brooke — second-rate artists, no doubt, but powerful players. And as for dramatists, what a contribution ! —Farquhar, Goldsmith, Sheridan—all of the very first and choicest class—with O'Keeffe, Murphy, even Sheridan Knowles.

* Anyone who is fortunate enough to have seen the late Samuel Phelps in the part—as I did often—has seen a unique and powerful performance. It was one of those creations which only one person in the course of several generations is likely to furnish. It *was* almost perfect. Figure, voice, accent, humour, ferocious tragedy, earnestness—nothing was wanting. The curious element was that Phelps seemed a revival of the author himself.

the country much as showmen used to do at the
fairs, willing to amuse anyone that would listen:
" Strollers " they were properly called—poor half-
starved creatures, often glad to divide as their profits
a few candle-ends. A raw turnip taken from a field
was often their dinner, as it was in the case of the
great John Kemble. Thus pressed by their necessities, they were regarded with suspicion and dislike in
the place which they invaded, very much as bands of
foreign gipsies are now. As " rogues and vagabonds,"
they were treated most unceremoniously. The
beadle was their enemy ; once so respectable a man
as Tate Wilkinson, manager of York, Hull, and other
theatres, was ordered by the magistrates to quit the
town with his followers and baggage.

" Macklin," Cooke tells us, " had collected a
company at the little theatre in the Haymarket, all
novices in the art, whom he undertook to instruct
in the principles of the drama, of whom Mr. Hill
gives an account in a work called ' On Stage
Recitation.' ' There was a time,' he says, ' when that
extravagance which has been recommended for farce
had its place in tragedy, both in action and delivery ;
the gestures were forced and beyond all that ever
was in nature, and the recitation was a kind of
singing.' "

It was during this venture at the " Hay." that
he offered an opportunity to the young Foote of
trying his powers. On February 6, 1744, it was
announced : " At the New Theatre in the Haymarket
a Concert, and after it ' Othello.' *Othello*—a gentleman
(Foote) ; *Ludovico*—a gentleman (one Mr. Hill) ;
Iago—Macklin. The character of Othello will be
new dressed after the custom of his country. No

money will be taken at the doors, nor any person admitted but by printed tickets, which will be delivered by Mr. Macklin." This was a device to avoid the penalties of trespassing on the patents of a great house, but it is astonishing how so palpable an artifice could have been tolerated. Macklin was, of course, responsible for the "new dressing" of the Moor.

" How a man so exclusively comic as Foote," says Cooke, " should think of a tragic part for his début, and one where all the contending passions of tragedy are so powerfully delineated as in ' Othello,' would be a matter of surprise, did we not consider that the prevailing passion of most of our stage candidates points to the *lover* and the *hero*. These seem to be the general pursuits of most young minds. . . .

" Though the generality of the audience received him with every degree of indulgence, and many of the first distinction cheered him, from personal and family knowledge, his performance on the whole was found to be too imperfect for either public or private patronage. Macklin, who was the Iago in this play, said on this occasion, ' It was little better than a failure.' "

Foote, Hill, and Macklin, appearing together on the stage, made a singular combination. Had they " clubbed " their strange adventurous lives, the result would have been bewildering. Hill came from a little apothecary's shop, to which he returned again after his failure. He dubbed himself a Knight, and was always known as Sir John Hill. One of his astounding performances filled twenty-six gigantic folios, and contained 1,600 copperplates ! We must be grateful to him for prompting Garrick to one of

the wittiest of epigrams.   A farce of his completely
failed, and he laid the blame on the manager, who
pleasantly retorted :

> " For physic and farces
>   His equal there scarce is :
>   His farces are physic,
>   His physic a farce is."

He attacked everybody, like his two fellow-per-
formers.

" This failure induced Foote to listen to the advice
of his friends, and to think of comedy as more suitable
to his figure, talents, and natural feelings ; but, unfortunately, the part in comedy which he adopted
seemed to be nearly as much out of his reach as
Othello was in tragedy : it was in no less a character
than that of Lord Foppington in ' The Relapse,' in
which he made his second appearance on the 9th
of April following. . . .

" The manager himself played Loveless (a gay, well-
bred man of intrigue), which was a part so little fitted
to Macklin's powers that it must have been either
uncommon vanity or the general poverty of the
company that could force him into it. . . .

" Disappointed in these two characters, his next
attempt was in Pierre in ' Venice Preserved,' which
turning out equally unsuccessful, at last induced him
to abandon for ever all thoughts of tragedy, and enjoy
himself in that element for which nature had so pre-
eminently qualified him.   In pursuance of this resolution, he engaged the next winter at Drury Lane
Theatre, where, turning his thoughts entirely to
comedy, he successively appeared in Fondlewife, Sir
Paul Pliant, Bayes, etc."

He may be considered to have had his first regular

engagement in 1745-46, under Lacy, in a company that included Woffington, Yates, Delane, the Macklins, and others. He made his first appearance on November 1, 1745, when he performed in "The Constant Couple," as Harry Wildair, supported by Mrs. Woffington. This was a great advance in so short a time, and showed that he had already taken a good position.*

The young fellow must have had energy and enterprise, for we find in 1744 that, though as yet

---

* At the Haymarket he played Lord Foppington, another light comedy part; on the 25th he was seen in "The Drummer" as Tinsel; on the 27th as Lord Foppington; on December 7 as Sir Harry; on December 13 as Bayes.

On October 13, 20, and 23, the play was repeated. On March 2 was the last performance of the season, "by a set of gentlemen for diversion, being the last time of their performing that play. On April 6 'The Relapse' was played, the part of Lord Foppington being taken by the gentleman who lately played Othello."

At his benefit on April 14 he played Sir Courtly. Mrs. Woffington, however, did not play for him, though he had played for her, and though she played for three or four benefits within that week. Perhaps there had been a quarrel.

These performances during his first season, with his many times of performance, show that Foote at once got to the front rank. Says Cooke : " His Ben in ' Love for Love,' though much followed for a time, was perhaps the worst of all his performances, except his Othello. It had none of the genuine naïveté and simple sprightliness of the sailor ; and, as if afraid of doing too much (his general failing), here he did too little. A contemporary writer (who, if unbiassed, was a competent judge of theatrical merit) says : ' It was as lifeless a lump of insipidity as I ever saw ; he had not even his usual confidence in the part, but shrunk from it, as under a timid impression of not doing it proper justice.' Yet, such is the caprice of public taste that his Ben was the great object of attraction for many nights in one season, and crowded boxes of beauty and elegance gave another proof how little fashionable criticism is to be relied on."

imperfectly equipped for his profession, he had set off to play in Dublin. Here again he was following Garrick's example, who had made a triumphant success in that city. He seems to have done fairly well, and had some good audiences. It will be seen later how much he was attracted to this capital, having visited it so many times in his course, viz., in 1744, 1757, and 1760. Owing to his showy personality, he was always looked on as something more than a travelling actor. He established the most familiar relations with his audiences, and in social life was heartily appreciated, while his wit and rough humour found admirers everywhere. No wonder that he ever thought kindly of his Irish friends.

Still, the new actor felt that, so moderate had been his success, he was not likely to make his fortune in the legitimate drama. As he humorously expostulated, "If they won't have me in tragedy, and I am not fit for comedy, what the deuce *am* I fit for?" Here we may note that shrewdness and sense that was always found in Foote. At once he drew the logical conclusion, saying to himself: "I must find some other department for which I *am* fit."

And what was the new departure that he meditated? Reckoning up his resources, he had boldly and recklessly determined to take a new and original line, and become a professional *mimic*. He would mimic all the world—notably public personages, with his friends and fellow-players among the rest. Among his companions at the Bedford and the coffee-houses, more probably at the Covent Garden pothouses, he had been obtaining great applause for his imitation of friends and boon comrades that were well known to the company, and it appears he "took them off" in a most vivid, striking way, and to immense applause. For nothing is so amusing as the mimicry of those we know well.

At starting I claimed for Foote an extraordinary originality of talent and methods, and this can be supported by the fact that he was the first to elevate mimicry into a regular profession or dramatic system, breaking into the ranks of society to secure material, and actually compelling society to furnish him with subjects. He could say: "Yonder is a public man of eccentric ways; I will have *him.*" "There is a man whom I know and all the world knows; he will do for me." This, as I said, is a different thing from the ordinary mimic's treatment. There is something dramatic here, for he "took off" the character of the man, showed what he would say and do in a new situation, serious or absurd. And then, the wonder that he was privileged to take these gross liberties, the victim submitting in most cases; friends and society generally looking on and applauding! We have never had such a state of things before or since, and it could only have been devised and carried out by an original genius.

The condition of the stage at the time was eminently favourable to this special style of exhibition. Dramatic work was practically confined to the two great patent theatres, where the old and old-fashioned "stagers" declaimed in a stilted, solemn fashion. We can recall the vivid description of Quin and his fellows, with their antiquated dresses and pompous methods. As is well known, the coming of Garrick as a player brought about a complete revolution, and his exertions as manager introduced a more free and natural treatment, with an order and decency behind the scenes which were sadly wanted. All the old conventions were swept away. Foote, who offered himself without training or schooling, was well suited to figure as reformer. He was unshackled by traditions, and, with his robust character, was fitted to strike out a line of his own. He had no respect for persons. He was "the sapper" of the stage, for whom "nothing was sacred."

From the days of Dryden it seems that this fashion of mimicking professional players was a suitable form of entertainment. Even the popular Garrick had been used to convulse audiences by imitating the stage dying agonies of Quin and others of the good old school; the victims were much hurt, and clamoured loudly. Foote, instead of dealing with this vulgar element in a casual way, determined to make a system of it. It should be a dramatic entertainment. Then he found, perhaps to his surprise, that he had yet another resource by him, the power of writing lively sketches of characters and amusing dialogue. At once he constructed some very lively scenes, which were a complete novelty for the public.

CHAPTER IV

MIMICRY

THE craving for mimicry has always been found irrepressible, and has constantly tended to encroach on the legitimate interests of the stage. It may be said that the origin of our "music-hall" entertainments is due to this relish for burlesque of the failings and absurdities of our neighbours. A certain indulgence, or even licence, has been extended to this species of enjoyment. There the mimic can revel in spontaneous antics, and draw the attention of a crowded house. He is stimulated by obstreperous laughter to "go one better." It is certainly a great temptation both for performer and audience. But to the cultivated or well-regulated mind it seems extraordinary that entertainment can be found in such things.

Even up to our time there lingered on at taverns such as the Coal Hole and Cider Cellars a sort of gross entertainment, given while the guests smoked, ate, and drank ; such as sham trials at law, etc. At these places some extraordinary perverted talent used to be exhibited. To-day at the music-halls nothing "goes down" so well as an imitation of some noted actor disloyally done by some clever brother.

There can be no doubt that this drawing from the life, or imitation, not merely of physical defects and oddities, but of traits of character, becomes under certain conditions of careful study and nice observation a valuable method of producing vivid and dramatic scenes or effects. All the great writers, either in dramas or novels, have used this method, and must use it. Many, either from haste or carelessness, have simply transferred the original to their work, the result being mere recognition of the original. But the genuine masters do not copy line for line or tint for tint. They search for the root or keynote of the character. This they make their own, and play upon it after their own fashion.*

When the function of the stage is found in study of intellectual work, the actor naturally acquires a certain nobility of character, and such high themes influence his nature. Nowadays the actor has become merely an element in a show made up of mimicry, buffooning, flourishing, grimacing, grotesque dresses, lime-lighting, paint, wooden structures, canvas, and the like, and must be affected by his surroundings. He is a portion of the theatrical mechanism. One result is that the low and uneducated find their way in. Anyone who stands at the stage-door and watches the strange miscellany that passes in becomes conscious of something inferior. Even the "carpenters," as they are called, have not the clean and honest air of the common mechanic. There is a suggestion of the public-house. This may seem harsh

---

* It was thus, we may be certain, that Boz developed his characters. In the case of the strange dialect of Mrs. Gamp, he may have heard one of these repulsive creatures "propoging" something, or declaring "which her name is Harris." From these scraps he could equip himself with an entire language, and could put her in new situations of his own devising.

and exaggerated, but it will be agreed there is some foundation for it.

When Foote, with Macklin and Wilkinson, introduced these fair-green methods, with the "rough and tumble" of the booth, the audiences began to lose respect for their entertainers. Hence the quarrels, disputes, interruptions, and the mixing up of audience and players. When the audience was brought on the stage by mimicry, it was natural that the player should go forth among the audience, and for a time convert the open street into a stage. This simple view really accounts for all the strange disorders and riots, the breaking of benches and chandeliers, the contentions between rival actors, and other disgraceful episodes. What sort of stage discipline or illusion could there be when, on a benefit, an amphitheatre was raised, which was crowded by fine ladies and gentlemen who could converse with the players?

Another form of this personal exhibition, now unknown and forgotten, was the once familiar and indispensable Prologue or Epilogue, filled with all kinds of familiar allusions. It was a sort of bridge between the stage and the pit, between the audience and actor, as, indeed, the place from which it was delivered — always in front of the curtain — clearly shows. The speaker half belonged to the stage and half to the audience, while what he spoke was in a sort of serious or familiar—often buffooning—strain. Audience and speaker thus came to be on the most intimate terms. There were jokes and topical allusions, and very little about the real matter in hand—to wit, the play. In the case of a prominent performer and proprietor such as Foote was, here was a rare opportunity for exhibiting his satire and ridicule. He even used to carry on

this extra business when the curtain went up, and did
not scruple to introduce "Mr. Foote" himself, manager
and actor, talking familiarly with his stage carpenters,
prompter, or candle-snuffers, who bore the names they
had in ordinary life.   All this was damaging to stage
illusion and to the proper dignity of the profession ;
and it is difficult to understand what sort of entertainment could be extracted from such exhibitions.
" Mr. Foote," however, was exhibited, and could, as it
is called, " show off " and fool it to the " top of his
bent."

This method of mimicry on the stage, and of mimicry
actors, was brought into fashion by that popular burlesque " The Rehearsal," written by the Duke of
Buckingham.   This the comedians grew to be fond
of setting off, in the mock tragic portions, by imitations of their fellow-players.   Resentment is almost
invariably excited by such mimicry.   No one, however good-humoured, can be pleased or indifferent at
seeing his ways taken off, even with a favourable colour.
Wilkinson's diverting memoirs are full of the quarrels
and bitter enmities engendered by these attempts.   I
think it was Mathews who was once performing in
this way, taking off his brethren, when he suddenly
recollected that a worthy old actor whom he had long
known—a personal friend, too—was actually present
while this ridicule was going on.   Greatly shocked, he
ran up to him and affectionately apologized.   The
other did not understand.   " My dear friend, did you
mean *that* for me ?   Don't distress yourself ; there
was not the least likeness."

In Foote's day, mimicry was a recognized accom-
plishment.   In social life, an " agreeable rattle " who
could " take off " a well-known acquaintance was in

much demand. Ladies and gentlemen, even, were accustomed to display their ability in this department at parties. Dr. Johnson spoke with praise of a well-known London lady who excelled in mimicry. " I believe," he added, perhaps significantly, " she has now gone mad."

It is well known that George IV., a Prince of many accomplishments, was an incomparable mimic, and used to convulse his friends by taking off his own Ministers, foreign visitors, and others, in the most humorous and life-like fashion. The Duke of Wellington, no indulgent critic of such " pranks," was compelled almost to wonder and admire. " He told me," says Mr. Croker, " that when he went with the Chancellor to accept the government, His Majesty was in bed groaning, and appeared very miserable and unhappy; but as the conversation went on he grew better, sat up in the bed, and began to describe all his communications with his late Ministers, mimicking them all to the life, and exhibiting such a drama, so lively, so exact, so amusing, that the Duke never saw anything like it—Goodrich, Lansdowne, and, above all, Anglesey, whom he positively made himself look like. I myself never saw anyone who exhibited the niceties of character with so much discrimination. As a mere imitator he has some superiors; but I have never seen his equal for a combination of personal imitation *with the power of exhibiting the mental character*."*

* In Edinburgh there was a famous mimic, Dr. Cullen, who is mentioned by Boswell. His reputation as such was truly extraordinary. Dugald Stewart declared that " he was the most perfect of all mimics"; and Lord Cockburn says that he could copy, not merely the looks, tones, peculiarities, etc., but " the very words—

Foote was not altogether original in his mimetic methods, for we can trace his system of mimicry and burlesque to Henry Fielding, who found profit and a regular substance in such pieces. Like Foote, he had ridiculed actors and authors, and brought public men, politicians, and others, on his stage. The familiar " Tom Thumb " became a vehicle for ridiculing contemporary writers. In " Pasquin," " The Historical Register," and other pieces, he introduced Ministers— Walpole as Quidam; and a further attempt, which was not successful, led in 1737 to the famous Licensing or Controlling Act, which gave the Lord Chamberlain supreme powers to authorize, suspend, or wholly forbid, any piece which was to be set upon the stage. Under this code the stage has been directed for some hundred and thirty years, and, it must be said, with great advantage : no excess in the way of personality has been tolerated, though there have been at times fits of occasional indulgence.

---

nay, the very thoughts "—of his subjects. Thus, in a tavern, sitting in one of the boxes, as they were called, he would take off Principal Robertson, giving indecorous toasts, speeches, and remarks, so that those on the other side of the partition went away perfectly shocked at the scandalous exhibition. This droll performance, however to be deprecated, gives a good idea of the higher class of mimicry.

Once one of the students at his college "broke out"—he was boarding with Dr. Robertson—when Cullen, arriving early in the morning, imitated the President's heavy step on the stairs, entered, and, sitting behind the curtain, gave the youth a severe lecture on his conduct, which brought him to a state of contrition and penitence, on which he was forgiven. By-and-by arrived the real President, who sat behind the curtain and administered a stern rebuke. The youth could only repeat his penitential assurances, but remonstrated against this double "jobation." "Ah," said the President instantly, " I see my friend Cullen has been here !"

And yet such personalities have ever had a strange, fascinating attraction. There can be little doubt at the present time that, were the Censor at all to relax his vigilance, and suffer delineations of well-known public men to be introduced under grotesque conditions, they would be welcomed with the keenest enjoyment, and even rapture. To see one we know well, clearly and accurately taken off, is a truly amusing, if unbecoming, entertainment, sure to engender perhaps the heartiest laugh of our experience. But all the time it is but an illegitimate form of being amused, and would speedily pall. The performer has to go on peppering and "peppering still higher," until the imitation becomes licentious.

It was extraordinary that at this moment the most disorderly and personal of all known satirists and mimics should come forward on the scene, and begin a successful career in defiance of this new and stringent law. In his case it would seem to have been a mere "dead letter." It was not to apply to this extraordinary being, this man of power who succeeded in at once amusing and terrifying the whole community, amusing the man of pleasure and the laughers, terrifying the timorous and weaklings. How this came to pass one may fairly wonder. But it was simply because Foote was a man of power, "incompressible" (it cannot be too often repeated), without sentiment, feeling, or delicacy; ready to trample on and "wipe his shoes" on anyone that attempted to oppose him. To such the community is ever ready to give way. They may condemn, but they admire all the time. Titmarsh, in an invaluable bit of practical advice, bids everyone go forward and roughly claim the best place or the best seat, when dozens will retire before him. Anyone with the proper air of authority will find that this is so. Foote knew his company perfectly. But, as I have shown, the severity of the Licensing Act was really intended for political offenders.

Foote's success in this "line" naturally engendered imitators, if not rivals, and he must have been a good deal disturbed later on by the rise of an entertainer, the novelty of whose methods secured him large audiences. The town began to run after George Alexander Stevens, who had really struck out something new. He appeared behind a long table, and was enclosed between two screens which met at an angle. It was a very clever and original performance. It was so pleasantly and even wittily put together that it could be read as well as it could be enjoyed on the stage. For it was issued as a volume, and passed through many editions. The lively author had prepared a number of modelled heads representing many types—politicians, writers, players, etc.—on which he commented in a very satirical and amusing way, introducing personal allusions that were eagerly caught up by the audiences. He in many points suggested the present Mr. George Grossmith, who takes off the various types of society—wise and foolish —in such brilliant fashion.

It would seem that a mimic of the first rank—that is to say, a mimic of genius—must be also an actor of the first rank. We can boast of but two performers reaching this standard, and both were actors of reputation. These exceptional men were Foote and Mathews the Elder. There was one similarity in their methods, but both furnished sketches of characters, both were socially successful. Mathews, of course, had none of Foote's obstreperous personality, and his

sketches were superficial enough. He was altogether
on a lower plane than Foote, and had too much
of the common "showman's" arts. It was strange,
too, that both these eminent mimics should have
closed their course in disastrous fashion. There is
nothing more piteous in stage annals than Mathews's
collapse both in health and fortune simultaneously,
he dying in a sort of wreck, everything lost, save
the tender and devoted wife and his faithful son.
Mathews too, like Foote, had lost the free use of one
limb owing to a frightful accident.

By the agreement of all the critics of his day,
Mathews possessed Foote's wonderful power of
realizing the *character* of the person he represented,
of becoming inspired, as it were, by all his thoughts,
feelings, and humours. Both had that miraculous
faculty of thinking or speaking upon a given subject
almost exactly as the person himself would think or
speak.

When Scott read the wonderful lines on Higgin-
botham's death in the " Rejected Addresses," he
seemed almost to recognize his own words, and declared that he must have treated the incident in the
same way. For this reason, Foote's talent must be
set far above mere vulgar imitation. It becomes the
inspiration of the actor. Foote always relied upon
this internal power, which helped him to reproduce
the mental and physical oddities of his subject ; but
here Mathews was inferior, for he relied on elaborate
make-up, as it is called, and he had, besides, the
natural power of altering his features and figure.
Finally, Foote had the power of dramatic creation: for
he could both write and realize the most original types
of character. Altogether, here were two very remark-

able persons, geniuses perhaps, who filled a large space in the life of the time.

The career of Foote, and that of other satirists who followed him, suggests the significant reflection that in our day such persons would have no opening for their talent—for the simple reason that there is no material. There is nothing for them to mimic. In Foote's time, oddity and *character* were found everywhere, almost in abundance. The lack of communication between the country and the towns left all the grotesqueness of provincial life unchanged, offering a rich store for the town satirist to work on.* We have only to read the comedies of Goldsmith, Colman, Morton, Reynolds, to see what a number of eccentric types were abroad and accepted. Now those steam-rollers of uniformity—communication by railway and the press—have crushed out all angularities and projections, and made one general smoothness. Quaint, natural oddity, once so relished, is almost thought an offence. Stranger still, it furnishes no amusement, because not understood; all is at one dead and monotonous level and one fixed pattern. And so it comes about that a brilliant delineator of

* These simple folk came to town, some with a favourite expression, which they brought constantly into their talk; others with odd gestures and odd clothes, which attracted no attention at home; some "sucked an oyster off their wrist," like Cadwallader, at every speech. These things made the town laugh. Foote found characters everywhere. Nothing is more curious than the reading of Colman's or Morton's comedies, with the amazing but highly amusing figures they contain: the two Rapids (father and son), the one always bidding the other to "keep moving"; Sir Abel Handy, the amateur inventor; the Country Lout, etc. Even the restrained comedy treatment of Goldsmith could not secure acceptance for his Croaker, a truly diverting character. Sir Antony Absolute, with his fits of rage, is looked on with a sort of antiquarian curiosity, for no father

Foote's pattern only finds that "the eyes of men are idly bent on him."

It was reserved for Foote to introduce a higher and more intellectual style, based on the study of the subject's character, placing him in new situations which called out a fresh and varied display of oddities. He would use these elements as a basis, and could create a sort of finished *character* under the very ribs of his mimicry. He had besides, as we shall see later, an incomparable dramatic gift, writing character scenes in the most dramatic fashion ; and it is rare to find a player possessing this double power. Here was Foote's true merit, and though he garnished his work with vulgar personalities and caricature, he appealed to the judicious by drawing a striking and interesting character. This brought him within the domain of art.

Connected with the changes in manners and taste is the singular phenomenon—which I have never even seen noted—of the complete extinction or disappearance of the "low comedian"—indeed, of low comedy itself. It is hardly an exaggeration to say that the present generation know nothing of broad comedy, have no taste for it, and, when some stray scrap of it is offered, do not recognize or understand it. Yet thirty or forty years ago, as many will recall, low comedy was a distinct branch—a loadstone of attraction. Every play had its low comedian. There was a whole corps of broadly humorous players, so well trained and practised that their mere glance or

---

nowadays thus menaces his son or flourishes his stick at him. In all the favourite pieces presented at the fashionable theatres, fathers, lovers, sisters, wives, move softly about the stage, do nothing violent, and do everything in the same way. And this seems a correct enough representation of the time.

laugh used to convulse the house : Buckstone, Wright, Compton, Toole, Paulton, Terry, John S. Clarke, Brough. Of these the measure was specially taken by the theatrical tailors, and plays were " written round " them. They had a rollicking heartiness, a thick rich voice, roguish eyes, a perpetual good humour, and a certain slyness of manner—as in the case of Compton—with much eccentricity. Such were the gifts necessary. All gone now ! It would be difficult to find anyone who knows the traditions of this " broad " treatment. Everything is done so correctly and genteely that even the servants are as deliberate and stately as their masters.

To this class Foote certainly belonged ; his acting was of the broad-comedy cast. All his characters have a certain energy, and require to be given with enormous spirit, filled out with play of feature, quaint glances, restlessness, gestures, grotesque dress, every resource, and, where possible, with well-studied mimicries.

CHAPTER V

1747

"THE DIVERSIONS OF THE MORNING"

WITHIN three years Foote could seriously think of taking the Haymarket Theatre as manager with a new entertainment. He ought to have anticipated the difficulties of such a step, for no house was allowed to compete with the two great theatres enjoying patent rights; and the world might have lost the apparition of Garrick's entertainment at Goodman's Fields had not the device, or trick, been thought of— of calling it a "concert." Foote had prepared a new and special "show" of his own devising. He had, as we have seen, long been practising his mimicries, and now announced an odd piece or show, which he called "The Diversions of the Morning"—a sort of "half play." Here was the announcement:

"At the Theatre in the Haymarket this day [April 22, 1747] will be performed a Concert of Musick, with which will be given gratis a new entertainment." The principal characters were by Foote, Shuter (who had come from Drury Lane to join Foote for the summer months), Costello, and others. There was a farce called "The Credulous Husband," from Congreve's "Old Bachelor"—Fondlewife by Foote—and an Epilogue, "to be spoken by the same performers as in the Bedford Coffee-House."

57

Here we have the beginnings of his long line of personalities.

This show of Foote's was really an original device. It was neither play nor monologue. A strange half-painter, half-actor, who hung loose upon the coffee-house, had a clever gift of taking off the various friends and characters who frequented this place. He did not merely simulate their oddities, but he gave a reproduction of the person. This struck Foote, who had much the same gift, and it occurred to him that he might work the mimicked person into a regular stage character. Then was suggested another device. He would have a set of living puppets—a few figures who were to say nothing and do nothing but what he told them, thus avoiding the monotony of a one-man recitation. Hence " The Diversions."

What was " The Diversions of the Morning "? Mr. Forster says it was never printed, so we must guess or " piece out " its purpose. But Tate Wilkinson has given an act of it in his memoirs, which supplies a fair idea of the treatment. It was clearly modelled on a portion of " The Rehearsal," just as Sheridan modelled his " Critic," or portions of it, on Foote's sketch.

He introduced a regular procession of popular players, ridiculing them as he went along.

Thus, in the case of Woodward, he was puzzled to find any trade he was fit for ; therefore he spoke the following speech, in his voice and manner, from Sir Fopling Flutter :

" Wherever I go, there goes a gentleman—upon my life a gentleman ; and when you have said a gentleman, why, oh ! [*here Foote dropped Woodward's voice and manner*] you have said more than is true."

He was also severe on Garrick, who was apt to hesitate (in his dying scenes in particular), as in the character of Lothario :

". . . adorns my fall, and chea—chea—chea—chea —chea—cheers my heart in dy—dy—dying."

It was remarkable that at starting, even, he preferred to mimic the physical defects of his brethren —always a rather cruel and unhandsome thing. Thus he exhibited Quin, from his sonorous voice and weighty manner, as *a watchman :* " Past twelve o'clock, and a cloudy morning."

Delane was supposed to have but one eye, therefore he fixed him as *a beggar-man in St. Paul's Churchyard :* " Would you bestow your pity on a poor blind man !"

And Ryan, whose voice for oddity and shrillness was remarkable, was exhibited as *a razor-grinder :* " Razors to grind, scissors to grind, penknives to grind."

Mrs. Woffington, who, though beautiful to a degree, had a most unpleasant squeaking pipe, was shown as *an orange-woman to the playhouse :* "Would you have some oranges—have some orange-chips, ladies and gentlemen ?—would you have some nonpareils ?— would you have a bill of the play ?"

Now, here was truly an extraordinary spectacle, one, too, of a disorderly and unbecoming sort. To realize its character, we have only to suppose that in our own day some smart forward fellow, well known at the leading theatrical club as a lively humorist and half-amateur actor, were to take a theatre, say the Haymarket, and announce that he invited all Londoners to come and hear him take off his brethren ! In all these variations he took a wide range, selecting some well-known oddities for treatment. The West-

minster Justice, Sir Thomas de Veil, with Cock
the fashionable auctioneer, were duly ridiculed. It
was amazing how patiently these folk suffered ; no
one thought of chastisement—for a time, at least.

He was not, however, without competitors. At
the time there were a number of vain, talking mount-
ebanks about, all struggling to catch the public eye.
Witness that eccentric being " Orator Henley," who
was presently " shown up " by Foote, though indeed
he himself, from his perpetual speech, just as well
deserved the title of " Orator Foote." This Henley
was a good specimen of the " tub-spouter"; he had
the full command of a foul and scurrilous tongue.
He had so-called " chapels " of his own, to which
people were drawn in the hope of hearing something
amusing.

Once, however, in this very year 1747, he and
Foote got into a dispute, both interchanging plenty
of gross " Billingsgate." The quarrel ended in the
orators appearing on the stage of the little Haymarket, where the pair fought to the enjoyment of
the listeners. Foote, however, was overmatched in
scurrility, and held to have the worst of it. He had
his revenge, for next year he introduced his opponent
into his " Auction."

" The Diversions " was a very free comment on
things in general, but prominently ridiculing the
familiar devices of the stage. Actors and writers had
long this fancy for exhibiting the rather repulsive
prose of life behind the scenes—a foolish proceeding,
as it destroys the air of mystery, diminishes the
public respect, and impairs the players' own dignity.
Coming forward as a manager, or rather as Foote
himself, he chattered away, giving his own mimicries,

and saying whatever came into his head as being likely to produce a laugh.

The humour of the thing was that the young man seemed to be accepted at his own valuation. The coffee-houses and taverns had stamped their seal on his mimicries. One who when a child could mimic his own father to his face was more than ready to mimic his brethren, in this wholesale and deliberate fashion. He made it a show, a means of earning his livelihood. It seemed extraordinary courage or impudence. Impudent or not, the attempt was entirely successful.

" He soon found," says Cooke, " that he reckoned without his host ; for, whether from the alarm excited in the theatres royal, or the resentment of most of the performers who smarted under the lash of his mimicry, the civil magistrates of Westminster were called upon to interfere ; and, under the sanction of an Act of Parliament, for limiting a number of playhouses, sent a posse of constables, who, entering the theatre, dismissed the audience, and left the laughing Aristophanes to consider of new ways and means for his support."

But Foote, ever irrepressible as incompressible, was not to be daunted. Within a few days he had devised a second scheme of an elusive kind, destined to be extremely successful and bring him much money. It furnished him with full opportunity for displaying his special view of humour and frolic. This was what he called his "giving tea " — a sort of colloquial "drawing-room entertainment," as it might be called. He affected to receive his friends and entertain them, not at a theatre, but at his own house.

Foote was thus victorious. He dared to oppose

these high powers, and fought the battle to the end. There can be no doubt that the law was violated, as he had produced a farce. This, however, he dropped.

On Friday, April 24, the town was informed that "On Saturday noon next, at 12 o'clock, at the new Theatre in the Haymarket, Mr. Foote begs the favour of his friends to come and drink a dish of chocolate with him: and 'tis hoped there will be a great deal of good company and some joyous spirits: he will endeavour to make the *Morning* as *Diverting* as possible."

No further interference was attempted; he proceeded with his work, growing bolder and more popular every day.

On June 1 it was given out, "At the request of several persons who are desirous of spending an hour with Mr. Foote, but find the time inconvenient, instead of chocolate in the morning, Mr. Foote's friends are desired to drink a dish of tea with him at half-past six this day, to-morrow, and Wednesday, at which time they are obliged to give over, most of the company being engaged to set out on Thursday for country expeditions. N.B.—Doors to be opened at $\frac{1}{2}$ after 4." Then followed: "June 6th, the 35th day and positively the last, at the desire of several persons of quality, Mr. Foote will give tea this day at $\frac{1}{2}$ after 6, having persuaded all the performers to postpone their journey till Monday."*

In this fashion Foote began his system of levelling

* It will be noted that here he anticipated our morning performances. With us half-past two, or two, is thought tolerably early, but noon seems somewhat inconvenient. We shall see later how he introduced the practice at Edinburgh.

the barriers between the stage and the public, and so finally introduced what might be likened to the coarse, happy-go-lucky methods of the seaside performances on Margate sands.

The imitation of Macklin and his oddities, in "The Diversions," is an admirable *tour de force*, and reads almost as well as though it had been recited before us. As a piece of humour it is excellent. He is presumed to be giving a lesson on Othello to his pupil Bounce:

"Begin at 'Othello's occupation's gone.' Now catch at me, as if you would tear the very strings and all. Keep your voice low—loudness is no mark of passion.—Mind your attitude. *Bounce.* Villain—— *Puz.* Very well! *Boun.* Be sure you prove my love a w—— *Puz.* Admirable! *Boun.* Be sure on't—— *Puz.* Bravo! *Boun.* Give me the occular proof—— *Puz.* Lay your emphasis a little stronger upon occ—occ—occ—— *Boun.* Occ—occ—occular proof—— *Puz.* That's right! *Boun.* Or, by the worth of my eternal soul, Thou hadst better been born a dog—— *Puz.* Grind dog—a d-o-o-g, Iag—— *Boun.* A do-og, Iago, than answer my wak'd wrath. *Puz.* Charming!—Now quick—— [*Speaking all the time.*] *Boun.* Make me to see it, or at least so prove it, That the probation bears no hinge or loop, To hang a doubt on;—or wo—— *Puz.* A little more terror upon woe—wo-o-e, like a mastiff in a tanner's yard—wo-o-o-e—— [*They answer each other*, W o-o-o-e, etc.] *Boun.* Upon thy life. If thou dost slander her, and torture me—— *Puz.* (*pushing him away*). Oh! go about your business—'twon't do—go, go—I am sorry I have given you this trouble. *Boun.* Why, sir, I—— *Free.* Oh! pray, Mr. Puzzle, let me intercede for him. *Puz.* (*as Mr. Macklin*). Zounds, sir! do you consider the mode of the mind, that a man's soul is tost, and lost, and crost, and his entrails broiling on a gridiron. — Bring it from the bottom of your stomach with a grind — as to-r-rr—— *Boun.* Torr—rture me—— *Puz.* That's my meaning. *Boun.* Never pray more; abandon all remorse—— *Puz.* Now out with your arm, and show your chest.— There's a figure! *Boun.* On horror's head—— *Puz.* Now out with your voice. *Boun.* Horrors accumulate—— *Puz.* Now tender. *Boun.* Do deeds to make heav'n weep—— *Puz.* Now terror. *Boun.* All earth amaz'd!—For no thing canst thou to damna—— *Puz.* Grind na-na, na, na, tion—— *Boun.* Na, na, na, tion add greater than that. *Puz.* Now throw me from you, and I'll yield.—Very well, keep that attitude.—Your eye fix'd—— There's a figure; there's a contrast."

All which is truly diverting, and must have had a droll effect.

Not content with this, he was longing to fly at higher game. He saw that his audiences would relish such an attempt.

In a letter written to Peter Garrick at Lichfield, and filled with theatrical gossip,* Windham described Foote as giving his " Tea," and as being determined " to bring out that very weak and abusive caricature " of the two managers, Garrick and Lacey. Lacey,

* From the Forster manuscript, and quoted in my " Life of Garrick." The generous owner, I remember well, used to allow me day after day to range through his valuable papers, and copy whatever suited my purpose. Forster told me that he always intended writing Garrick's life, having such a rare mass of materials by him, but that he cheerfully handed it over to his friend.

he said, was infuriated, and swore that he would break Foote's neck. He also complained to the licenser. But the prudent Davy sent to him privately to tell him that he did not at all object, and that "Mr. Foote was quite welcome" to deal with him. He was afraid that it would be given out that the step was taken at his instigation, so courteous was he. This, however, shows that Johnson was not the first to threaten the mimic with a cudgel, and it would seem, indeed, that the threat had availed.

"The Auction" was the next form of his humour —a rambling commentary on persons and things in general, with humorous comments and mimicries after the pattern of his "Diversions." There is no copy of it in print, so we cannot learn exactly what it was like. Foote described his "show" as being held at "the Auction Room, late the little Theatre in the Hay"—a device probably intended to baffle the censors. On April 18 he gave out a performance "for the sufferers in a late calamity, when Mr. Foote will exhibit a choice collection of pictures." On June 11 there was "Foote's Sale" for the thirty-fifth time, and on the 14th and 16th there was "Tea"—last times of performance. During next season "The Auction" continued to draw. On January 2 he was announcing a charitable perform-ance for the Lock Hospital.

On the 14th Foote's "The Auction" was to be "per-formed, positively last time"—a fallacious announce-ment; for on January 25, " by particular desire, Foote will exhibit some entire new lots, consisting of a poet, a beau, a Frenchman, a miser, a tailor, a sot, two young gentlemen, and a ghost—two of which are originals, the rest copies from the best masters. With

5

an oration, and a dance called Prince Eugene's
March. Places for the boxes to be taken at the
auction room; the auction to begin at half-past six."
From this it is clear that Foote was about to enlarge
his system, and extend his ridicules from his own
fellows to the outside world. His announcement
meant that he would be "general" in the case of all
save two. One of these can be identified. There was
a quack oculist—Chevalier Taylor, as he called himself—who was skilful in his art, and wrought cures,
but who combined with his science a vast deal of
absurdity and quackery. He was introduced and
ridiculed.

Woodward, that brilliant comedian whose portrait
by Grisoni, in the Garrick Club, is itself a speaking
comedy, resenting Foote's freedoms with his brethren,
contrived what he called a little "retaliatory" piece,
which he called "Tit for Tat," in which were the
lines:

> " Called forth, see poor I appear
> To try one fall with this famed auctioneer."

And in the character of Foote, he said:

> " But when I play'd Othello, thousands swore
> They never saw such tragedy before."

Foote heard that this skit was to be produced
at Garrick's theatre, and actually wrote a sort of
insolent, threatening letter to the great manager,
warning him at his peril not to allow it. He cared,
he said, as little for the actor's attempts as he did
for the manager's "passive wit," but he might
mention that he had a plan for a short farce, which
would be wormwood to some, entertaining to many,
and very beneficial to Samuel Foote. In conclusion,

he removed himself from the free list, saying, " If the bookkeeper returns this he will be cheating you of five shillings—a sum not very contemptible to you. This insulting stroke shows that Foote had already " taken his line " as to Garrick—viz., that of hectoring and intimidation. And he knew how well it would answer, for in judging character he was infinitely shrewd. Not to our surprise, we find Garrick writing to him in the mildest, most conciliatory way. How could he be offended at the character?—" that of a smart, pleasant, conceited fellow and a good mimic "; and there were some amiable vices " which can never be applied to you." This was a compliment in return for the sneer. Thus began their long bickering. While Foote insulted, Garrick ever temporized. The result proved that the last was the wiser policy.

Foote now offered " some new lots "—a poet, a beau, etc. Woodward on his benefit night returned to the attack, and publicly threatened him with " a dish of his own chocolate with an addition of *one mew at his cats*." Foote wrote in the papers that the Italian cats would not do, so he had disposed of them to Drury Lane. He promised to exhibit a portrait of Harry the Smuggler (so he called Woodward) as he looked at his trial—that is, " when begging pardon as the Prodigal Returned "; the Smuggler Foiled, etc. How incredibly puerile are these squabbles of the mummers, and the supreme vanity of these appeals to the public to decide ! One thinks of Johnson's contemptuous verdict on the rival claims of two inferior poets — " Sir, there is no settling the precedence between a flea and a louse." Woodward, however, was not to be intimidated, and Garrick did not

interpose.   So when he took his benefit on March 18,
" by particular desire "—an old-standing dramatic
falsehood, but a useful one—Woodward announced
that he would present his very good friend the
Auctioneer with " Tit for Tat," or one dish of his
own chocolate.   And when Shuter and Costello took
their benefit at Old Drury on May 15, they presented
" The Auction " and " A Smuggling Episode called
Tit for Tat, or the Smuggler Foiled at his Own
Weapons."   There was also a portrait of " Harry the
Smuggler as he looked at his own trial."   Why he
was called the Smuggler, or what his trial was about,
we cannot guess.   Thus early was the young man
embroiled with his comrades, and through one of these
he had ventured even to challenge Garrick.   People
were already somewhat in awe of him.

On January 16, after the last performance of " The
Auction," a strange riot took place at Foote's theatre,
arising out of the " Bottle Hoax," or exhibition of a
conjurer who " undertook to enter from the stage into
a quart bottle without equivocation, and there sing a
song."   An extraordinary excitement was caused by
this announcement.   It was firmly believed that the
thing would be attempted.   However, the conjurer
not appearing, a dreadful riot broke out, in which the
interior was quite demolished—furniture, boxes, etc.—
the disorder being led by the Duke of Cumberland.
An attempt was made to show that Foote had nothing
to do with the speculation, on the ground that he had
taken possession of the money, in order to return it
to such as claimed it, should they have destroyed his
house.   It looks very much as though it had been one
of Foote's choice practical jokes.   There was a " fast "
Duke also concerned with it.   Ten days later a play

was given, so the playhouse could not have been seriously damaged.

In this new venture, Foote's deportment to his assistants was ingenious enough, and helped the dramatic illusion. He generally put them to act as what they really were — that is, untrained novices whom he instructed in presence of the audience. He knew how to turn their mistakes and bashfulness to account. This prompted many of his humorous speeches and allusions. But he always remained the attraction, the one and only Foote. People "*went to see Foote*," not his play. And it is to be feared that here is one of the fixed abuses or corruptions of the stage : for even nowadays people "go to see," or used to go to see, not the play, but Irving in the play, Lewis Waller, Martin Harvey, and the rest.

This system of Foote's was really an invention of his own. The purely monologue entertainment, where a single person bore the whole on his shoulders, was always monotonous and required relief. Still, our modern showmen have always clung to it. But it occurred to Foote that he might supplement his efforts by having a few passive assistants, lay-figures as it were, on whom he might exercise his wit, who would suggest to him remarks and commentaries. There was ingenuity and dramatic interest in this idea, but it required a man of much readiness and cleverness to carry the idea out.

CHAPTER VI

1749—1752

FOOTE'S FIRST COMEDY, "THE KNIGHTS"—ELOPEMENT
TO FRANCE

As I have said, the surprises offered by Foote were
to be never-ending. He had not yet found what
suited him: tragedian, comedian, mummer, and mimic
—he had tried all; but though the mimicry had
"caught on," it was but a limited field, for he had
presently exhausted all the grotesque types about
him. Yet he had learned to portray types of character. He could analyze, discriminate, and colour
all kinds of oddities in the most admirable way.
What if he now tried his hand at a regular drama?
And presently this energetic man had written a very
spirited and amusing comedy of a farcical sort,
showing full knowledge of all stage devices. And
though but a first attempt, both Goldsmith and
Sheridan did not disdain to draw some inspiration
from it.

This piece was entitled "The Knights," for it dealt
with the oddities of two eccentric knights. One of
the leading characters, Sir Penurious Trifle, a rather
far-fetched name, was played by Foote himself.
There is an extraordinary *mechanical* defect in the
treatment of this character, who never appears, but

is described; and then Foote, as Hartop, another of the characters, simulates him with all his curious phrases, mannerisms, etc. There is something false and *un*scenic in this notion, though Foote no doubt very cleverly contrasted the two characters, Hartop and Sir Penurious. The spectator must have been confused, and scarcely able to distinguish between Foote himself, Hartop, and Sir Penurious. And the more perfectly and elaborately the last was given, the more certain one would be that in real life no one could mimic thought and eccentricity of mind so fully.

Considering that it is a first attempt, it causes surprise at the power and force displayed in the two leading characters, whom he had " picked up " on a journey. Sir Gregory, in particular, has strange oddities of phrase, betokening, not, as in the case of Dickens, superficial eccentricity, but real mental obliquity and confusion.* Witness this little display : Says the knight : " Mr. Jenkins, I am your humble servant ; a strange town this, Mr. Jenkins ; no news stirring, no papers taken in ! Is that gentleman a stranger, Mr. Jenkins ? Pray, sir, not to be too bold, don't you come from London ? *Hart.* But last night. *Sir Greg.* Lack-a-day ! that's wonder-

---

* Apropos of this second knight, " Sir Gregory Gazette," a person apparently so named because he was fond of reading newspapers, how amazing it seems nowadays that anyone in nature should be called Sir Anthony *Absolute*, or Mrs. Candour, or Surface, or Snarl ! Who can even conceive of such a monstrosity as a person called *MacSarcasm*, or Sir Pertinax MacSycophant !—it bewilders one even to think of it. Yet even Boz in these later days used to devise names of the same character : Lord Frederick Verisopht and Sir Mulberry Hawk. Incredible ! As though giving a burlesque name to a person would help him in the least to produce any sort of effect in the world.

ful!——Mr. Jenkins, introduce me. *Jenk.* Mr.
Hartop, Sir Gregory Gazette. *Sir Greg.* Sir, I am
proud to—— Well, sir, and what news? You
come from—— Pray, sir, are you a Parliament-
man? *Hart.* Not I indeed, sir. *Sir Greg.* Good
lack! maybe belong to the law? *Hart.* Nor that.
Sir Greg. Oh, then, in some of the offices—the
Treasury or the Exchequer? *Hart.* Neither, sir.
Sir Greg. Lack-a-day! that's wonderful! Well, but,
Mr.—— Pray, what name did Mr. Jenkins, Ha——
Ha—— *Hart.* Hartop. *Sir Greg.* Ay, true!
what, not of the Hartops of Boston? *Hart.* No.
Sir Greg. Maybe not. There is, Mr. Hartop, one
thing that I envy you Londoners in much—quires of
newspapers! Now, I reckon you read a matter of
eight sheets every day? *Hart.* Not one. *Sir Greg.*
Wonderful! then, maybe you are about Court; and
so, being at the fountain-head, know what is in the
papers before they are printed. *Hart.* I never trouble
my head about them.—An old fool! [*Aside.*]
Sir Greg. Good lord! Your friend, Mr. Jenkins, is
very close. *Jenk.* Why, Sir Gregory, Mr. Hartop
is much in the secrets above; and it becomes a man
so trusted to be wary, you know. *Sir Greg.* May
be so, may be so. Wonderful! ay, ay, a great man,
no doubt. *Jenk.* But I'll give him a better insight
into your character, and that will induce him to
throw off his reserve. *Sir Greg.* May be so; do, do;
ay, ay! *Jenk.* Prithee, Jack, don't be so crusty—
indulge the knight's humour a little; besides, if I
guess right, it may be necessary for the conduct of
your design to contract a pretty strict intimacy here.
[*Aside.*] *Hart.* Well, do as you will.

Next let us turn to the other knight, Foote's

character, one of the most extraordinary displays of
eccentricity that can be conceived.   His ideas travel so
fast, and grow so jumbled, that he has to leave them all
inchoate and undeveloped :

"*Hart.* Where did I leave off, hey, you Dick ?
Tim. About coffee and tea.   *Hart.* Right, you,
right ! true, true ! so, God, you knight, I used to
breakfast at this coffee-house every morning ; it
cost me eightpence, though, and I had always a
breakfast at home——no matter for that, though
there I breakfasted, you Dick, God, at the same
table with Lord Tom Truewit :—you have heard of
Truewit, you knight ; a droll dog ! you Dick, he told
us the story and made us die with laughing :—you
have heard of Charles the Second, you knight ; he
was son of Charles the First, King here in England,
that was beheaded by Oliver Cromwell : so what
does Charles the Second, you knight, do ; but he
fights Noll at Worcester ; a town you have heard of,
not far off ; but all would not do, you ; God, Noll
made him scamper, made him run, take to his heels,
you knight ;—Truewit told us the story, made us die
with laughing ; I always breakfasted at the coffee-
house ; it cost me eightpence, though I had a breakfast at home——so what does Charles do, but hid
himself in an oak, an oak-tree, you, in a wood called
Boscobel, from two Italian words, *bosco bello,* a fine
wood, you, and off he marches : but old Noll would
not let him come home ; no, says he, you don't come
here !—Lord Tom told us the story ; made us die
with laughing ; it cost me eightpence, though I had
a breakfast at home——so, you knight, when Noll
died, Monk there, you, afterwards Albemarle, in the
North, brought him back ; so, you, the Cavaliers ;

you have heard of them? they were friends to the
Stuarts; what did they do, God, you Dick, but they
put up Charles in a sign, the royal oak; you have
seen such signs at country alehouses. . . .   It made
us all die with laughing! Lord Tom told the story;
I always breakfasted at the coffee-house, though it
cost me eightpence, and I had a breakfast at home
——hey, you knight! what, Dick, hey!"

All this is really wonderful, from its *tumultuousness*,
as I may call it, and confusion.   How original the
interjections!   The use of " you," etc., is as amazing
as original.

With a lack of dramatic propriety, or craze for
mere buffooning, Foote spoiled his work by adding
an unmeaning parody of an Italian opera, giving what
he announced as a " Cat's Opera."*   This, however,
was omitted after a few performances.

As was to be expected, this erratic being was now
preparing one of his " surprises."   Here he was with
a managerial burden on his back, a regular theatre,
a clever corps of actors engaged, and a fairly successful piece, when of a sudden it was learned that he had
disappeared—had fled to France, and was not likely
to return!   It has not been said that he wished to
escape from creditors; it may have been that he had
just now inherited one of the fortunes that came

* " On the last rehearsal Harris was missing; and as nobody knew
where he lived, Shuter was prevailed upon to find him out, if
possible.   He inquired in vain for some time; at last he was
informed that he lived in a certain court in the Minories, but at
what house he could not exactly learn.   This information was
enough for a man *of congenial talents* like Shuter; for the moment
he entered the court he set up a *cat-solo*, which instantly roused
his brother musician in his garret, who answered him in the same
tune."—*Cooke*.

to him, and that, tired of work, he wished to enjoy it—that is, *spend* it.   There was much talk and speculation, but the matter was soon forgotten.

A couple of years and more went by, but his shifting career was still of sufficient interest to attract public curiosity.   One strange report was accepted for a time : that " he had been hanged " in France for some offence—a strange, odd shape for it to assume, considering the family history.   But all such stories were set to rest by his sudden appearance in town.

The wonder was that his absence seemed to have made no difference in his position.   Most persons when they fall out of a profession find it difficult, if not impossible, to recover their old place ; but here was Foote in far better case, having even improved his condition, installed at Old Drury, the manager subservient, and a new comedy called " Taste " accepted !   What was his power over the great actor ?   How did he so suddenly attain the supremacy over him which was never shaken ?

Foote might well protest in his preface that he would ever "retain the most grateful remembrance of his assistance, assiduity, and kind concern at the broken progress and *untimely end* of this my last and favourite offspring."   The piece did come to an untimely end, and, meeting with opposition for some nights, was withdrawn.

It must have been a little humiliating for the great David to come forward dressed as an auctioneer, announcing himself thus :

> " Before this court I, Peter Puff,* appear,
> A Briton born, and bred an auctioneer."

---

* It is not clear why Puff should be described as an auctioneer, as he seems to have been no more than a picture-dealer, or " faker,"

There was a good deal of wit, however, in some of his strophes. Thus, alluding to the craze for buying " curios " :

> " Oh ! think on us what various ills will flow
> When great ones only purchase what they know."

> " I here declare on oath,
> I never yet sold goods of foreign growth,
> Ne'er sent commissions out to Greece or Rome ;
> My best antiquities are made at home.
> I've Romans, Greeks, Italians, near at hand,
> Three Britons all, and living in the Strand."

This, however, was merely the text for Foote's piece.

The comedy was no more than a bald framework which he covered over almost entirely with mimicries and personalities. The Chevalier Taylor, as he was called (or as he chose to call himself), was again a conspicuous figure, and offered a subject for ridicule. He was known as the " Itinerant Oculist," for, though he had much skill in eye cases, he affected the ways of a charlatan, going about the country making speeches, etc. One of his patients was Gibbon. Odd to say, he himself was to die blind. Johnson said of him that " he was an instance of how far impudence will carry ignorance." One Langford was said to be the original of " The Auctioneer."

In a fit of generosity he claimed to have written the piece to benefit James Worsdale—a sort of half-artist, half-actor, and in social life a licensed droll.

who attended sales. " Auctioneer " may have been used in this sense—that he was a go-between and agent for the amateurs. A fine mezzotint by MacArdell was published of " Mr. Garrick " in the character of an auctioneer, so the impersonation must have obtained some popularity.

This Worsdale must have been a quaint rascal, for, having been colour-grinder to Sir G. Kneller, he set up a claim to be his natural son—an original stroke! He was also supposed to take the credit of theatrical pieces written to his order. His family was not much, but he was an amusing comrade— no doubt this was his claim to Foote's patronage. Worsdale acted Lady Pentweazle, which later became a highly popular and effective character.

But the piece was a failure. Foote was deeply mortified, as is evident from his sneers at the ignorance of his audience. "Juno Lucina, Jupiter Tonans, with other gentlemen and ladies of antiquity, were, I dare to say, utterly unknown to my friends of the gallery; nor do I believe they had many acquaintances in the other parts of the house."

The name of this piece was "Taste," and it was intended to ridicule the craze for buying antiques. Puff, the fashionable auctioneer, is a truly amusing character, and, had he been in "Sherry's" hands, would likely enough have uttered many of his sayings. His foreign jargon is very original. Thus: "I was come to bid for paints for de Elector. Oh, dare are good pieces; but dare is one I like mightily : the off sky and home track is fine, and the maister is in it." "What is the subject?" "Dat I know not. Vat I minds, vat you call the draws and the colours." Noticing a "lillee swelf" (little swelling) on Juno's half-foot, Puff pronounces that it "looks like bad proportion." Still, "Dat is fine ; the maister is in it."

There are many pleasant touches, such as : "Squire Felltree has been, and insists on Miss Rachel's picture being immediately finished and carried home ; as to his wife and children, he says you may take your own time."

Puff asks : " Are the antique seals come home ?" " No, but they will be finished next week." He also asks : " Where is de Hercules' Calf ? Upon my word, 'tis a very large calf—big, big, big all de way up, all de way down. Lord, I believe this Hercules was an Irishman !"

" Here, gentlemen, here's a curiosity—a medal, the only one in the visible world ; there *may* be some underground." Lord —— takes it up. " Fine indeed ! *Will you permit me to taste it ? It has the relish.*"

Granted the topic of a fashionable taste for mutilated antiques, nothing could be more pleasantly or even wittily played with. As I said, we have an anticipatory echo of Sheridan. Play or action there was none. The dealers and their confederates talk over their plans, the victims arrive and talk, and finally the trick is exposed. The cast was wonderfully strong—Palmer, Yates, Cross, Blake, Shuter, Taswell, Worsdale, and Costello—all supplied from his stock company. But it did not go down. Perhaps it was too good, though " the maister is in it."

Foote could not disguise his vexation at the failure of his play. He puts it, as we have seen, on the ignorance of " my very good friends of the gallery." The Latin allusions must have been unknown.

That Foote was witty as well as humorous, that he could delineate strokes of character with the best, there can be no doubt. The personages he introduces never flag ; if he supplies a witty person, he is always witty when the occasion calls, though *everything* that he utters be not witty. We feel that they *could* say it, though they do not. Our moderns know nothing of this reserve. We have in our time *soi-disant* " witty dialogue," as it is called—a number of smart things artificially strung together; but we have no writer who can conceive a really humorous character, independent of written talk. The significant note of the incident was the incipient influence of Foote upon Garrick.

This domination of a pushful young man over another of established reputation is so strange a phenomenon, and opens so much concerning the relations of the pair, that it is worth considering in detail.

CHAPTER VII

FOOTE, GARRICK, AND JOHNSON

LONG and rarely interrupted was to be Foote's connection with this " abridgment of all that was pleasant in man," the brilliant and ever-engaging Garrick. Who could dislike such a being, or annoy him, or libel or ridicule him ? No one, indeed, save those whom he had laid under serious obligation. The elder Dumas once astonished a party by announcing that he had written to a friend to lend him a sum of money, " and, would you believe it," he said, " this man, to whom I have never refused anything, and on whom I have conferred innumerable benefits, *has actually sent the money!*" There was a deep philosophy in this. Garrick never relaxed his kindness to Foote ; his money, his theatre, his service, were always ready. But Foote was an everlasting thorn in his side. This seems unaccountable. Gibes, sneers, abuse, threats of exhibition on the stage, quarrels—such was the return ; but nothing could ruffle or interrupt the prudent Garrick's kindnesses. I say the " prudent," for the manager felt deeply all these attacks ; but he was really in terror of his " friend," and hoped against hope to conciliate him. The astute Foote also knew this fact well, and never abated his animosity. This offers a curious spectacle of human character; for one would imagine that it would have been to his interest to conciliate Garrick, who was so profitable a friend. What, then, could have been his motive? I suppose that a constitutional dislike, and, it must be said, a jealousy of the other's superior success, must have triumphed over his own interest. It was intolerable to him that a being so much his inferior, as he conceived him to be, should enjoy such advantage and live in the "lap of luxury"; while he, a poor struggling fellow, of infinitely greater talent, wit, and general ability, was compelled to use all sorts of shifts to "keep his head above water" and his place in social life. Garrick's assured superiority was not to be shaken; but Foote could at least *disturb* his course, and in their private relations could assert *his* superiority by making his friend tremble before him. And he could also bring him down to his own level by gibes and aspersions. He was "the meanest hound" and "the stingiest of men." All which seems rather ignoble. Still, it may be considered that by his own follies and recklessness he was in miserable straits; that his "trade" was the maligning of everyone, friend or enemy; that his mind was soured and jaundiced; and that, in short, *il faut vivre.* And this was his way of earning his living. It is altogether an extraordinary phenomenon : the undisturbed relations of the two men—intimate friends, yet enemies ; with kindness on one side, abuse on the other ; with benefactions repaid by sneers and calumnies.

It will be noted that all our great and leading performers have been personages of mark off the stage as well as upon it. Garrick, Foote, Kemble, Mrs. Siddons, Kean, Macready, Irving—all these were

6

playing to double audiences : to one before the stage,
to another outside the theatre.   It will be said that
the outside audience is due to the one within, but this
is disproved by the exceptions ; for in the case of
retiring natures the public does not trouble itself
much.   In Foote's case, it is hard to fix on the line
that divided his stage from his common life.   He, in
truth, was appearing on many stages—as a satirist, as
a joker ; now as a manager, now as an actor, now as
a writer ; but everywhere talked of, applauded, or
quarrelled with.   What Mr. Foote thought, said, or
did, was all-important.   We can gather the value
of this importance from the extraordinary impression
left by him on Dr. Johnson.   It is difficult not to
enroll Foote in the list of recognized actors ; it might
almost be said that he worked his way to the front
rank.   This is proved by his steady appearance
during a long course of years at the leading theatres
as a legitimate performer.

Both were quite young men, and nearly of the
same age ; but Garrick was older in his experience,
in his wonderful prudence and restraint—never, in
familiar phrase, "giving himself away."   This the
other was always doing ; though by a sort of jugglery
he contrived to get back what he had given.

The praises of Garrick have been sung by many
admirers and biographers.   His was a fine, high-
souled temper ; he was above meanness, was generous,
forgiving of injuries.   But there were some strange
elements in his character—a curious dread of opponents, a lack of courage in confronting them, a
nervousness, together with a sort of jealousy that
disturbed his repose.   It seems difficult to conceive
of this amiable man being so intimidated by Foote

as to allow respectable players of his own and other theatres to be mimicked and ridiculed on his stage. And by-and-by, when an opening came, we find him, with smiling reluctance and enjoyment, consenting that Foote himself, who had caused him such worry, should in his turn be mimicked and ridiculed. How demoralizing, therefore, was this system, which cankered, as it were, all the honourable traditions of the stage !

The relations of this remarkable pair, both men of exceeding wit and talent, are so interesting and piquant that the spectacle becomes a sort of stage entertainment, which we follow with amusement. It really makes a portion of Foote's life. The society round them watched their contests with daily enjoyment. Both were men of the world, but with different systems—Garrick always cautious and reserved, never " giving away " his interest or " burning his boats "; Foote thinking only of a momentary victory, sparing no one, not even that all-important person, Foote himself; and recklessly sacrificing his interests on the slightest suggestion of advantage. Then would come alternations of good humour and the most intimate friendship, to be succeeded by threatenings and menaces; by money borrowed and returned in a new fit of ill-humour. They were certainly two extraordinary men, but the success on the whole was with Garrick, who was ever amiable, good-tempered, and forgiving. At the close he had the general advantage ; was still popular and admired, while the hapless Foote sank to the bottom, for ever ruined in character and fortune.

Was this treatment of Garrick by Foote—consistent, so to speak, in its inconsistency—mere

waywardness and capriciousness ? or was it deliberate ?
In common life we often meet persons of this temperament, who are subject to fickle " humours "—who are
now pleasant and friendly, and now of a sudden
turn "nasty" and hostile without reason. Such
people are really unstable, "infirm of purpose,"
because they lack self-control. But I am afraid it
looks as though this behaviour of Foote's was a
deliberate and settled policy. He had taken the
measure of the actor's timorousness, and saw that he
could work on it to his interest; and this by showing no such weakness as gratitude or kindness, but
by keeping him " under his thumb," as it were. The
result proved his sagacity, and for a long series of
years he terrorized him to his own profit and interest.

No one knew so well as Garrick the inestimable,
precious value of the astute Talleyrand's maxim :
" Pour jouir de la vie il faut glisser sur beaucoup "—
that is, you are to ignore trifling irritations and disputes ; raise no questions of inferior importance, but
put them aside. In every transaction with Foote we
can see this principle applied ; even when Foote was
coarsely insulting, Garrick smilingly affected to think
it a mere good joke. He was not to be provoked.
Anyone with the firmness and restraint necessary to
carry out this policy will find his way through the
world smooth, and will subject many things and
persons to himself.

The relations between the pair, as I have said,
make up quite a serious portion of Foote's life ; it
even shaped his whole character.

It will be interesting to hear the pleasant, candid,
plain - speaking Tom Davies, Bozzy's introducer
to Johnson—that pleasantest of all known introduc-

tions—on this vendetta. His life of the great actor is
a very agreeable one, written in a clear, limpid style,
and full of information.

"It is almost impossible," he says, "to date the
origin of Foote's settled malevolence to Mr. Garrick;
however, we may venture to say that it did not break
out with any degree of violence till after the Duke
of York had obtained a patent for him of the Haymarket Theatre. They were then rival managers. . . .
Whatever were Mr. Garrick's real thoughts of Foote,
he continually spoke of him as a man of very great
abilities, and the most entertaining companion he
ever knew. He, notwithstanding, could have no
affection for one whom, in his heart, he feared; all
the praises which he bestowed on Foote were, for
that reason, suspicious; they were indeed thrown
away upon him, *for he constantly railed at Mr.
Garrick in all companies. His abilities as an actor,
he questioned, in contradiction to all the world; his
compositions as a writer, he treated with scorn;
virtues, as a member of society, he had none; he was
covetous and tricking; in short, according to his
opinion, he was everything that was mean and unworthy of a gentleman. Neither his family, his friends,
nor acquaintance, were spared by this strange wit, who
ran a-tilt at everybody, and was at the same time
caressed, feared, admired, and hated by all.**

"In the meantime these rival wits would often
meet at the houses of persons of fashion, who were
glad to have two such guests at their table, though

---

* I have put these lines in italics because they seem to me one
of the most singular and unique drawings of a character that we
can conceive of. It is something almost terrible to think of, and
yet is as true as it is admirably delineated.

they certainly should have entertained their friends separately; for Mr. Garrick was a *muta persona* in the presence of Foote—he was all admiration when this genius entertained the company, and no man laughed more heartily at his lively sallies than he did. It must be owned that he tried all methods to conciliate Foote's mind; so far, at least, as to prevail upon him to forbear his illiberal attacks upon him when absent. The more sensibility Mr. Garrick discovered, the greater price the other put upon his ceasing from hostilities. Lord Mansfield was not unwilling to silence such a battery of ridicule as Foote could raise against him, or any man, the greatest and the wisest in the kingdom, and often invited him to his table."

Foote's termagant temper was constantly goaded almost to fury by this jealousy of his friend, inflamed by the spectacle of his constant success and his ever calm restraint. At times, mollified and repentant, he made such amends as he could; but presently there would come a fresh outburst. Here is a typical scene. Garrick has just come in, fresh from one of his noble titled friends, and eager to let drop particulars so as to impress. Now might Foote say to himself: "I will take him down a peg!" And he begins to tell of a new performer whom he had heard that day, and who would eclipse them all! No one came near him. Garrick all the time is on thorns; anything of a new actor worried him visibly. He gave himself away. Foote, after thus torturing him—"twisting the hook in his gizzard," as he put it—bursts into a loud laugh, and tells him that he was only speaking of Mr. Pitt, one of whose great orations he had just heard. Garrick he thus played upon again and again. But what will be said of the actor's weakness in accepting such treatment ?

Foote was never tired, it must be said, of thus torturing him. When a hat went round for contributions, and the collection was very successful: " If Garrick hears of this, he will certainly send us *his* hat !" If he were looking fruitlessly for a guinea which he had dropped : " Where on earth can it have gone to ?" " To the devil, I think," said Garrick. " Let you alone for making a guinea go farther than anyone else," was the reply. When the actor was dining with him, and Mr. Garrick's servants were announced, Foote would say, *sotto voce :* " See that the plate is locked up." This was a joke, but certainly a gross, unmannerly one.

" Garrick lately invited Hurd," said Foote to a friend of Rogers, " to dine with him in the Adelphi, and after dinner they walked up and down. As they passed and repassed the dining-room windows, Garrick was in a perfect agony, for he saw a thief in one of the candles ; and yet Bishop Hurd was of too much consequence to be left, to save his tallow." How characteristic of Foote to furnish this tale, or rather his interpretation of it ! It is impossible that it could have happened. The proprietor of a house where a candle is left to itself in this state may feel a little nervous. But as for " saving his tallow," that was all Foote's invention.

It was the redoubtable Doctor who repeated one truly clever speech of his. " There is a witty, satirical story of Foote," said Johnson. " He had a small bust of Garrick placed upon his bureau. ' You will be surprised,' he said, ' that I allow him to be so near my gold, but you will observe *he has no hands.* ' "

Witty and satirical indeed ! Mr. Forster sees in it " a
tribute of affection and a friendly goodwill," for he
urges that, if Foote disliked Garrick, he would not
have allowed his bust to be so near him. But this is
being a little too "literal."

Once Foote was giving a dinner at which were
young Mr. Lyttelton, a fashionable scapegrace, and
two other gentlemen. Garrick used to tell the story,
beginning always, "For *you must know that Foote
hates me*," said he. The young man began describing
the actor as " so mean " to one of the gentlemen,
who defended Garrick in spirited fashion. The
other then said that it was his father's opinion also.
The discussion became warm, but the host said not a
word. Garrick was deeply wounded. It was easy to
carry off this treatment lightly, as being Foote's
way, and the way he treated everybody. But it
harassed the victim and became a sort of persecution. The amiable Mrs. Garrick, sitting for her
portrait to Reynolds, complained to him that this
ceaseless, unaccountable hatred was embittering their
lives. Reynolds, who had always a low opinion of
Foote, comforted her, and said that he behaved so
because he felt his inferiority, and tried in this way to
put himself on a level. Davies tells us that Garrick
in society shrank from competition with Foote, and
remained silent. " The reason was," said Reynolds,
" that he disdained to compete with one whose style
of talk and wit was vulgar merriment, indecency, and
impiety.

The forbearance and regard shown to Foote by
Garrick was indeed almost a letter of recom-
mendation. But there was one other greater than
Garrick, whose appreciation may be considered a

patent of nobility.   This was Dr. Johnson, that
other " Sam," whose cordial admiration for Foote's
great gifts seemed to be unbounded.   Whenever
Foote was discussed before him, he was prompted to a
sort of outburst of praise, accompanied by a fine
criticism of his versatility and spontaneous power—a
criticism expressed in the happiest phrase.   The
subject had an extraordinary attraction for him, yet, at
the same time, for Foote's character he had nothing
but reprobation.

I confess there is something piquant in this
appreciation, extorted as it were from this great man.
Boswell has furnished many brilliant portraits and
sketches of notable men, but it may be doubted if
there be one drawn with more power and pains both
by Johnson and by his follower than the series of
Foote sketches.   They stand out and linger in the
memory.   In these relations to the sage we have
Foote's whole course and character drawn in a few
rapid strokes.

Thus, at the " Mitre," Boswell found fault with his
practice of turning his visitors and guests into
ridicule.   " It was making fools of his company," he
said.   The sagacious Doctor, always a man of the
world, replied : " Why, sir, when you go to see Foote,
you do not go to see a saint ; you go to see a man
who will be entertained at your house, and then bring
you on a public stage.   Sir, he does not *make* fools of
his company ; they whom he exposes are fools already :
he only brings them into action."   How true and
sensible was this, and how fair to the actor !

And how often did they come back to this topic,
as though it had an absorbing interest for both !
" Foote," said Boswell, " has a great deal of humour."

Johnson agreed. "He has a singular talent of exhibiting character." "Sir," said Johnson, "it is not a talent—it is a vice; it is what others abstain from. It is not comedy, which exhibits the character of a species, as that of a miser gathered from many misers; it is farce, which exhibits individuals." How acute is this criticism, which goes to the very root of dramatic action—mere imitation, as the Doctor put it, being a vice, not a talent.

When Johnson heard of Foote's disastrous ride, Boswell reminded him that this accident would help Foote to mimic George Faulkner more closely; on which the Doctor was prompted to invent a new and grotesque word. "George," he said, "will rejoice at the *depeditation* of Foote." Thus was the actor ever stimulating the wits of the pleasant pair.

Foote must always have dreaded Johnson's sayings at his expense, they were so vigorously telling and so well seasoned by the Doctor's wit. How racy, for instance, was the comment when he was told that Foote "had been kicked in Dublin!" We can speculate what an ordinary man would say: "Serve him right —a good lesson," etc. But Johnson was ever original. He paid him a seeming compliment: "I am glad of it. He is rising in the world. When he was in England, *no one thought it worth while to kick him.*" The best part of this jest was its truth, and the contempt must have hurt more than the kicking. We may indeed wonder how Foote always contrived to escape without chastisement. No doubt the saying was repeated to the wit, and rankled.

During their travels they were constantly talking of Foote. Indignant with a Highland host who had "entertained them meanly," Boswell suggested that he would do for one of Foote's farces, and that "the best way to get it done would be to bring Foote to be entertained at his house." The old Doctor agreed. "*Sir, I wish he had him.* I who have eaten his bread will not give him to him ; but I should be glad if he came honestly by him."

When the Doctor was depreciating the artificial methods of actors, his friend urged that in a room you would respect Betterton far more than Foote. Johnson betrayed his admiration. "Why, sir," was the retort, "if Betterton were to walk into this room with Foote, Foote would soon drive him out of it. Foote, sir, *quatenus* Foote, has powers superior to them all."

This is really excellent. Nothing can be better than his account of the wit when he was exhibiting himself : "Foote being mentioned, Johnson said : ' He is not a good mimic.' One of the company added : ' A merry-andrew, a buffoon.' *Johnson.* But he has wit, too, and is not deficient in ideas or in fertility and variety of imagery, and not empty of reading ; he has knowledge enough to fill up his part. . . . Then, he has a great range for wit ; he never lets truth stand between him and a jest, and he is sometimes mighty coarse. Garrick is under many restraints from which Foote is free. *Wilkes.* Garrick's wit is more like Lord Chesterfield's. *Johnson.* The first time I was in company with Foote was at Fitzherbert's. Having no good opinion of the fellow, I was resolved not to be pleased—and it is very difficult to please a man against his will. I went on eating my dinner pretty sullenly, affecting not to mind him. But the dog was so very comical, that I was obliged to lay down my knife and fork, throw myself back upon my chair, and fairly laugh it out. No, sir, he was irresistible. He

upon one occasion experienced, in an extraordinary
degree, the efficacy of his powers of entertaining.
Amongst the many and various modes which he tried
of getting money, he became a partner with a small-
beer brewer, and he was to have a share of the
profits for procuring customers amongst his numerous
acquaintance.   Fitzherbert was one who took his
small-beer ; but it was so bad that the servants
resolved not to drink it.   They were at some loss
how to notify their resolution, being afraid of offending their master, who they knew liked Foote much as
a companion.   At last they fixed upon a little black
boy, who was rather a favourite, to be their deputy
and deliver their remonstrance ; and having invested
him with the whole authority of the kitchen, he was
to inform Mr. Fitzherbert, in all their names, upon a
certain day, that they would drink Foote's small-beer
no longer.   On that day Foote happened to dine at
Fitzherbert's, and this boy served at table ; he was
so delighted with Foote's stories, and merriment, and
grimace, that when he went downstairs he said: 'This
is the finest man I have ever seen.   I will not deliver
your message.   I will drink his small-beer.'"

Foote took pride in repeating to his friends a
testimonial of Johnson's appreciation : " For loud,
obstreperous, broad-faced mirth, I know not his
equal."   Admirably chosen words these, and Foote
might well be proud.   Who can forget one epigrammatic passage, one of the finest things Johnson ever
said?   In the Hebridean tour he compared Foote and
Garrick, alluding to their habits of mimicry.   " Garrick
is restrained by some principle, but Foote has the
advantage of an unlimited range.   Garrick has some
delicacy of feeling ; it is possible to put him out ;

you may get the better of him. *But Foote is the most incompressible fellow I ever knew ; when you have driven him into a corner, and think you are sure of him, he runs between your legs or jumps over your head, and makes his escape.*" An admirable, vivid, dramatic passage, discriminating, and one which never leaves the memory. Yet another occasion furnished the same phrase in a varied form : " One species of wit he has in an eminent degree—*that of escape.* You drive him into a corner with both hands ; but he is gone, sir, when you think you have got him, like an animal that jumps over your head." It is hard to say which of the two forms is to be preferred, both are so picturesque and witty, and the distinctions made are so acute. And again, on another occasion, he said that, " though he made you laugh, he had the air of a buffoon paid for entertaining the company." He indeed well deserved his hire. " By his fashion of telling a story he subdued avarice and roused stupidity." There is a subtlety in this which might not be understood at first. To unloose purse-strings and win over the miser by tickling his midriff—here was evidence of high powers and charm. Rousing stupidity was even more difficult ; but that he did in the case of the black boy, who would, he swore, drink his small-beer.

Still, the Doctor, as I have said, though appreciating Foote's talent, had but a mean opinion of his moral character. When Foote told him anything, he said he always dismissed it as a shadow. When he was reminded that Foote's aim was only to supply images and pictures, Johnson said roughly " that he was quite impartial, for he tells lies of everybody." He told Mr. Cradock that " when you are in Foote's

company you have no right to look for truth." How
epigrammatic the form, "no right to look for"!

The allusion in Johnson's anecdote to Foote's having
at one time taken to the calling of brewing beer—and
of bad beer, too—suggests the odd shifts to which the
actor was reduced in search of a living.* It is plain
from the story that Foote's friends had to order this
inferior article from the histrionic brewer, who
laughed, and sent them so bad an article that the
servants revolted. As a matter of course, the experiment was but short-lived, and the actor tried his
friends' good nature with something else.

The pleasant "Bozzy," who sympathized with anything that was really humorous, gives a pleasant
sketch of Johnson, Sheridan, and Foote, all in a
group. Here is the way he puts it: "He laughed
heartily when I mentioned to him a saying of his
concerning Mr. Thomas Sheridan, *which Foote took
a wicked pleasure to circulate :* 'Why, sir, Sherry is
dull—naturally dull; but it must have taken him a
great deal of pains to become what we now see him.
Such an excess of stupidity is not in nature. So,' said
he, 'I allowed him all his own merit.'" One cannot help
liking the sketch of Foote going about and retailing
this truly comical speech, *"taking a wicked pleasure"*
—a happy phrase of "Bozzy's"—in doing so. We like

---

* At the last moment I have come upon a passage in the *New Newgate Calendar* which helps to explain matters. Charles Price, better
known as "Old Patch," a notorious swindler, issued an advertisement, inviting persons to contribute £500 to a scheme that was
certain to "secure a large fortune within a very short time." Foote
caught at the bait, which proved to be a brewery, but which failed,
as was described by Johnson. The schemer proposed to him to join
in a bakery, to which the humorist is said to have replied, "No, as you
have brewed, so you may bake ; but I am cursed if ever you bake as
you have brewed."

Johnson " laughing heartily " at his own wit, and we like " Bozzy's " pleasant appreciation of the whole.

Foote's good taste as a critic is shown by a little incident in Murphy's early life, when he was conducting the *Gray's Inn Journal.* He was in the country with Foote, and said he must go to town to arrange the next number of his paper. His friend said : " Why go ? Here is a French magazine with a very pretty little Oriental tale ; translate it and send it up." Murphy did so ; but the story proved to be one translated from the *Rambler.* This led to Murphy's acquaintance with Johnson.

The Doctor had but a poor opinion of his mimicry, and, indeed, of mimicry in general. " ' It is amazing,' said Boswell, ' how a mimic can not only give you the gestures and voice of a person whom he represents, but even what a person would say on any particular subject.' *Johnson.* Why, sir, you are to consider that the manner and some particular phrases of a person do much to impress you with an idea of him, and you are not sure that he would say what the mimic says in his character. *Boswell.* I don't think Foote a good mimic, sir. *Johnson.* No, sir ; his imitations are not like. He gives you something different from himself, but not the character which he means to assume. He goes out of himself, without going into other people. He cannot take off any person unless he is strongly marked, such as George Faulkner. He is like a painter who can draw the portrait of a man who has a wen upon his face, and who therefore is easily known. If a man hops upon one leg, Foote can hop upon one leg. But he has not that nice discrimination which your friend seems to possess. Foote is, however, very entertaining with

a kind of conversation between wit and buffoonery."
This is all accurately and acutely distinguished.
And yet the two men all but came to blows! Foote
longed to ridicule his admirer, while Johnson calmly
checked him by a firm and decided menace. This
situation, however, did not alter their relations ; and,
on the news of Foote's death, the Doctor declared
that " he was a fine fellow."

Boswell tells the story in his usual happy fashion :
" Foote, who so successfully revived the old comedy
by exhibiting living characters, had resolved to
imitate Johnson on the stage, expecting great
profits from his ridicule of so celebrated a man.
Johnson being informed of his intention, and being
at dinner at Mr. Thomas Davies's the bookseller,
from whom I had the story, he asked Mr. Davies
'what was the common price of an oak stick'; and
being answered sixpence, ' Why then, sir,' said he,
' give me leave to send your servant to purchase me
a shilling one. I'll have a double quantity." Who
will not respect the sturdy, gallant old fellow ?

Johnson's utterances on the subject of Foote
show how deeply, in its various capacities, Foote's
character and abilities had impressed him. In the
case of no other does he expend so much critical
refinement, so lively and ever willing a spirit of dis-
quisition, as he does in that of this singular man.
The whole forms a very accurate and telling delineation of Foote done by a masterly and sympathetic
hand. And yet behind all there is a good-natured
indulgence. He really admired the man; we seem
to be looking at one of Zoffany's spirited and vividly
coloured portraits, such as hang in the Garrick Club.
They form, as it were, the true official recognition of

Foote's general talent, which has certainly received a fair measure of appreciation from his contemporaries; but none of these have the value of his deliberate judgment delivered by one of the great critics of his time.   It is, perhaps, a unique specimen, for the sage has not spoken with such deliberate pains or sympathy of Garrick or Goldsmith or any of his other contemporaries.

When Foote went to Paris, where he often found himself, he was always in the best company.   Once it chanced that, while he was there in 1775, Dr. Johnson arrived.   Foote used to give amusing descriptions of his odd figure, dress, etc., which he says perfectly astonished the French—the old brown coat, plain shirt, etc.   He described him as inveighing against actors, French or others, likening them all to " dancing dogs."   " But you will allow, sir, that some are better than others ?"   " Yes, as some dogs dance better than others."   Angelo, that vivacious fencing-master, when on a visit to Paris, met Foote, who was figuring away in the best theatrical set, giving dinners to Préville at his hotel in the Rue Colombier.   For this artist he exhibited his imitations of Garrick and others.   Préville enjoyed these portraits, and in his turn gave the French players.   As all were laughing heartily at the Garrick mimicry, he turned to the young Angelo, and said : " If you go home and tell Garrick, you young dog ! I'll have you broke on the wheel."

Foote was no " family man," but we rarely find in the chronicles of literary characters so complete an obliteration of all the domestic feelings and associations.   It may have been that his family cast him off, but, whatever be the reason, we hear nothing of the

7

worthy old Cornish squire and his family all through
the son's erratic and even meteoric course.

His father and mother lived to see his prosperity,
though their own, in spite of luck, appeared to
have decayed. In fact, we hear odd tales of his
mother in London suffering from debt and other
privations : but we do not hear of the father, who
was alive at the time. She is described as having
written to him from a debtors' prison, begging assistance : " DEAR SAM,—I am in prison. Come and see
me and help me," etc. To which he replied : " DEAR
MOTHER,—So am I, which prevents his duty being paid
to his loving mother by her affectionate son, SAM
FOOTE." There can be little doubt of the truth of this
incident. He could not resist the jest, which is quite
in keeping with his character. But he wished merely
to give her a fright, just as Tony Lumpkin drove his
mother round and round her garden. For he adds a
" P.S.," telling her that he is sending his attorney to
help her, and adds seriously : " In the mean time, let
us hope for better days." This is, I think, inconsistent
with a manufactured story.

It seems impossible to explain this complete
collapse of a well-to-do county family which had
inherited a fortune. But one might reasonably
suspect that the dissolute Foote had somehow contrived to get control of the estates, which may account
for the story of three fortunes coming to him. He
was so rough and powerful that his family were not
likely to have resisted his masterful pressure. Incompressible himself, he could fatally compress
others.

Foote had a brother who, to make the family
party completely grotesque, adopted the clerical

profession, which he cannot be said to have adorned
or followed.　He seems to have had the full irregu-
larity of his brother without any of his talent;
" *a humdrum*, quiet kind of man," Cooke describes
him, who went through life " mostly unbeneficed in
his profession "—a happy turn.　This contrast between
the brothers must have been amusing to lookers-on.
Foote had to support him, allowing him £60 a
year—somewhat irregularly paid, we may suspect.
He good-naturedly gave him " the run of his theatre,"
where this odd parson was always to be seen gossip-
ing in the green-room and " fussing " about.　One
night the Duke of Cumberland asked his name:
" Who is that little fellow in the shabby plush coat ?"
" Oh, that's my barber," said Foote.　But the Duke
found out later that it was his brother, and taxed the
actor with the deception, which Foote put off with a
humorous excuse.

Here arises a question which has never been clearly
resolved, and for which evidence is curiously lacking.
In the case of most literary men, it is known for
certain that they had been either married or un-
married ; but it is characteristic of this erratic being
that he should have contrived to leave the matter
quite uncertain.　It would seem that this was the
most convenient arrangement for him.　In the
official books there is no trace of a wife or her name-
connections.　Mr. Forster declares positively that
Foote was never married ; yet it is all but certain
that he was.　For anyone who has gone carefully
through his life must arrive at the conclusion that he
was married.　His friend, "co-drinker," and biographer,
assumes the fact as a certainty, and relates various
anecdotes about the much-tried lady.　Had he had any

doubt, he would certainly have questioned his friend upon the point, and his friend would have readily furnished a comic account of the lady. A reckless young fellow such as Foote was, who had tried everything in life that brought excitement, and had not omitted taking any foolish step that could be committed, was not likely to omit that of an improvident marriage.

We may take it as a certainty that he found some girl whom he fancied, married her, and then became repentant of his folly. For this folly he was to punish her, as though it were her own fault, by prompt neglect and dismissal. This was Foote's way in most things.

This poor lady must have had a weary time of it with her too exuberant husband. She is described as being mild and tolerant, and gently accepting her treatment. He was fond of making her the butt of his broad humour. His biographer is even minutely particular in his statement. "He married early in life," he says, " a lady in Worcestershire, a choice that met with the approbation of his family. They had no children, and she died early." He then gives a rather ghostly story, which Foote was fond of rehearsing, how on their wedding tour, at Truro, they one night heard a concert of music, which they fancied was some sort of charivari in compliment to their arrival, but were assured that no one knew anything of the matter or had heard the music. Foote went on to relate—and he told the tale often—that he had marked down the day and hour, and found later that it was the day and hour of his uncle's murder. No doubt an hallucination of some sort, but it will be noted how Foote's wife figures in the matter. If we accept the dates, the young man must have been very precipitate in his marriage, as indeed we might have expected. Not unlikely is it that the lady may have brought him the money which he was so lavishly squandering in making a figure in town.

"This lady," Cooke tells us, "was kept so much in the background by the gay, licentious, eccentric life of her husband, that little is known of her history, except that she was the very reverse of him. Mildness and forbearance seemed to be the leading features of her character; and these qualities could serve as no lasting checks upon a man of his temper. . . .

"Dr. Nash of Worcester, being in town one spring not long after Foote's marriage, intended to pay his old fellow-collegian a visit, but was much surprised at hearing that he was in the Fleet Prison. Thither he hastened directly, and found him in a dirty two-pair-of-stairs back-room, with furniture every way suitable to such an apartment. The doctor began to condole with him, when Foote cut him short by turning the whole into raillery: 'Why, is not this better,' said he, 'than the gout, the fever, the smallpox, and

"The thousand various ills
That flesh is heir to"?

'This is a mere temporary confinement, without pain, and not very uncongenial (let me tell you) to this sharp biting weather.' . . .

"Laughing on in this manner, the doctor perceived something stir behind him in the bed, upon which he got up, and said he would call another time. 'No, no,' said the other; "sit down: 'tis nothing but *my Foote*.' 'Your foot!' said the doctor; 'well, I want no apologies—I shall call another time.' 'I tell you

again, it is my Foote,' and then, going over to the
bed, revealed the poor shrinking lady."

At last he tired of her and dismissed her. The
unhappy wife of the great and popular wit was
thrown upon her own resources. Friends now remonstrated, and at last induced him to receive her again.
An inferior Irish player named Costello, one of
Foote's " laughing junto," was accordingly despatched
to bring her to Blackheath, and this fellow, who was
driving, contrived to overset the vehicle, and the
poor lady's face was much injured and disfigured by
the accident.

There was to have been a sort of dinner to celebrate
her return, at which Murphy assisted. On his arrival
he asked, " Had the lady arrived?" when Foote
broke out into one of his coarse jests. " You will
find her in the drawing-room, and, if you like, can
study geography in her face, which is now a regular
map. You can see the Blue Mountains, the Black
Forest, and the Red Sea, and also," touching his
forehead, " the Scilly Islands." It was idle to look
for good taste or self-respect from this irrepressible
jester.

One of Foote's smaller satellites in his coterie was
Arthur Murphy, a clever Irish adventurer, who
worked his way to importance by a threatening use
of his pen, intimidating when he could not convince
or attract. Garrick was to experience his harassing
persecution. He was a sort of theatrical free-lance,
a man of great and various abilities, critic, dramatist,
wit to a certain extent, a pleasant convivial companion. His comedies have high merit from their
genuine spirit and vivacious characters. But, like
Foote, he was an adventurer, and constantly " in hot

water," always prompt to resent fancied or real
grievances. Miss Burney gives a pleasing sketch of
him in her agreeable " Diary." When he was touched
or offended he became a bitter foe, as Garrick found
to his cost in their dispute about the authorship of
" The Clandestine Marriage." The literary society
of the time owed a great deal of its dramatic spirit
and animation to pleasant Irishmen, who by their
talents, alternate good-humour and quarrels, increased
the public stock of harmless pleasure. Without such
a figure as Goldsmith, with his amiability and naïveté,
Burke, Murphy, and others, Boswell's incomparable
work would have lost much of its attraction.*

Courage in dealing with persons of Foote's type,
who assail and ridicule unoffending persons, is the
surest protection. The trading satirist has to rely
on bullying methods, and tries to " carry it off " by
intimidation. But Foote was occasionally to be
confronted with calm, resolute men, who pressed him
into a corner; then his methods forsook him, and he
became reasonable. He was several times in this
mortifying situation, but on the whole he escaped
with comparative impunity. His most signal defeat
was at the hands of Dr. Johnson, an awkward
customer to tackle. But Johnson knew his man,
and—quite an unusual thing in the case of such
victims, with whom Foote took French leave (that
is, no leave at all)—Johnson's sanction had to be
obtained.

* Murphy contended that he was present at Boswell's introduction to Johnson in Davies's bookshop. Boswell proves clearly
by his account that this could not have been the case. The
mistake is characteristic of the imaginative cast of Murphy's
countrymen, which often thus confuses different seasons and
localities.

Murphy was seven years at St. Omer's Catholic college, a circumstance which did not escape Churchill in his scathing lines. Though he died a Commissioner of Bankrupts, both Gray's Inn and the Temple declined to receive him, on the ground of his having been on the stage. Lincoln's Inn showed him more liberality. He wrote some thirty pieces for the theatre. Adventurer as he was, he was exceedingly clever and decorous. In Miss Burney's " Diaries," as I have said, he is shown forth as a good-natured, important, and rather stately personage. He died in 1805, when seventy-five years old. Foote had his quarrels with Murphy ; they seemed to be allies and enemies alternately ; but Foote never forgot his interest and profit, and never pushed a quarrel beyond the possibility of reconciliation.

Churchill seems to have loathed him, and to have been possessed with a peculiar rancour against him. He describes him as one " Whom dulness only kept from being mad." He went on :

> " What though the sons of nonsense hail him sire,
> Auditor, Author, Manager, and Squire . . .
> When motionless he stands, we all approve ;
> What pity 'tis *the Thing was made to move !*

> " The hopeful youth a Jesuit might have made,
> Bred at St. Omer's to the shuffling trade ;
> With various readings stored his empty skull,
> Learn'd without sense and venerably dull,
> His name had stood in City annals fair,
> *And prudent Dulness marked him for a Mayor.*"

He then asks :

> " What then could tempt thee in a critic age
> Such blooming hopes to forfeit to the stage ?
> Could it be worth thy wondrous waste of pains
> *To publish to the world thy lack of brains ?*

"Or might not Reason e'en to thee have shown
Thy greatest praise had been to live unknown?
Yet, let not vanity like thine despair:
Fortune makes Folly her peculiar care."

These insulting taunts must have rankled, and
what a sensation they must have caused! We have
only to think of someone addressing such personalities
to a popular actor of our day. A cry would rise up
from end to end of the kingdom, followed by a
police-court case, or an action for swinging damages,
or both.

Foote, after his return, thought he could turn his
foreign experiences to profit. With his usual keen-
ness, he had taken note of the ridiculous behaviour
of his country-folk in France, and their absurd
attempts at aping foreign ways and habits. The
piece was a sort of farce, called "The Englishman
in Paris," and was, indeed, a well-cropped acreage
of absurdities. It must be said that he treated it
with a boisterous humour and gaiety. Later, he
good-naturedly made it a present to his old friend
Macklin, and "wrote up" the female character for
Macklin's daughter. It is likely that he offered the
piece to Garrick, but, as it happened, it was produced
at Covent Garden on March 17, 1753, with great
success. We can almost follow Garrick's nervous
caprices and changes by watching the bills, for after
a few months we find the new play and its author at
Drury Lane. He may have fancied, perhaps, that
he had lost a good thing.

Foote himself, when at Drury Lane, took the
character of Buck on October 20, and induced his
friend Garrick to supply a special prologue of a
personal and familiar character, setting out various

adventures, or rumours of adventures, which had
befallen Foote in Paris. These familiarities read
strangely now, but the audiences then relished hearing such details about their favourites.

It is astonishing to see how Garrick obsequiously
attended on his wishes. The return of this *vaurien*
he thought should be celebrated. He was ever
ready to write for him one of his welcoming prologues, and even to speak it. Before now he had
written another for one of his friend's pieces; when
Foote, with his usual coolness, came forward and
spoke these lines about himself:

> " *Sir Peter Primrose*, smirking o'er his tea,
> Sinks, from himself and politics, to me.
> ' Paper! boy.'—' Here, sir, I am.'—' What news to-day ?'
> ' Foote, sir, is advertised.'—' What! run away ?' "

It goes on:

> " ' No, sir; he acts this week at Drury Lane.'
> ' How's that ?' (cries feeble *Grub*) : ' Foote come again ?
> *I thought that fool had done his devil's dance :*
> *Was he not hang'd some months ago in France ?'*

> " Upstarts *Mac-bone*, and thus the room harangued :
> ' 'Tis true, his friends gave out that he was hang'd ;
> But, to be sure, 'twas all a hum ; because
> I've seen him since ; and after that disgrace,
> No *Jontleman* would dare to show his face.' "

> " To him replied a sneering bonny Scot :
> ' You reason right, my friend ; hang'd he was not ;
> But neither you nor I can tell *how soon* he'll gang to pot.' "

This is surely undignified. We cannot but wonder
at Foote's delivering such speeches all at his own
expense.

Murphy, noting the success of this piece, which
offered a fine opportunity for Foote's mimicries, wrote

a sequel, which was to be called "The Englishman
Returned from Paris," and in his effusive confidence
entrusted his friend with the details of his plan, the
plot, characters, etc.   The wily Foote listened and
noted, and with all speed worked these very materials
into a piece of his own with the same title, which
he at once brought out at Covent Garden, to the
amazement and indignation of his friend !

This piece of sharp practice—or bad faith, as some
might call it—was largely characteristic of Foote—it
belonged to his methods ; and yet on this occasion
he was not as lawless as usual, and something could
be said for him.   The original idea and the original
piece were his own, and he might fairly claim the
exclusive right of adding a second part.   Murphy
was a trespasser, and was stung to fury at what
he considered a treacherous breach of faith.   A
violent quarrel followed.   Foote's sequel was successful, Murphy's—who had so foolishly hesitated in
preparing his version—a failure.   Infuriated by these
misfortunes, he wrote a sort of farce called "The
Spouter," into which he introduced Foote, Garrick,
and some others who had injured him ; treating
them with the coarsest ridicule.

Rancorous as were now these enemies, and irreconcilable, we find them in a short time on the
best of terms and joined in management.   Murphy
always followed Foote's tactics in the case of Garrick,
worrying and harassing him till he cried for quarter.
A slight dispute with Garrick as to the authorship
of a character he worked up into an almost ferocious
encounter.   By-and-by, after many of these tussles,
the asperities were worn away, and we find Murphy
enjoying the society of Johnson and the Thrales—

looked up to with respect, and apparently become a moderate, placid man.

It can hardly be said that gratitude was one of Foote's assets. Macklin, his old patron, now retiring from the stage, on which he had lived in constant turmoil, was taking farewell benefits, etc., and announcing a strange scheme of a tavern in Covent Garden with which was to be combined a lecture-hall, where he would instruct the public in the oratorical art and other subjects. His idea was that the lecture would induce the hearers to repair to the tavern and restore their strength with dinner and drink. Foote, as was to be expected, ridiculed the old actor, and went about—and heartily enjoyed going about—prophesying that he would not keep to his engagement of retiring, and would, further, be made bankrupt by the tavern—in both of which prognostics he proved to be right. The strange thing was that he found such relish in poor old Macklin's scheme that he began a sort of persistent persecution. Accordingly, when the actor had started his show and begun his lectures, his old friend stood at the bottom of the hall making ridiculous remarks, interrupting and putting awkward questions, to the infinite annoyance of the lecturer, who, out of patience, would say, "Sir, do you understand what you are talking about?" "No, sir, *do you?*" was the retort.

Once, Macklin was expatiating on the memory, and the methods of strengthening it by repeating strings of words, when his persecutor is said to have written down a grotesque passage which he gravely challenged the lecturer to get by heart on the spot. This was the famous "nonsense" speech :

" So she went into the garden to cut a cabbage-leaf

to make an apple-pie, and, at the same time, a great
she-bear, coming up the street, pops its head into
the shop. ' What, no soap ?' So he died, and she
very imprudently married the barber ; and there
were present the Picninnies and the Joblillies and
Garolillies and the Grand Panjamdrum * himself,
with the little round button at top, and they all fell
to playing the game of Catch-as-catch-can till the
gunpowder ran out at the heels of their boots." †

It was much praised as a piece of Gilbertian
nonsense, but I confess one can scarcely join in
Mr. Forster's extreme admiration.   It is grotesque,
no doubt, but it has always seemed to be rather

---

* With the use of the word Panjamdrum as personifying
some lofty or magnificent person I lately found myself connected in
a rather curious way.   Sir J. Murray, the gifted editor of the great
English Dictionary, was treating the word with illustrations, etc.,
when it was found that I—humble I !—had used it in the year 1860,
and it would seem this had been the earliest instance of its use as
a description.   This I was inclined to doubt, and search was made
for the book in which it appeared.   I could, however, give no aid,
as, after so many years, my mind was naturally a perfect blank on
the matter.   So it was duly registered in the dictionary in this
general way : " Great Panjamdrum—*Fitzgerald.*"   A year or two
later the place occurred to me, but it was then too late to amend.
" But what Fitzgerald ?" future readers will ask.

† This is not altogether so incoherent as it affects to be.   The
Irish wit and orator, Curran, once made use of it to set down a
foolish man who was chatting in confused fashion with " dull "
incongruous stories.   He got into " a bog " in the middle of one of
his stories : " And so and so—no—and so, it being dark—Sir John
said—no, the cook said——"   " Stop, sir !" roared Curran ; " I
will finish your story for you.   *So*—they wanted a rush-light ! and
—so—the great *she*-bear was walking about the town—so—he
popped his head into the barber's shop, and said : ' What ! *no soap ?*'
So—he died—*she* married the barber—the powder blew out of
their shoes, etc."

a manufactured jest and lacking in spontaneousness. There are some other natural specimens of
incongruity which are more telling. The grave
nonsense of " Alice in Wonderland " has never been
surpassed for its all but convincing absurdity. No one
ever can help smiling, even after endless repetitions, at
the Judge's rebuke : " Prisoner, you have had a good
education and been brought up by pious parents,
instead of which you go about stealing ducks " (or
some form to that effect).

This bit of grotesque seems to have made its first
appearance in print in 1825, in Miss Edgeworth's
story " Harry and Lucy," and she names Foote
as its author. The story, however, is not mentioned
in either Foote's or Macklin's memoirs. It has been
also attributed to Quin the actor, who is said to have
devised it to provoke Foote.* This egregious piece
of nonsense has appealed even to classical scholars,
and we have versions in Latin and Greek. Thus in
the former—viz., " Tweed of Oriel "—of which here
are some telling lines :

> " Jamque aderat studio ludorum accensa juventus
> Jobiliana cohors, Garanini æqua catervœ.
> Impubesque manus Picaninnia quos super omnes
> Panjamdri regale decus, etc.

Foote, with all his smartness, could not have
improvised an elaborate composition of this kind.
It was too good for that. But is it not likely that
all this was a confederacy ?—for a droll scene
occurred in the piazza of Covent Garden, that
elegant structure of Inigo Jones, half of which

---

* There is an Irish version also, slightly varied. See " Book of
Quotations," by W. Gurney Benham, p. 449.

was pulled down many years ago.   The actors were
fond of using it as a promenade before dining at
the Bedford or other coffee-houses.   Here Foote
and Macklin used to meet, each with a party of
friends, passing and repassing.   Foote was all the time
railing at Macklin, ridiculing him to his own party in
a loud voice.   Macklin retorted, to *his* friends, and the
encounter was pursued for some time with contending
animosity.   Finally the actors went off to dinner,
leaving the two leaders behind, when, to the surprise
of Murphy, who witnessed the scene, both advanced,
and, on Foote's proposal, went off to a tavern to dine !
Murphy told this story to Taylor the journalist, and
it shows how little such apparent quarrels in the
profession are to be taken seriously, especially where
mutual interest depends on harmonious relations.

CHAPTER VIII

TATE WILKINSON

To an eccentric yet interesting being we owe some
of the most important details of Foote's life and
character.   There is such a dearth of authentic
and intimate information concerning him that we
must welcome this history with something like
gratitude.   Tate Wilkinson's career was all through
associated with that of Foote : he was his pupil
and a sort of henchman and satellite ; he was his
devoted friend at times, and often his enemy.   He
lived with him, travelled with him, was one of his
company, affected to be his rival, at times hearing
the welcome cry, " Foote outdone !"   He knew
him thoroughly, and no one has more skilfully
depicted that strange character, a compound of
talent, meanness, jealousy, bluster, tolerance, and
good-nature.

The form in which this record* is set forth is
unique and original.   No other book can be compared to it for form or matter.   Too much praise
cannot be given to its natural vivacity, or to the
amusing scenes it sets forth—above all, to its ad-

* " Memoirs of his own Life," 4 vols., York, 1790 ; " The
Wandering Patentee, or History of the Yorkshire Theatres ;" and
" The Actor's Tablet," 1795.

112

mirable delineations of character, which are almost convincing. The dialogues, incidents, all are *sui generis*
and most amusing. But what shall be said of the
style, the English—so rude, full of strange incoherent
utterances, yet not unpicturesque? There are sentences without formal beginning or end. Yet the
whole effect is not bad, but persuasive and interesting,
often eloquent. Foote, however, is the hero; we see
him here as we see him nowhere else. We hear him
talk and jest in his rough style. The situations in
which he is made to figure are really diverting, and
told with infinite spirit. At the same time, it may
be admitted that there is an amount of colouring
which must be allowed for. For this Wilkinson was
a small-minded creature, envious, jealous, mean, and
even revengeful; and his accounts often reflect these
unpleasant feelings. But it is easy to separate these
clouding elements; and he remains always an acute
observer.

How strange, then, that the one modern critic,
an admirable and well-schooled writer of the old
pattern, who has attempted a serious, deliberate
sketch of Foote's life, should have so completely set
aside these valuable contemporary memoirs, dis-
daining to use them in any fashion! "They are
worthless," he used to say to me. He did not
think it was even necessary to show that they were
worthless. Like Podsnap, in his friend's story—
drawn, it is said, from this model—"he waved it
out of existence." Now, I have gone over all the
statements and details carefully, and found them
wonderfully correct. If the whole be a fiction, Wilkinson becomes a genius of high mark, from his
capacity of devising or inventing all these comedy

8

scenes, dialogues, and strokes of character, the mere
reading of which convinces us of their truth.

Next to Foote the figure of Garrick stands out.
We have a perfect picture of his various qualities,
drawn admirably. His good-nature, easy conquest
by flattery, apparent stinginess in trifles,* generosity
in great matters, are all set out with much acuteness.
The scene of his visit to Portsmouth is described
delightfully, and leaves a pleasing picture of the
great man's condescension to the poor strolling
actor with whom, arm in arm, he walked about in
town.

As these scenes display Foote's character and
methods in a most dramatic fashion, and carry
forward the details of his life, I shall lay them before
the reader at length in the very words of the chronicler.

Wilkinson obtained an introduction to the great
man Garrick, and was invited to wait on him at South-
ampton Street to display such gifts as he had. He
was allowed to give some of his impudent mimicries,
and, knowing the manager's weakness, adroitly
introduced one of Foote, which caused the great
actor's brilliant eyes to flash with enjoyment.
Wilkinson was treated with much favour and
bidden to call again. When he presented himself,

* Take, for instance, that capital trait at Portsmouth when he
admired a roquelaure of Wilkinson's, and asked him to order him
one like it; then, his slight testiness and annoyance when
reminded of the debt. Another characteristic trait at a Drury
Lane rehearsal was his surprisingly coarse and indescribable
criticism of Tate's acting, intended as a stroke of humour, and
as such circulated in the theatre as a bon-mot, even the ladies slily
enjoying it. This adroit form of flattery was known to be pleasing
to the great man. That the incident is true, no one who reads it
can doubt.

"Mr. Garrick said, 'Young gentleman, I have seen Mr. Lacey, and we have determined to put you on the books at thirty shillings per week the ensuing season. . . . As I am on the wing, do oblige me with a repetition of what you recited last Saturday.' I readily complied, and executed it with spirit. From the imitation of Foote I proceeded with great alacrity to several others ; and when I came to those of Mr. Barry and Mrs. Woffington, as Macbeth and Lady Macbeth, I was obliged to stop, he seemed so truly entertained. I thought it very comical, and, that the joke might not be lost, I laughed too ; but on the merriment ceasing, I perceived a concealed third laugher—the Lady Teazle behind the screen, which greatly puzzled me ; when on a sudden a green cloth double door flew open, which I found led to a little breakfast parlour, and discovered a most elegant lady—no less a personage than Mrs. Garrick, who had, it seems, been purposely posted there for her secret opinion of my imitations of Foote. . . .

"Mrs. Garrick apologized for her rudeness and intrusion—confessed she had taken possession of that snug spot unobserved, at the desire of Mr. Garrick, as, from his account of my imitations on the Saturday, she expected to be much gratified ; but when she heard the tones of Mrs. Woffington, the ridicule was so strongly pointed that it was not in her power to refrain from laughter, by the pleasure and great satisfaction she had received. If it had happened otherwise, Mrs. Mouse would not have appeared, but kept snug in her hole."

He was thereafter regularly installed at the theatre, and tells us what followed : "The last week of Mr.

Foote's playing in Drury Lane, previous to his intended trip to Ireland, he was accidentally with Garrick, after his performance of Kitely, as was Mr. Holland and others. The conversation by chance turned on imitation. Garrick said, 'Egad, Foote! there is a young fellow engaged with me who I really think is superior to either of us at mimicry. I used to think myself well at it, but I actually give him the preference. He has tried to resemble me, but that will not do; though Mrs. Garrick says she is sure he will be like me.' 'Damn it!' says Foote, 'I should like to hear him.' Holland, with Garrick's approbation, came immediately to inquire for me. I was soon found in the green-room, and escorted to the manager's cabinet, he assuring me that Mr. Garrick wanted to see me on particular business. My heart panted with fear, doubt, and hope, on this unexpected summons; after an awkward entrance and a silence of a few minutes, my suspense was eased by Mr. Garrick very good-naturedly saying that he had spoke well of me to Mr. Foote, and desired I would satisfy that gentleman with a taste of my quality, such as first struck my fancy; adding that he expected I would do my best in order to convince his *good* friend, Mr. Foote, that his assertions of my merit were not exaggerated. I complied, and (as the phrase is) *took off* several performers—Barry, Sparks, Woffington, Ridout, Sheridan, etc.—received high encomiums and thanks, made my bow, and retired from the august assembly. . . .

" The next day a friend who was intimate with Foote waited on me with that gentleman's compliments, intimating that he was going to Dublin for a few weeks in five or six days' time. He had

observed Mr. Garrick thought me only fit for his
Hobby Horse in the Rehearsal, and if I wished to be
released from such tyranny, he would be glad of my
company to Ireland at his own expense, and he
would fix me on genteel terms with Mr. Sheridan
—that I should appear in Othello, and he would act
Iago.   This was a cheering cordial elixir to my
drooping spirits, and to my still more drooping
pocket."

Nothing could suit Foote better ; the young man
was exactly what he wanted.   The arrangement was
duly made, and the curiously assorted pair started
together for Dublin.

The old system of stage touring, when the actor
set forth on a toilsome journey for a short engagement
in the North or South, was a useful and amusing
form of discipline.   He was thrown on his own
resources and among strangers—hostile or jealous
comrades—and had to exert all his energies.   Some
of these peripatetics developed great spirit and gifts.
The provincial managers were rare folk, often highly
eccentric, such as Wilkinson later at York, and
Mrs. Baker on the Kent " circuit."   From this lady,
Boz, who had read the old memoirs, very likely
adapted the worthy, mirth-moving Mrs. Crummles.*

The success of the venture depended a good deal
on personal character.   Foote—one of the social
" hustlers," as the Americans have it—wherever he
went was likely to carry all before him, and to engross
all attention as the central figure.   His obstreperous
voice, bustling, overpowering ways, and roguh jokes,
were irresistible.   On his various tours, notably to

* The reader of Dibdin's and Charles Mathews's memoirs will
find her portrait well drawn.

Dublin, he made large sums, besides being joyously entertained ; and he was now making a descent on that jovial capital.

To any diligent reader of the old memoirs dealing with the eighteenth century, nothing seems so surprising as the comparative ease and frequency with which long journeys were accomplished. People seemed to think little of starting for Paris or Dublin or Edinburgh, and endured the fatigue and discomforts of the coach or chaise as a matter of course. Actors particularly seemed to be continually on the road. The journey to Paris could be made in about three days, and those to Dublin and Edinburgh in about the same time. The cost must have been serious. We can imagine the discomfort of forty hours in a coach or chaise. But, really, it might be said that people set off then with the same carelessness as they do now on a railway journey, and thought as little of the business.

Tate now proceeds to recount their adventures on the road : " I met Mr. Foote at the Bedford Arms, and in one hour after set off with him in a post-chaise, and his servant on horseback. We only travelled that night to his little cottage at Elstree, in Hertfordshire. . . .* On the following day we went with Captain Bonfoy for Park Gate, as the Captain said he would sail that afternoon. Here we were detained with several persons of fashion, who had been impatiently attending on the caprice of the wind —Mr. Hill, an elderly gentleman, Lord Macartney, Mr. Leeson, now Lord Milltown, and several others. We all went on board, but all returned as the wind

---

* Could this have been the scene of the later notorious murder of Weare by Thurtell ?

continued obstinate. We all messed together; for Foote's company, as he was well acquainted with each, was the only treat that truly dreary place Park Gate could afford. Our patience being exhausted, it was unanimously agreed that we should proceed to Holyhead. Horses were hired; this was early in November, and was not pleasing. . . . I thought we were all to have set off together; they went at seven o'clock in the morning, requesting Foote's company at each house they stopped at; but Foote and myself remained behind, and on my asking him the reason of his delay, he answered that it was a rule of his, and worth my observation—that whenever he met with persons of distinction and fortune on the road, travelling to small inns (as was, and is, the case on the Welsh roads), he made it a rule always to be half a day behind or before them, as, with all their politeness, they expected the best accommodations, or, if they were so kind as to offer you a preference, you could not in policy or good manners accept such an offer. . . .

" And at nine at night, all dark and dismal, did we roll in the boat belonging to the pacquet, over waves most dreary to behold; for the whiteness of the breakers shone double from the darkness of the night. When handed into the pacquet, I asked for a bed; but they were all secured, not even one for Mr. Foote, as plenty of cash from the great people had made that request impossible to be complied with. The cabin was wedged like the Black Hole at Calcutta. The tumultuous moving of the ship soon made my inquiries after a bed of down quite needless. . . . The storm increased, but the wind was fair for Ireland; as to death, I was so truly sick that I was very indifferent whether I sunk or swam. Mr. Foote was tolerably well, and walking most of the night from place to place.

"Thank God, we arrived safe in Dublin Bay about twelve o'clock, and by one were taken in a Dunlarey hoy to Dublin Quay. A coach conveyed us to a tavern in College Green, where we were regaled— I say we, though I continued very sick and much out of order. . . . In about an hour Mr. Foote went to the lodgings provided for him, and left me to take care of myself. I inquired for a hotel, and was directed to one on Essex Quay, to which place I took coach ; where, overpowered with illness, sickness, and fatigue, I went to bed and lay till Monday noon."

Here the youth fell seriously ill of a fever, and lay for some weeks in a precarious way. Some Dublin friends, however, found him out and took care of him. But he complains bitterly that he was completely forgotten and abandoned by his principal.

Foote's behaviour to this certainly unhappy youth whom he had brought over in his train does seem unfeeling and heartless. Still, he had heard that the young man was suffering from a dangerous fever, and no doubt thought that he must give up all hope of reaping any benefit from his services, or was in dread of the contagious disease. Wilkinson was deeply indignant at this neglect.

But from his rather prejudiced account it is clear that the actor's behaviour was really more thoughtless and careless than unkind. He came at once when he was sent for, and then showed himself inclined to look after his protégé. In his position as a star actor, much sought after, he had little time to be hunting through Dublin for a follower. "Will you believe it," Tate tells us, "that all this time of my severe suffering, notwithstanding Mr. Foote must have heard I had left the hotel and tavern with evident marks of indisposition, he never once (to the disgrace of Christianity be it asserted) made inquiry whether I was living or dead; or if living, whether I had decent necessaries. . . .

"Before I was able to go abroad, or even to leave my apartment, I sent my compliments to Mr. Foote, to acquaint him where I was; for Mr. and Mrs. Chaigneau were so offended at such brutality of behaviour towards me, that neither of them had given him any intelligence concerning me. Mr. Foote, by way of apology, said he could not see me for three or four days for fear of catching the infection from the fever; professed himself anxious to supply my wants, which he was informed was at that time quite unnecessary. After that he waited on me as my most *anxious* friend, and in about three weeks I recovered."

Sheridan was then the manager at Crow Street.

"It was appointed for me to appear the Monday following in Mr. Foote's 'Tea,' in the character of a pupil under Mr. Puzzle, the supposed director of a rehearsal; Mr. Puzzle by Mr. Foote. It was agreed that I should appear as Mr. Wilkinson (his pupil) when called upon, and repeat just what I could select to please myself—not any regular character. When the night came, Lord Forbes, Mr. Chaigneau, and all my friends, went to encourage and support me, and engaged all they knew for the same purpose. One lucky circumstance was, my not being known as a performer; therefore I had their wishes and pity in a high degree—but great fear of my not being able to succeed. . . .

The bill ran thus :

After the Play

MR. FOOTE will give TEA.

MR. PUZZLE (the Instructor), MR. FOOTE.

FIRST PUPIL by a YOUNG GENTLEMAN
(*Who never appeared on any Stage before*).

By eight in the evening I was in full dress behind the scenes. I had never been there before ; the company were all strangers to me. . . . I, on reflection, soon grew weary of my solitary seat in the green-room—alone in a crowd—and between the play and farce looked through a hole in the curtain, and beheld an awful pleasing sight—a crowded, splendid audience, such as might strike the boldest with dismay.

" The farce began, and Mr. Foote gained great applause, and roars of laughter succeeded. In the second act my time of trial drew near. In about ten minutes I was called—' Mr. Wilkinson ! Mr. Wilkinson !' Had I obeyed a natural impulse, I was really so alarmed that I should have run away. But honour pricked me on ; there was no alternative. My brain was a chaos ; but on I went, and must have made a very sheepish, timid appearance, as from fear, late illness, and apprehension, I trembled like a frighted clown in a pantomime ; which Foote perceiving, good-naturedly took me by the hand and led me forward, when the burst of applause was wonderful, and apparently that of kindness and true benevolence. But it could not instantly remove my timidity ; and I had no prompter to trust to, as all depended on myself.

" Foote, perceiving I was not fit for action, said to

his two friends on the stage (seated like Smith and
Johnson in ' The Rehearsal ') : ' This young gentleman
is merely a novice on the stage ; he has not yet been
properly drilled.   But come, my young friend, walk
across the stage ; breathe yourself and show your
figure.'   I did so ; the walk encouraged me, and
another loud applause succeeded.   I felt a glow,
which seemed to say : ' What have you to fear ?
Now, or *never !* This is the night that either makes
you or undoes you quite.'   And on the applause
being repeated, I said to myself : ' That is as loud as
any I have heard given to Mr. Garrick.'   I mustered
up courage, and began with Mr. Luke Sparks of
London (brother to Isaac Sparks, then in Dublin)
in the character of Capulet.   Most of the gentlemen
in the boxes knew all the London players.   They
were universally struck with the forcible manner of
the speaking, and the striking resemblance of the
features—a particular excellence in my mode of
mimicry.   A gentleman cried out : ' Sparks of
London ! Sparks of London !'   The applause re-
sounded, even to my astonishment ; and the audience
were equally amazed, as they found *something* where
they in fact expected *nothing.*   Next speech was
their favourite Barry in Alexander, universally known
and as universally felt.   I now found myself vastly
elated and clever ; fear was vanished, and joy and
pleasure succeeded : a proof what barometers we are
—how soon elated, and how soon depressed !   When
quite at ease, I began with Mrs. Woffington in Lady
Macbeth, and Barry in Macbeth.   The laughter
(which is the strongest applause on a *comic* occasion)
was so loud and incessant that I could not proceed.
This was a minute of luxury ; I was then in the

region of bliss. I was encored ; yet that lady had
declared in London, on hearing I was to go with
Foote to Ireland : ' Take me off—a puppy ! If he
dare attempt it, by the living G—d, he will be stoned
to death !'* Here the lady was mistaken ; for, on
repeating the part, the second applause was longer
than the preceding. A sudden thought occurred ; I
felt all hardy, all alert, all nerve, and immediately
advanced six steps ; and before I spoke I received
the full testimony of ' true imitation.' My master,
as he was called, sat on the stage at the same time ;
I repeated twelve or fourteen lines of the very prologue he had spoke that night (being called for) to
the author, and he had almost every night repeated.
I before Mr. Foote presented his other self ; the
audience, from repetition, were as perfect as I was ;
his manner, his voice, his oddities, I so exactly hit
that the pleasure, the glee it gave, may easily be conceived, to see and hear the mimic mimicked ; and it
really gave me a complete victory over Mr. Foote,
for the suddenness of the action tripped up his
audacity so much that he, with all his effrontery,
sat foolish, wishing to appear equally pleased with
the audience, but knew not how to play that difficult
part. He was unprepared ; the surprise and satisfaction was such that, without any conclusion, the
curtain was obliged to drop with reiterated bursts of
applause. . . .

   " When the farce, called ' Tea,' was concluded, I
had great congratulations paid, seriously and ironically.
Mr. Foote affected to be vastly pleased, but in truth
it was merely affectation, so differently do we feel for

* Bernard the actor describes very minutely the whole, but says
that Peg herself was present in the boxes.

ourselves when ridicule is pointed at us ; but he said
it was perfectly well judged to make free with him,
yet he did not think it very like himself, for it certainly was my *worst* imitation, but he rejoiced at my
good fortune.   In truth, Mr. Foote got the cash—
not me ; what I did was for him, as he acted on
shares, and the fuller the house, the greater was his
profit.   He was piqued and chagrined ; but as he had
kept within no bounds himself, and made free with
all characters whatever—stage, pulpit, bar, public
and private peculiarities, benefactors, patrons, friends
as well as foes—he could not, with any degree of
sense, appear displeased or censure me for what I
had done, but kept his resentment locked up for a
more proper and convenient opportunity, as he considered the repetition of himself in my imitations was
to his advantage, by the evident partiality the public
had shown me.   He made himself, therefore, tolerably easy, and may be truly said to have *pocketed*
the affront.

"The conversation the next day, particularly of
all my eager, partial friends, was an universal cry of
'Foote outdone ! Foote outdone !—the pupil the
master !'   And this was greatly assisted by their
agreeable disappointment ; for I do not believe any
one of them, however warm they might have been in
their wishes for my welfare, but trembled for the
event.   They felt unhappy lest I should make a
despicable attempt and be universally disapproved,
and then reflected within themselves : 'Good Heaven !
what is to become of this poor youth ?   What can he
do for a subsistence ?' . . .

"Mrs. Woffington, being so well known to all
ranks and degrees, was of infinite assistance to me as

an imitator. After the first night of my performance,
Mr. Sheridan appointed me a salary of three guineas
per week, and requested, with my approbation (which
was readily obtained), that Mr. Foote would write to
Mr. Garrick to grant permission for my continuance
in Dublin till the end of February. Foote was
obliged to go to England with all speed, as he had
stayed beyond his time; but I was left behind."

It was not surprising that Foote cast off his young
supporter; for it was an outrageous piece of impudence to mimic his master in his own presence before
a crowded audience, and the cries of "Foote outdone!" could not have been palatable. There was
something piquant in the notion of the mimic being
mimicked; but it is even more piquant to find that
all through the Foote who terrorized others was himself beginning to be in dread of the new mimic, and
at once began to conciliate him.

It was said, in a letter from Dublin, that he had
set up as a fortune-teller, with a room hung with
black and a dark lantern. Sending out handbills, he
wrote his visitors' fortunes without asking them any
questions. No one guessed that this was the great
comedian, and he is said to have cleared some £30
a day at 2s. 6d. a head.

CHAPTER IX

1758

DRURY LANE CONFUSION

FOOTE, having achieved what success he could, but
somewhat discomfited, presently returned to England,
leaving his unexpected competitor behind him. The
latter unscrupulously seized on Foote's pieces, and
had a very good season indeed, for he had become
decidedly popular. The sympathies of the vulgar
went out to the impudent youth who had ventured
to beard the eminent comedian, and make him
ridiculous. By-and-by he also returned to town.
There he might have expected to be pursued by the
animosity of the man he had so insulted. But nothing
of the kind followed. Bitter as Foote could be, his
bitterness was ever restrained by the sense of his
personal interest. He reflected that the youth was
engaged, as he was himself, at Drury Lane, and that
his wisest course would be to conciliate him.

We now find him at Drury Lane Theatre as
viceroy over his half-friend, half-enemy. There can
be little doubt that Foote had expressed what with
another would be a desire, but with him was an
imperative demand, that this should be arranged.
So there was to be the incursion of not one but two
disorderly mimics into a stately, well-regulated house

—conducted on lines that suggest the antique Théâtre Français—who were to reduce all to confusion. Garrick, we may be certain, was helpless in the matter. The junior mimic supplies a most diverting picture of the *émeutes* that broke out almost at once.

" I was pursuing my walk," he says, "when a strong voice issued from a dining-room window with great vehemence, calling out : ' Wilkinson ! Wilkinson ! Wilkinson !' I looked round, and soon spied my Master Foote, as he was termed. . . .

" He eagerly repeated his astonishment at not having seen or ever heard from me ; he was quite anxious to know what I had been doing since he last saw me in Ireland, and what and when I was to appear at Drury Lane, not having a doubt of my success, let the character be what it would. He had the repeated pleasure of meeting with his friend Colonel Thornton . . . who told him that he was acquainted with me at Portsmouth, and had been much entertained with my performances at that theatre. Mr. Foote insisted on my staying dinner, which invitation I could not refuse ; after dinner, and while the glass was circulating, he intimated a wish I would make my first appearance at Drury Lane, as his pupil, in a farce he had newly furbished up, and titled ' The Diversions of the Morning '; and added : ' You must, Wilkinson, plainly see and be convinced that dirty hound Garrick does not mean to do you any service or wish you success ; but on the contrary he is a secret enemy, and if he can prevent your doing well be assured he will. I know his heart so well, that if you give me permission to ask for your first attempt on his stage, and to be in my piece, the hound will refuse the moment I mention

it ; and though his little soul would rejoice to act
Richard III. in the dog-days, before the hottest
kitchen fire for a sop in the pan, yet I know his
mean soul so perfectly that, if, on his refusal, I with a
grave face tell him I have his figure exactly made
and dressed as a puppet in my closet, ready for
public admiration, the fellow will not only consent
to your acting, but, what is *more* extraordinary, his
abject fears will lend me money, if I should say I
want it.' This, I must own, seems a severe picture,
but the traits are from the life, and a true delineation
of character. . . .

"With very little thought I assented to Mr.
Foote's proposal, which I just now mentioned, of
playing in his farce ; and verily believe, if I had not,
that I never should have had an opportunity of
appearing on Drury Lane stage, unless in some part
totally unfit for me, when Mr. Garrick would have
said and published he had really out of charity done
all he could to serve me, but found it was impossible
to make anything to the purpose of such a blockhead."

The scenes of disturbance and tumult that followed
at Drury Lane are as diverting as they are dramatic ;
for the pair of mimics succeeded in throwing the
whole well-ordered interior of Garrick's theatre into a
state of tumult and confusion. As usual, we must
rely on the vivacious Tate for the details. His
picture of the unhappy Garrick tossed about among
these licentious elements is truly piteous.

Whether the manager found his attraction failing,
and that it was necessary to supplement his regular
répertoire by some broadly farcical exhibition, it is
difficult to decide.

9

" Measure for Measure," a heavy Shakespearean drama, was to open the ball, to be relieved by the boisterous " fun " of the pair. Foote thought of his old " show " with which he had opened the " little Hay.," and which had " caught on " so famously in Dublin. It was an elastic performance enough, and could be shaped in many ways, depending on a kind of master teaching his pupil stage elocution. He tacked to it a sort of first act or opening from his recent piece " Taste." There was an overflowing theatre ; everyone was eager to see and hear the pair ; for it was known that the entertainment would be singularly droll, and, above all, marked by strong personalities. Mrs. Woffington in particular was to be " taken off." The news speedily travelled to the lady, and then the confusion set in. " Soon after this farce was known by the town to be in rehearsal, some Mrs. Candour gave my friend Mrs. Woffington the alarm, who still lived and existed on the flattering hopes of once more captivating the public by her remaining rays of beauty (born to bloom and fade) ; and who declared she was astonished on hearing I had survived my presumption in Ireland, in daring (to be the devil in her likeness there) to take her off. Colonel Cæsar of the Guards, who it was whispered at that time was secretly married to Mrs. Woffington, had been, as mentioned, at Portsmouth the night of my benefit, when the Duke of York and most of the principal gentlemen of the army in the kingdom were at that time assembled, and were most forcibly struck with the sudden and high entertainment they received by seeing their favourite Woffington where she was so little expected ; and, indeed, the exactness of manner rendered it certainly, as a performance of that kind, far beyond mediocrity. . . . When she was first made acquainted with my appearance in 'Queen Dollallolla,' she declared by the living God she was amazed 'the fellow was not stoned to death in Dublin!' . . . She then deputed Colonel Cæsar to wait on Mr. Garrick; he related his objections in point of delicacy and honour concerning any affront, however slight, reflectedly thrown on that lady. He said to Mr. Garrick he should not be surprised if young Wilkinson had success on such an attempt. . . . His intention as a visitor to Mr. Garrick was to inform him, if he permitted such procedure or achievement from Mr. Wilkinson on his stage, he must expect from him (Colonel Cæsar) to be seriously called upon as a gentleman to answer it. Mr. Garrick immediately not only acquiesced, but expressed a detestation of any such performance (*bless his good nature !*), and I actually believe would not have been displeased with receiving an order from the Lord Chamberlain. . . .

" The day before the piece was to be acted he summoned both Foote and me before him, and told us these particulars. He informed us that his word and honour was engaged to Colonel Cæsar that Mr. Wilkinson should not take the liberty to make any line, speech, or manner relative to Mrs. Woffington, or presume to offer or occasion any surmise of likeness, so as to give the least shadow of offence, on any account whatever. This I subscribed to on Mr. Garrick's commands, and Mr. Foote became my bail for the same; for Garrick was really on this matter very uneasy with Foote and Wilkinson—his d——d exotics. . . .

" ' The Diversions of the Morning ' was at length produced in October, and to an overflowing theatre.

9—2

Curiosity was universally raised, to see Mr. Foote's pupil, as I was called, and indeed by many believed to be. Mr. Foote's acquaintances were numerous, and of the first circles; and he took every precaution and care for his own sake (for fear of failure or party) to have me strongly supported, and he blazed forth Wilkinson's wonderful merit, as on my success he intended what he put into execution, which was, to give me the labouring oar and make myself a number of implacable enemies; and as to the money I brought, he judged it only safe and fit for his own emolument. . . .

"The scene between Mr. Foote and myself went off with great éclat; on my departure from the stage, while he did his puppets, etc., the audience grew very impatient by seeing my exit, and judged that was all the new actor was to do; and feeling a disappointment, from murmuring they grew impatient, and at last burst out into vehemently asking for Wilkinson, and desiring to be informed if that was the only performance they were to expect from that young gentleman. This loud interruption was not paying him his accustomed attention, and he seemed much nettled; however, he bowed, and said the new performer was only retired for a little respite necessary for his following part of the entertainment. This answer was approved, and Mr. Foote was proceeding, but the little clamour had reached and disturbed the minds of the gods, and John Bull . . . again repeated: 'Wilkinson! Wilkinson!' Foote at this second interruption grew really offended, and having secured the lower house, he stopped and said to Mr. Manly (Holland, who was on the stage with him): 'Did you ever hear such fellows? D—n it, they want the

fifth act of a play before the second is over!' And
as what he said generally passed current, this occasioned
an universal roar, and all went on peaceably, and with
great good humour, till the appointed time for my
second entrance, which was near the conclusion—the
people eager to applaud they knew not why or what,
but full of expectation that some strange performance
was to be produced. . . . The farce finished with my
performance, and Mr. Foote on my bow made his
own, not attempting to proceed, and was himself in
great raptures for reasons before hinted at ; but when
the curtain was down he went on and assured the
audience he was much honoured by their approbation,
and with their permission would the next night repeat
the same piece again, which they had expected he
would do, and returned the usual tokens of their
approbation."

As to Garrick's " vanity "—really, his genuine consciousness of his own superior merit—no one who has
followed the course of this amiable and unselfish man
could say a word. This vanity, such as it was, was
really founded on a nervous timidity of anything that
might disturb his supremacy. Indeed, in ordinary
cases, what is thought to be a leading actor's jealousy
is really but an apprehension that a rival's success will
shake his position and destroy his fortunes. For
popularity seems to be a fixed quantity, and when a
new-comer secures it, the older favourite has to share
with him. Wilkinson has furnished a really brilliant
sketch of Garrick's character from this point of view.
The analyses of the conflicting emotions are revealed
by some admirable touches. I doubt if Boswell himself could have done it better. It proves, however,
what an easy business it was for Foote to play upon

this sensitive being, the "stops" of whose nature he knew so well.

Nothing can be more acute or true to character than the following sketch by this shrewd observer of these two eminent men and their relations : "Foote was irresistible, spontaneous, and not confined to manner or character ; for wherever he aimed his humour and raillery he shot the object as it flew by his quick fancy, and all with a superior degree to his opponents.

"When Mr. Garrick was at the noon rehearsals, he ever was on the listen, and, if he heard Foote and the performers joking, would enter all full of whim and *affected* easy affability and equality, and made himself one of the laughing group, and at every jest of Foote's appeared to pay particular tributes of surprise, applause, and attention ; but when in turn he related what he had studied and prepared as *very* comical, if the same repetition of approbation as had gone before attendant to Foote's humour was wanting to his, he has been cut to the soul at finding Foote's superiority, which was generally the consequence when both were pitched for battle and eager for victory at the game of repartee and sparring sarcasm. . . .

"One great reason, as a man of wit, for Foote's superiority in such convivial meetings was that he, like the American, felt bold, knew his superiority, which was raised by the perfect knowledge of Garrick's fears, and which made Foote assail him : for he gave not himself the trouble to hate. Mr. Foote would frequently say to Mr. Garrick, ' Bless me ! we have been laughing away our time ; it is past three o'clock ; have you and Mrs. Garrick enough for a third, without infringing on your servants' generosity, for I know they are on board wages ? besides, the

kitchen fire may be gone out if it be one of your
cold meat days ; or if one of Mrs. Garrick's fast days,
I cannot expect a dinner on emergency.' On Foote's
repeating such a whimsical jargon, Garrick would act
a laugh like Bayes, though all the joke lay, like
Mr. Bayes s, in the boots.

" Many meetings have I been at between those two
great geniuses, and truly enjoyed them from that
time to the present. But Mr. Foote's knowledge of
Garrick was but superficial when compared with
Mr. Murphy's ; for Mr. Murphy's cool and sensible
penetration made him a perfect judge of the whole
inward soul of Mr. Garrick, while Foote, without
perplexing himself with the fatigue of thinking, was
contented with slighter materials to garnish his merriment—which amply satisfied his love of satire and
cheerfulness. To speak seriously of these gentlemen
—why Foote should have entertained such an inconceivable disgust to Mr. Garrick I cannot devise,
unless from that implacable attendant, more or less, in
the human breast, called *envy*, which ever haunts
a theatre. That Garrick had much reason to be
offended with Foote is certain, and that he inwardly
hated him is as certain ; nor is that to be a matter of
surprise, as Foote was ever endeavouring to expose,
and even, if possible, to injure him. He gloried in it,
and seized every opportunity to have a cut at him
and serve him up as the maimed, not perfect Garrick
—unless to acknowledge perforce, like Colley Cibber,
who allowed (but with great difficulty) to Mrs. Bracegirdle, that really Garrick, he believed, had merit, but
Foote never introduced his deserts, or heard of him as
an actor with pleasure, or allowed him any credit for
his theatrical abilities, but wished the conversation

was over ; or, if obliged to give his sentiments, would
conclude with, ' Yes, the hound had a something
clever ; but if his excellence was to be examined,
he would not be found in *any part* equal to Colley
Cibber's Sir John Brute, Lord Foppington, Sir Courtly
Nice, or Justice Shallow.' . . .

" But Justice bids me say in favour of Mr. Garrick,
that to my knowledge he often assisted Mr. Foote
with sums of money, not trifling, and Foote always
attributed the favour done from fear, not generosity ;
yet it certainly was an obligation, and that service
tendered when Foote has been in awkward situations
for want of cash, and to relate facts on all sides I am
here answerable. . . .

" The next night," he says, " the house was jammed
in every part—the morning of which it was strongly
rumoured that the actors of Covent Garden were
highly enraged—that Mr. Sparks in particular was
really disordered on the occasion—Mr. Holland called
at the theatre and informed Mr. Garrick and
Mr. Foote he had actually heard that Mr. Sparks was
so much hurt and unhappy, that he had taken to his
bed and was dangerously ill ; Foote immediately
replied (in his laughing manner) that it could not be
true, or, that it must be a d——d lie ; for he had met
his wife with two pounds of mutton-chops on a skewer
for her husband's dinner.   This impromptu occasioned
a hearty green-room laugh."

" At night the house was what we of the theatrical
tribe like to see, and term *chuck full in every part*. . . .
On my first entrance there were marks of disapproba-
tion, and on my second sounded to me at such an
alarming height, that I thought all was over ; but the
multitude of well-wishers, and the number whose

curiosity had been raised, longed to be satisfied, and bore all before them.

" This little piece went on in a most flourishing state till about the fifth or sixth night, when Mr. Sparks, of Covent Garden Theatre, felt himself so wounded by my attack on his acting (which truly was a very picturesque one, and those who remember him and me at that time will allow what I have here said) that he waited on Mr. Garrick, and requested he would not suffer him, as a man of credit in private life, and an actor of estimation in public, to be destroyed by such an illiberal attack on his livelihood; and, as it struck at his reputation, hoped he would not permit it in future as far as regarded himself, whom it had rendered miserable. Garrick said: ' Why, now, hey, Sparks! why now, hey, this is so strange now, hey, a—why, Wilkinson, and be d——d to him, they tell me he takes me off, and he takes Foote off, and so—why, you see that you are in very good company.' ' Very true, sir,' says Sparks, ' but many an honest man has been ruined by keeping *too good company* '; and then Sparks made his bow and his exit. Mr. Garrick, however, came to the theatre at noon, paraded with great consequence up and down the stage, sent for me, and when I obeyed the mighty summons, he was surrounded by most of the performers. . . . ' Now, hey, d——n it, Wilkinson!— now, why will you take a liberty with these gentlemen the players, and without my consent? you never consulted or told me you were *to take off*, as you call it; hey, why now, I never take such liberties—indeed I once did it, but I gave up such d——d impudence. Hey now, that is, I say—but you and Foote, and Foote and you, think you are managers of this

theatre. But to convince you of the contrary, and
be d——d to ye, I here order you, before these
gentlemen, to desist from taking any liberty with any
one of Covent Garden Theatre; and I think it necessary to avow and declare my abhorrence of what you
have done, and at the same time to disclaim my
consent or knowledge of it: I do not allow myself
such unbecoming liberties, nor will I permit them
from another where I am manager; and if you dare
repeat such a mode of conduct after my commands,
I will fine you the penalty of your article.' . . .

"Presently entered Foote, loudly singing a French
song to show his breeding, and on seeing such a
group of actors on the stage, pronounced like Wit-
wou'd: 'Hey day! what, are you all got together
here like players at the end of the last act!'—then
said he had called at Mr. Garrick's house, and was
informed he should find him at the theatre; for
he wanted to fix on two or three plays wherein he
would act on the nights of his 'Diversions of the
Morning.' Mr. Garrick then assumed much serious
consequence, and related to Mr. Foote the state of
affairs—that he had received strong representations
from Covent Garden Theatre, and had, from motives
of humanity and consideration, resolved to put a stop
to Wilkinson's proceedings, and that Mr. Tate must
that night perform the part of Bounce only, and
at his peril to disobey his orders; and that after
his exit as Mr. Bounce, the piece must finish with
Mr. Foote's performance, and no more Wilkinson.
'If indeed, now — if Wilkinson could have taken
me off, as Mrs. Garrick says, why, now, as to
that I should have liked it vastly, and so would
Mrs. Garrick. But I again enforce Wilkinson's not

appearing on my stage a second time'—and to my astonishment Foote assented. But had I been entrusted or acquainted with chicanery and the mysteries behind the curtain of a London theatre (though to this hour I am not above half perfect), my wonder would not have been so great. . . .

"As the evening approached, I went and prepared myself for Bounce only, according to order, and when Bounce was finished retired to the green-room; but am certain both Mr. Garrick and Mr. Foote had planted persons in the house to call for Wilkinson, because Mr. Foote had not gone through half his performance when the call for me was universal; which could not have been the case, as it was a repeated piece, and the time not come for my second appearance as usual, had not some subtlety been used in the business. . . . I thought Mr. Foote had been prepared with sufficient reasons for the omission, and that he would have explained them to the audience, and the farce be no more repeated. The clamour continued when Mr. Foote retired from the stage, and Mr. Garrick ordered the lights to be let down, which consisted of six chandeliers hanging over the stage, every one containing twelve candles in brass sockets, and a heavy iron flourished and joined to each bottom, large enough for a street palisade. This ceremony being complied with, Mr. Garrick said it would, with the lamps also lowered, be a convincing proof to the audience that all was over; but this only served, like oil thrown on flames, to increase the vociferation. On Garrick's perceiving this, he came to me in the green-room, and with seeming anger and terror asked me how I had dared to cause a riot and disturbance in his theatre, and

send a set of blackguards into the house to call for
me. All I could urge in my horrid situation was,
asserting my ignorance of the matter, but which was
of no avail; and while I was proceeding with my
asseverations in *piano*, the *forte* broke out into outrageous tumult. What was to be done? I replied,
I would run away; but that, Mr. Garrick said, as
matters stood, could not be suffered. 'Foote!
Foote! Foote!' was echoed and re-echoed from
every part of the house. He had been standing
with the most perfect ease, and laughing all the
time; but being thus loudly summoned, obeyed the
call of duty, and on the stage instantly presented
himself; and when there was interrogated, Why
Mr. Wilkinson's part of the farce, that had been so
well received, was omitted? Mr. Foote made an
harangue, and observed, if honoured with their
patience to hear him, he would endeavour to explain,
and he hoped to their satisfaction. On this silence
ensued. He said he was exceedingly sorry to have
given cause for being called to an account for any
motive of their displeasure; begged respectfully to
assure them that, as to the omission of Mr. Wilkinson's latter performance, it had only been introduced
by way of entertainment, not with intention of injury
to any individual whatever; for a harmless laugh was
all the young gentleman had aspired to—nor could he
have meant more, and by so doing to add a trifle for
the entertainment of the public; and Mr. Wilkinson
had desired him to remit his grateful acknowledg-
ments for the kind indulgence they had honoured
him with. But, very unfortunately, what had only
been humbly offered as harmless had been basely
misconstrued into wickedness. . . .

" This declamation, instead of pacifying, was treated with marks of anger and contempt, and an universal cry for ' Wilkinson ! Wilkinson !' On which Mr. Foote advanced once more, and said, as for his own peculiarities, if they could afford the least entertainment, Mr. Wilkinson was at full liberty to exercise his talents to their utmost extent; and then added, *archly* (for the which, I have reason to think, the manager did not find himself in the least obliged), he believed, nay, was assured, Mr. Wilkinson might as far as respected Mr. Garrick, without any restrictions, take the same freedom. The cry was for me immediately to appear, and that without delay ; Mr. Foote promised I should be instantly produced, and took leave with a general plaudit. On Mr. Foote's return to the green-room, he laid hold of my arm, and said I must go on the stage that moment. 'And what must I do when I am there?' says I. 'O !' replied he, ' anything—what you like, and treat them with as much of me as you please.' ' Ay,' but says I, 'what does Mr. Garrick say? for without his orders I cannot proceed.' 'Hey—why, now—hey !' says Garrick, ' why, now, as they insist, I really do not see that I am bound to run the hazard of having a riot in my theatre to please Sparks and the rest of the Covent Garden people ; and if they are not satisfied with your serving up Mr. Foote as a dish— why, it is a pity, as I to-day observed, but you could give me ; but that, you say, is not possible with any hopes of success. Why, now—haste ! they are making a devilish noise ; and so, as you have begun your d——d taking off, why, go on with it, and do what comes into your head, and do not in future plague me with your cursed tricks again.' So Sam Foote

popped the 'Exotic' on the stage ; there was no time
to be lost, as they feared bad consequences.   I was
afraid to go on, but on the stage I was actually
pushed by Mr. Garrick and Mr. Foote, and my hair
did stand on end like quills upon the fretful porcupine.
The curtain was dropped, and the branches also down
on each side.   My fright was apparent, but Mr. *Town*
soon cheered my spirits, as there was not one dis-
senting voice in the whole audience.   I began, and
very freely with Mr. Foote, and then was for retiring,
but the cry was ' No, no—go on, go on !' and many
said aloud, ' Damn it, take them all off !'   I took the
hint, and was encouraged at so furious a rate that
I went through a long course of mimicry with great
éclat, having permission, as I thought.   My distress
of the morning all vanished, and was exchanged for
the most delightful feelings in the evening ; being all
elated, and, on a short reflection, relying on Garrick's
declaration, as the words of truth, when he had twice
declared nothing could please him or Mrs. Garrick
more than a well-executed likeness of himself as an
actor ; but note, good reader, in this point I had not
acted with honour, but duplicity ; for whenever he
had jokingly asked me 'What sort of a subject I
could make of him ?' I always answered : ' I never
could form any resemblance whatever; for his
manner and tones were so natural, and his voice
so melodious, that any imitation was impossible.'
This he greedily swallowed and believed (charming
flattery !), but in the close of my performance that
remarkable night the audience were wonderfully
surprised and tickled on beholding so unexpectedly
a resemblance of the incomparable Roscius, which increased my spirits to such a degree that . . . I deter-

mined to give the audience a good meal ; and finding
my first attack had made a favourable impression in
their opinions, I advanced without mercy, cried havoc,
and produced Mr. Garrick in three characters. . . .

" And at the last line I made my finish and exit
in his manner, with loud acclamations, and was all
alive, alive O! But for me personally to recite
these peculiarities would give a much better idea
than even the ablest pen can possibly describe.

" After this night all opposition or affront was
dropped, and the enraged performers were advised
to let me die a natural death, as the most prudent
method ; for by opposite means they rendered
Wilkinson popular, and by not taking umbrage he
would sink into insignificance. The farce was continued and gained additional force ; and Mr. Foote,
as he reaped the profit, was highly enraptured, and
said Wilkinson was very clever. He was the general,
receiving high and honorary rewards, whilst, in fact,
I was merely held in rank but as a poor subaltern
at low pay, for standing to be shot at. . . .

" All this time I received not *one* guinea as a
present, or as a bribe, from either Mr. Garrick or
Mr. Foote ; nay, from that whimsical night Mr. Garrick was so hurt and offended with my representation
of his likeness, that almost during the remainder of
the season he never deigned to let his eye grace
me with its observance, and of course not a single
word to comfort me from his royal lips ; all conveyed, whenever I met him, austerity, anger, and
dislike. Indeed, he felt himself inwardly hurt with
the liberty I had taken.

" Foote, by the practice of seeing me take him off
every night, as I kept within the bounds of decorum,

let it not a whit disturb his repose ; for, as he obtained
the golden fleece—why, let the world laugh and be
——. And so far it became his sole business and
interest, while that farce lasted ; but as to his good
friendship for me, though very pleasant at the time,
it only extended to—*No longer pipe, no longer dance.*"

Altogether a strange sketch of free-and-easy stage
manners, while the manager had to look on, tolerating
it all.

CHAPTER X

"THE AUTHOR"—VISITS TO SCOTLAND

WE may again wonder how the correct and orderly
Garrick could have brought himself to tolerate these
unworthy exhibitions and undignified tumults. The
reason, it is clear, was that he was compelled to
accept them by his domineering actor, Foote. We
find the latter back again at Drury Lane during the
season 1756-57, when the manager, undeterred by
the previous failure, was induced, or felt himself
compelled, to accept another comedy, "The Author,"
whose attraction was a clever but gross caricature
of a harmless private gentleman, a personal friend
of Foote's. Garrick was now to experience a whole
series of further troubles arising out of this unfortunate connection.

There was a well-to-do Welsh Squire named
Aprice—or Apreece, as it became later—evidently a
simple, credulous sort of provincial who wished to
"get into society," and who to his misfortune came to
know Foote. He was an eccentric, had a grotesque
way of speaking and of saying aloud what was passing
in his thoughts, illustrated by all sorts of odd
ejaculations. Foote was much struck with him,
asked him to dinner, where he studied him at his

leisure, and at last "got him." The result was the amusing, truly farcical figure of Cadwallader, which caused roars of laughter, and for years was acted all over the kingdom.

We may imagine this poor simple country gentleman going on his way quite unconscious that he was, as it were, being measured, and destined, obscure as he was, to furnish laughter to the whole town. Foote worked away at his canvas, and drew him to his own satisfaction. At last "The Author" was produced, and Mr. Cadwallader—Foote himself— stepped upon the stage in a grotesque dress, copied, though exaggerated, in the minutest details from the victim. For our manager, to secure accuracy, would stoop to buying an old suit from the valet. Let us conceive the poor country gentleman, brought to the house, placed by Foote in a good box to see the play (he fancied, no doubt, that he was being paid a compliment), and listening to the shouts of laughter. It was said that he enjoyed it most of all, and he was of course pointed out by Foote's chosen friends as the original. It must have been a play in itself to see the victim laughing and applauding through the night, unconscious that he was being laughed at. He little knew, poor soul! that for the next five or six years he was to be the laughing-stock of the kingdom, that people would be stopping and turning round in the street to look after him, saying: "There he is! That's he! Eh, Becky, Becky!"*

* This unlucky Mr. Aprice I find attracted Foote's notice some years before; for in "The Knights" he has a very gratuitous allusion to "a collateral branch by his mother's side, the Aprices of Laubridon, and we have ever since quartered on an escutcheon of pretence the three goats' tails rampant, divided by a chevron, field argent, with a leek pendent."

As I have said, the plot was of the slightest. A youth who had turned bookseller's hack was in love with Cadwallader's sister. A colonial Governor disguises himself as Tartar Ambassador to "get over" Cadwallader, reveals himself, forgives his son, and the lovers are made happy. But Foote so enriched the part with comic touches, so luxuriated in bustle and eccentricity, said and did such odd things, never flagging for an instant, and, above all, so permeated the character with diverting mimicries of a living person, that he carried all before him. Above all, he was supported by the exuberant spirit of the admirable Kitty Clive in the part of Becky. We of our time have little or no idea of this tumultuous spirit, such as used to be exhibited by Wright or Buckstone, whose very look, with the twist of his droll mouth and the tone of his voice, threw the audience into convulsions of merriment. Broad, comic acting at this moment is virtually extinct.

The more we consider Foote's treatment of his contemporaries, and even friends, the more perplexing is it to understand. Here was a man on intimate terms with conspicuous men, meeting them constantly at clubs, dinners, and convivial suppers, writing them friendly letters, and yet all the time taking notes of their manners and penchants, either bringing them on the stage, or preparing to do so. This was well known, and yet we find him treated, not as a spy or treacherous guest, but accepted as a personage of such importance that he is to be propitiated or kept in good-humour. In our time, a popular or funny man who was known to be giving anything like mimicry of his acquaintances at his "show" would find that it led either to law or to personal chastisement. Or supposing him to be one of those agreeable persons who were asked to entertain parties, and that he introduced some of his friends, their dress, etc., into his songs, he would certainly be "dropped," "cut," or avoided. In Foote's case none of these results followed, the reason being that all felt his power, and that he was not a man whom it was safe to offend.

I have mentioned that Foote had an amazing gift of conveying personal oddities and tricks of speech in suitable words. He was more than successful on this occasion, and set before his audiences a perfect portrait of a most diverting eccentric, who was so eager and exuberant that he made use of every aid —gesture, tones, ejaculations—to express his feelings. His contentions with his Becky, his sudden appeals to her, caused infinite amusement. To call for Becky became a common form. His favourite utterance was "Hold! hold!" uttered in the most comic cadence.

"*Cad.* Well, what say you, Mr. Cape? Let's have it, without equivocation; or hold, hold, hold, mental reservation. Guilty or not? *Cape.* Of what, sir? *Cad.* Of what? Hold, hold, of making love to Bell. *Cape.* Guilty. *Cad.* Hey! how? Hold, zounds! No, what, not with an intention to marry her? *Cape.* With the lady's approbation and your kind consent. *Cad.* Hold, hold, what, my consent to marry you? *Cape.* Ay, sir. *Cad.* Hold, hold, hold, what, our Bell? To mix the blood of the Cadwalladers with the puddle of a poet? *Cape.* Sir? *Cad.* A petty, paltry, ragged, rhyming—— *Spri.* But Mr.—— *Cad.* A scribbling, hold, hold, hold—garreteer, that has no more clothes than backs,

no more heads than hats, and no shoes to his feet.
Spri, Nay, but—— *Cad*. The offspring of a dunghill !
Born in a cellar, hold, hold, and living in a garret—a
fungus, a mushroom.   *Cape*. Sir, my family——
Cad. Your family ! Hold, hold, hold—Peter, fetch
the pedigree."

As the season had closed and the novelty had
passed away, Foote fancied that he was perfectly
assured.   The Apreece family may have thought that
it would be wisest to take no notice of the matter.
Three months of the season had gone by when, on
December 18, the family, on opening their paper,
were disturbed to find that Foote (for his benefit
night) had selected this obnoxious farce or comedy,
and that the tide of personalities was to be set flowing
once more.   The victims at last turned and resolved
to check the abuse at once.

Foote had prepared a rather taking bill.   It seems
extraordinary that he should run the hazard of
attempting Shylock, a part one would have thought
him wholly unfitted for.   No doubt the contrast
with the obstreperous fun of Cadwallader would
attract.   Wilkinson relates the sequel :

" An additional scene was wrote for me.   The
character was entitled and called Mrs. O'Shocknesy ;
all was ready, rehearsed, and perfectly prepared for
our royal exhibition—when, O dreadful to relate !
or, as Mrs. Inchbald's epilogue to ' Such Things Are '
expresses it, ' Down came an order to suspend the
ball !'   In plain English, a peremptory mandate from
the Lord Chamberlain to inform Mr. Garrick that
Mr. Aprice, a gentleman of family and fortune, had
made personal application to him as highly aggrieved,
and had urged that, at the united voice of all his

connections, he desired the farce of 'The Author' might
be expunged from the list of theatrical pieces, they
having all concurred in one general opinion that the
character of Mr. Cadwallader was purposely written
and drawn out by the writer to render ridiculous
Mr. Aprice, his manner, and his peculiar oddities,
which made him a topic for public laughter and
satirical joke and mummery—himself and wife could
not go along the streets without being insulted with,
' My dear Becky, and here comes Dicky,' etc.—which
allegations were strictly true : in short, he urged that
they were become common objects for laughter and
affront by Mr. Foote's audacious freedom ; and
though he honestly confessed he had with his wife
Dolly seen the farce, yet they could not find a
similitude, but his family felt injured as well as all
their friends, who insisted on a curb being laid on
Mr. Foote's licentiousness, and the only proper and
immediate removal of grievance rested on the sense,
feelings, justice, and honour of the Lord Chamberlain
for instant *redress*.   His lordship . . . gave his verdict
against Mr. Foote : being at the very crisis, and not
put in force till the day of performance, all appeal, all
interest to counterbalance, was in vain ; he would
hear no petitions ; that day was the final will and
pleasure. . . . This sudden and fatal decree was
irrevocable, and Mr. Foote, as the command came so
unexpectedly, even while I was actually rehearsing
the new scene, was thrown into a consternation and
panic not to be described. . . .

" Mr. Foote appeared shocked, pale, and dejected,
for in ' The Author ' he had depended on honours flowing thick upon him, which this hasty killing frost not
only nipped, but cut the root, so as to prevent its

being for that year a tree-bearing fruit; nay, even
Mrs. Clive was melted, who hated him, and had said
but an hour before, ' You play Shylock, Mr. Foote!
how the devil should you know how to act Shylock,
who never could play a character well in your life!'
' Why not, madam?' replied Foote ; ' how can you
tell I can't act Shylock till you have seen me?'
' Why,' replied Clive (with a woman-like reason),
' because I am certain you don't know how to speak a
line of it.' . . . This tender Catherine (and there she
was clever) almost sobbed for her dear Foote when the
author was prohibited, and his lordship, who sent the
decree, did not escape her deprecations; but the
secret lay here : Becky—I mean Mrs. Cadwallader—
her part in the farce being stopped, was as great a
disappointment to her as an actress, as the author
being silenced was to Mr. Foote.   He felt like Shylock, which he had been rehearsing, and regretted the
money this stoppage would lose him, three thousand
ducats in that, besides other precious jewels.   The
incomparable Clive outwardly grieved for Foote, and
acted it very well, though tragedy was not her forte,
but was inwardly assisted by her anger, and all her
tenderness being really moved for the loss of her dear
Mrs. Cadwallader ; and certainly very few such instances of great acting ever were or will be produced
in competition with her performance of that character.
She there (as Cibber says in his preface) outdid her
usual outdoings.   She was the terror of poets,
managers, actors, actresses, and musicians—O rare
Kate Clive!—there was no resource left but to change
the farce, stick up fresh bills, explain the unavoidable
necessity for so doing, and request the usual indulgence.   As to what farce—the stale ' Diversions of the

Morning' was the only substitute.* These precautions
taken, Mr. Foote went home to dinner as sheepish
and with as little appetite as I had done some weeks
before on my general lecture day, and I dare answer
for him with as little relish ; for those who are blessed
with superabundant spirits, when once they are sunk,
are quite chop-fallen."

It was amusing to find how speedily chastisement
followed Wilkinson, and overtook him at unexpected
moments and places. Years later, he was busy
arranging his benefit in the country. On the morning
of the performance a number of gentlemen entered
during the rehearsal, and a young man, walking up
to him, made an unexpected address. After saying
that the piece " written by that scoundrel Foote " had
been stopped six years before, in December, 1758,
" My name, sir," he said, " is Aprice, and the character
you mean to perform is an affront to the memory of
my father, who is now dead. As his son, by——, I
will not suffer such insolence to pass unnoticed or
unpunished ; therefore if at night you dare attempt or
presume to play this farce, myself and friends are
determined, one and all, not to leave a bench or
scene in your theatre. So, Mr. Wilkinson, your
immediate and determinate answer." The manager
was called in, and, being timorous, the play was withdrawn and another piece substituted. No announcement of the change was made, and there was, naturally,
great confusion in the audience. But the night was

* Genest says that there is a manuscript note in the British
Museum which states that Foote came forward during this night of
troubles, and defended himself from the Apreece charges. Garrick
was too partial to these "exotic" exhibitions. During this very
season he allowed a farce to be played by children.

got through without disturbance. It was a strange coincidence that brought Aprice's son on the scene, but a fitting retribution.

This successful personality established Foote's gross system on a firm and permanent basis. It was now known that he would in the future supply his stage *regularly* with this form of attraction. Henceforth no well-known person endowed with a stock of oddities was secure from the manager—a terrible prospect for some. Many might wonder where was the licenser—his Act of 1737 being only a few years old, and assumed to have been passed to check disorders and protect the public. Foote virtually made it "a dead letter." His rampant methods had intimidated all. No one dared to interfere with him, for fear of worse. The licensers—the Lord Chamberlains—were his intimate friends, to whom he used to dedicate his pieces.

But there is another view. The Act was passed to check *political* licence—ridicule of Ministers and persons in high office. Had Foote dared to touch them, he would have been promptly restrained. The mere ridicule of ordinary members of society was as nothing to the officials. It was a strange, curious state of things, but a wonderful tribute to Foote's vast power.

Wilkinson goes on: " Mr. Foote's benefit, though he was disappointed of his farce of ' The Author,' was, it is true, very beneficial ; but his career was stopped, and our ' Diversions of the Morning,' though it had afforded good dinners, suppers, etc., for several weeks, would not any longer produce even tea for breakfast, particularly on a sharing plan, as, like most things in this world, it had had its day. So Mr. Foote, the

poet, had by the approach of January, with perfect
ease, squandered away all the profits which arose
from our diversions, and as easily the massy sum of
his benefit night ; so all the extravagant rarities which
he had enjoyed in November and December were, in
a comparative view, to be devoured by a real good
stomach, by imagination, with fancied delicacies, like
his own poet Mr. Crambo ; and Mr. Foote therefore
in earnest felt the January blasts, which cut him
through and through.

" A single joint of mutton was his fare, of which I
often partook, and he generally had one or two to
dine with him ; but humble port and Lisbon were the
only wines at dinner—no claret or Madeira, for the
credit had waned with the pocket. He never could
work till his genius was put to its wits' end. . . . I
must allow myself at that time much obliged to his
good breeding, as he ever seemed glad to see me at
his table, and seemed to study to make that table
agreeable ; and, indeed, he never showed himself to
more advantage than when making his guests welcome, as he seemed the generous, hospitable, cheerful,
and sincere friend of every person who partook of his
fare, which was always of the best, whenever the best
could with convenience be procured.

" He was soon after his benefit in such a state
of poverty that all parties at the Thatched House,
Bedford Arms, etc., were obliged to be given up.
He appeared vexed whenever I was indispensably
engaged—unless, indeed, he could get much better
company, such as Mr. Murphy or Mr. Macklin. But
they were not always to be had, nor were they ever
hand and glove ; for whenever Macklin and he had a
tiff, though I believe Mr. Foote might be the aggressor,

yet Mr. Macklin on such broileries would treat him,
not only very cavalierly, but very roughly.

"At the time my company was so welcome, many
happy, laughing evenings have I had in James Street
with himself, Messrs. Murphy and Macklin. Often,
as the circling glass went round and warmed my vain
heart, Mr. Murphy and Mr. Macklin would com-
municate their intentions of proceeding on a play or
farce, or some lucky thought. Foote got all the
information he could, and, like Mr. Bayes, pop! he
clapped it down and made it his own."

During their affectionate intimacy Foote had
promised his young friend to play for his benefit, and
the latter counted on this as a chief attraction :

"As to Mr. Foote's acting for me, I really thought
it a duty, as well as a debt of honour. Mr. Foote
came to town in a few days ; and in my bills and
advertisements were published both play and farce,
but luckily (as it proved) I had not inserted Mr.
Foote's name. I called to see him, and had reason to
believe he was denied ; I called a second time, and
was then admitted. I congratulated him on his
return, and informed him of my reliance on his ful-
filling his promise by performing for my benefit,
which was to be on the 14th of May ; and on that
full dependence I had advertised 'The Diversions of
the Morning,' and had the pleasure to inform him my
boxes were all taken. Foote, after coughing and
taking a quantity of snuff, and plucking his chin with
tweezers—a constant habit of his in private life—at
length coolly replied : 'That as a young man he
wished me success in the world ; but was hurt to
observe, the publishing of his farce was an unwarrant-
able freedom. His health was very indifferent, and

would not permit his assisting me at my benefit. The
infinite services and favours he had conferred on me,
by introducing me to the public notice of the London
and Dublin audiences, were a full or more than an
equal compensation for such trifling, immaterial assistance as I had given him, or that my vanity might
have supposed to have added to the success of
his piece by performing in it.' Then again added:
'He was not well, and besides he had letters of
consequence to despatch, and no time to trifle away,
therefore must wish me a good-morning.' I was
truly astonished, as may be easily supposed, at such
an unexpected, mean, despicable behaviour ! It was
ingratitude in every sense of the word.

"The reader will recollect what a winter of confusion and turbulence I had undergone. The money
I had certainly drawn by the sweat of my brow. He
had feasted on my labour, and had lived in clover,
while I was merely buffeted from pillar to post. I
desired he would not by any means neglect his health
or his letters of consequence, for that I not only took
my leave of him for that day, but was determined
never more to trouble him with a second visit.
However, to try him further, I said, as the farce was
advertised, my loss would be irreparable if not performed, and hoped he would not add additional
cruelty by inflicting a punishment unmerited, by the
refusal of the copy of his farce. He sternly replied,
indeed he should ; he had a reputation to lose, and
would not hazard the representation of any piece of
his not printed, to be mutilated, spoiled, and condemned by my ignorant bungling. Here the visit
ended, and I left him most truly with an honest
contempt, and said to him, when at the door, 'Fare-

well, Mr. Foote!' and determined never more to
renew our acquaintance.

"In this dilemma some management was necessary
how to cook up my bill of fare, as the 14th of May
required strength to make the night fashionable. My
best and only resource seemed to be the waiting on
Mr. Garrick and entreating the favour of his hearing
the relation of my wrongs, as I could not think of
any expedient for relief, unless he would for once
advise and assist me. This intention I put into
instant practice, and Mr. Garrick received my tale
of ill-treatment with more attention and good-nature
than I could possibly have expected from our long
distance and quarrels. In fact, he inwardly rejoiced
at the destroying my connection with Foote, as he
thought that together we were two mischievous
devils, and capable of giving him great uneasiness.
He stepped forward, and said : ' Well, Tate' ('Oh,'
thought I, 'if it is *well, Tate,* all will be right'), 'you
will now be convinced of your error in offending me,
and you will learn in future, I hope, to distinguish
between your real friends and your professional ones.'
I thanked him, and urged my wish for the continuance of the farce (which I had long in secret secured ;
it was correctly wrote out for me by Mr. Brownsmith, under-prompter to Mr. Cross, of that theatre).
' Why, now,' says Garrick, ' that is, if you have a true
copy—why, but what would you do with it for want
of Foote's characters being supplied ?' ' Oh,' says I,
' do not fear that, sir, for I mean to do them myself ;
and in those characters I will make such an example
of *good* Mr. Foote, by fair imitation, as shall cause
him to remember giving " Tea " as long as he lives.'

" Garrick's eyes sparkled with pleasure, and betrayed

a satisfaction he wished to conceal. He inwardly
hated Foote (and not altogether without reason);
he wished to frown, but, with all his ingenuity and
cunning, he was not an actor equal to the task, for he
could not hold back any longer his consent, and said
he was really unhappy at the ill-usage I had received
from ' that Foote.' Foote owed me a recompense for
my great services ; but if I had lost a false friend, I
should find in him a true one ; but he must observe
that he expected I would not make a bad use of his
kindness, but plant my mimicry against Foote alone,
as he was a proper object, and he wished every
success to my benefit and performance. Nay, he was
so generous that he insisted on a bottle of wine being
brought, and after the second glass he asked me if
I would drink any more, but carefully at the same
time put the cork into the bottle. ' No more, sir.'
Nay, he was so generous on that occasion as to give
me a neat new edition of ' Othello,' worth one shilling
and sixpence, which I have to this day preserved, and
have piously transmitted it to my son. When parting
with him, he assured me that he was so much hurt at
the ill-treatment I had received from Foote that he
never would make any future agreement with him—
merely words to please me on our reconciliation. . . .
I promised him not to introduce any mimicry that
might tend to the least likeness whatever of the
performers of either theatre. . . .

   " The wished-for night arrived. A splendid and a
crowded house ; Lady Granard, Lady Tyrawly, Sir
Francis Delaval, the Duke of Portland, the Captains
Dives's, the Hanways, Mrs. Jones Skelton, etc., had
secured all my boxes. My acquaintance, with such
particular interest, aided by public curiosity, a full

theatre cannot be a matter of great surprise to relate. . . .

" My Lady Pentweazle went off with every success
my most sanguine hopes could wish for ; but when I
came on in the very dress Foote had worn, and as
Mr. Foote, the audience seemed actually astonished ;
and, from that point being gained, I really was for
the remainder of the evening persuaded by the height
of fancy that *I was Mr. Foote*. I gave all the particulars he had done, with the imitation of his puppets,
and a new Italian burletta of my own composing, in
the manner of the favourite burletta-singers then at
the Opera House ; and what most highly pleased was
the conversation scene between Mr. and Mrs. Cadwallader as Mr. Foote and Mrs. Clive, which cheered
the audience, as they had not seen it for two years.
Peals of laughter attended the performance, and, I
may add, shouts of applause at all my strokes on
Mr. Foote. . . .

" When Garrick came to the theatre on the Tuesday
morning . . . Mr. Austin said that he greatly enjoyed
all Wilkinson's strokes upon Foote. Garrick, then pretending to be angry, said : ' Now, why, Austin, now,
what d——d tricks has this friend Tate of yours been
at ? Well, and now you want him to be at his tricks
again on Wednesday next? Well, now, really, Austin,
I will have no more to do with these d——d exotics !
But you say he really trimmed Foote well—ha ! ha !
ha !' In the midst of this cheerful scene came a letter
from the Lord Chamberlain, couched in severe terms,
for Mr. Wilkinson's taking the liberty on Monday
night to restore and act a scene from ' The Author '
which had been prohibited ; it had given great offence
to Mr. and Mrs. Aprice, and therefore it was expected

no such rude infringement should be again repeated. Mr. Garrick was now really angry at being called to an account for my breach of his theatric laws ; but I had thought it vastly clever, as it supplied that part where my imitations of the performers were usually given.   Mr. Austin brought me the intelligence, but it chagrined me much ; for, as I had executed that part so well, it was taking a principal feather from my gaudy newly-acquired plume.   However, high authority had laid its weighty commands, and I was obliged, though much against my will, to submit.

" The farce was nevertheless acted, but with the Lord Chamberlain's cruel lopping off a principal limb ; it went off vastly well, but not with such acclamations as on my own night."

The luckless Foote was now so " pinched," as his friend called it, that he arranged a sort of comic lecture to be given at the Haymarket early in December. It seems to have been a kind of rambling discourse, " rather defective and lame, but in that whimsical delivery and oratorial situation in which Foote was unrivalled ; as he had great spirit, fire, and volubility, and was very equal and collected in a situation so difficult." It was ill-prepared, too. However, all his friends mustered strongly for the exhibition.   He ridiculed the two managers, Rich and Garrick ; the latter, he said, " not even allowing the writers to pick up the crumbs that fell from his table "—an unfair charge, as he had been lavish in presenting Foote's pieces and Foote himself.

By the time he came to the second portion of his lecture, he found that he had " dried up " and had nothing more to say.   " He seemed to have no resource, and was reduced to beg leave to sit down at a table with

two candles and read his new piece, called 'The
Minor,' which was in a very mutilated, unprepared
state, and, though enforced by him, was very languid
to a larger audience.   He soon found his experiment
weighed as heavily on himself . as on his hearers,
and therefore broke up the assembled court rather
abruptly, apologized for the hurry, bowed, and
departed with neither token of approbation or disgust, for each party seemed pleased with their
release." All this seemed disastrous enough. But
he was still Foote, the incompressible. Wilkinson
tells us of the next scheme that occurred to the re-
sourceful Foote :

"As January, 1759, had pinched, so February,
instead of being more calm and quiet, made the air
of Covent Garden far from being softened, for it
nipped the wit with increasing severity.   Therefore,
as a resource, he wrote to the manager at Edinburgh.
Callender (as near as I can remember) was the name
of that commander ; the theatre at that time in
Scotland was only a smuggling vessel, but now it is
enlarged and dubbed a royal man-of-war.   Mr. Callender wrote Mr. Foote word that himself and his
company would be proud of his assistance for a few
nights, and assured him it was a compliment his
coming.   At that time birds of passage from London
to Scotland were experiments unknown, for it was
judged impossible for a London theatrical sunflower
to survive the chillness of such a barbarous Northern
clime." All this reads curiously now, when the
Scottish capital is a favourable hunting-ground for the
travelling player.   Foote, it will be seen, was bold and
enterprising.   The late modern system is, however,
quite opposed to such individual visits ; it declines to
receive the profession save, as it were, *en bloc*, when

the whole play, scenery, properties, and company, to use the proper term, "goes on tour." The old system was unquestionably a true and healthy one, the local stock company being fit and ready to welcome the passing guest.

When he had settled on going to Scotland, of which he talked as familiarly as though he were going to Drury Lane, he said airily: "But where's the means? Damme, I must solicit that hound Garrick." He did so promptly, and the actor at once promised him £100. "But then he lent it *like* Mr. Garrick, and could not omit his love of parade," but enjoined formalities; such as that he should see Pritchard, the treasurer, on the matter, and Foote might send up in the evening, when the money would be handed to him. We may be sure that all this was quite true, for it was the careful Garrick's mode of making—and very properly, too—the disorderly Foote feel that it was a serious obligation. On the other hand, Foote could not relish being sent to an underling, so he got his friend Tate to take his note and receive the cash. "He was now in such high spirits that it seemed a moot point with him whether he should continue in London and spend the money, or undertake the journey in search of more. But for a wonder prudence prevailed, and a chaise was ordered for the following morning. On that evening he not only feasted on Mr. Garrick's cash, but, by way of returning thanks, *told more ludicrous stories of him than at any other time I can ever recollect*. He ridiculed him much as a poet, saying: 'David's verses were so bad, and he was so fond of writing, that if he died first he dreaded the thought of his composing his epitaph.' But wits must be forgiven for such little sallies." This is an amusing scene, with

some pleasant traits of character, and about the whole
there is a convincing tone of truth.   We can feel and
see the struggle that was going on in Foote's mind,
and the way in which he strove to indemnify himself.

" Foote at Edinburgh (to use McRuthen's words)
was *quite a phenomenon.*   Everyone in London stared
at his strange disposition, to adventure from the
metropolis of England, a journey of 400 miles, to
Edinburgh, and wondered that an actor of eminence
should venture to a place where at that time a £60
benefit was a treasure."

He reached Edinburgh on March 15, 1759, and on
the 20th made his bow to a Scotch audience, in the
Canongate Concert Hall, with a sort of " fit-up "
theatre.   The scheme turned out far better than was
expected ; he was handsomely received, played in all
his own pieces—in Shylock, besides Bayes' Sir Paul
Plyant.   The morning performance—the first given
in Scotland—on Friday, March 30, was a genuine
morning performance, doors opening at eleven, curtain
to draw up at twelve.   He was welcomed, and entertained hospitably.   He remained until May, and then
returned to town.

In the year 1770, Foote, who always inclined to
bold, ambitious schemes, conceived the idea—a perfect
novelty then, but much practised later—of taking his
whole company into " the provinces " as far as Edinburgh.   He entered into negotiations with Ross,
manager of the Theatre Royal, a new house that had
been opened in Shakespeare Square only the year
before.   Foote took a lease of it for three years, and
the season began about November 10.   The venture,
however, was not successful ; he tired of it, and,
disposing of his lease, went back to London.

And indeed he had a most disastrous journey, being snow-bound at Moffat, at the King's Arms.* A facetious Scot, one Mr. McCulloch of Ardwell, who was at the head of the Customs, fixed to Foote's chaise window some lines in the name of Boreas :

> " Return your steps, I say ;
> Let not one Foote, 'tis my request, profane
> The sacred snows that lie on Erickslane."

Foote was amused, and told the writer " he himself was game for all, as he took anyone for game that suited, as of course." They became friends, and had many a jovial night together.

Foote had brought Woodward, that brilliant comedian, with him, also Robson, Dancer Weston, Mrs. Didier, Mrs. Baker, Mrs. Jewel—about a dozen in all. Rather a contrast this to the modern tourist train with its hundred or so of passengers !

On his return he settled his plans for a visit to Dublin. He little dreamed that his henchman was there before him, already contriving a fresh intrigue for his annoyance. He would have been still more surprised had he known that his good friend—or foe— Garrick was at the moment indirectly concerned in the plot, or favouring it indirectly. Here again is an amusing episode which illustrates Garrick's strangely mixed character.

To Tate Wilkinson.

" I thank you, my dear sir, for your congratulations on my arrival in Scotland, where, by-the-by, I have encountered more perils than in a voyage to the

---

* The accounts of the two journeys to Edinburgh are a little confused, and this and other passages may refer to the first journey.

Indies, not to mention mountains, precipices, savage cataracts, and more savage men. I was locked up for near a week in a village—dirty, dismal, and desolate—by a deluge of snow.

" I think of quitting this town in three weeks at the farthest, and shall certainly pay my homage to you in your kingdom of York ; but not with the least design of becoming your subject : all my campaigns shall end with this place, and my future operations be confined to my own principality. I am glad to find that your theatre stands its ground, though you are so unfortunate as to hobble a little.

" I shall let you know by a line on what day I shall be likely to see you. I beg my compliments to your amiable queen, and the whole royal brood.

" Believe me, sincerely yours,

" SAMUEL FOOTE.

" EDINBURGH,
    " *February* 16."

CHAPTER XI

FOOTE seemed always to revel, as it were, in scenes of confusion; and his presence on one side or the other was sure to stimulate the disorder. He was going to Dublin to repair his finances, where a strange condition of things prevailed.

During the season of 1759-60, a fierce contest was raging between Barry's and Mossop's theatres, to the utter ruin of both. Foote was engaged by Barry, and was to appear as Bayes in "The Rehearsal," which he was to enrich with his favourite mimicries. Macklin, that ever-tempestuous spirit, violent as Mossop, and a tempting enough object from his eccentricities, was marked down for ridicule. The scenes that followed are so racy and entertaining that I cannot resist introducing them for the pleasure of the reader; they also show to what disorder and confusion this licentious spirit led.

The whole city ranged itself into factions taking part with one side or the other; ladies of rank supported their favourites. Barry, Sheridan, and Woodward, at Crow Street, were opposed to Mossop at Smock Alley, There was no money—only noise, combat, and riot. As the contest was a life-and-death one, no missile that could damage was neglected, and when Wilkinson, at Christmas 1759,

166

arrived, each party determined to secure his aid as
a mimic, either with or against Foote.

It must have been a scene of rich comedy when
Foote, already goaded to fury by the petty persecu-
tions of Wilkinson, discovered on arriving that " the
fellow," the "d——d pug,"as he called him, was already
there, and engaged at the rival house. But what would
he have thought, or done, had he suspected that
Tate had been stimulated by Garrick to follow him ?

Foote had a great relish for Irish humour, and
understood it as well as did Thackeray. He did
not care for the hackneyed stage stories, the blunders,
or the bulls. He used to relate admirably tales in
which there was something really witty. They
inspired him with wit—witness his familiar tracing
of the origin of the Irish beggars' clothes. He liked,
and was amused by, the Irish. Long after, in one of
his prologues, he pays a friendly compliment to Irish
humour. A letter from Garrick appeared in the
Dublin papers. The letter ran :

" I have detached Foote's pupil to help you to pull
down those mighty Kings. God send he may have
better success than the Ostrich ; for that, I am told,
never drew enough to pay its freight. He is all I
can spare at present—a d——d clever fellow, and
will work their buff. If he should fail he will be no
loser, for he is continued on my pay. I beg you will
be kind to him. These cursed burletta people I took
from Marybone have done nothing ; I wish the devil
had them. For God's sake let me know if you think
they would go down in Dublin, and I will hustle
them off to you immediately. Tell the poor people
to keep up their spirits, for they may depend upon
every assistance that can be spared by," etc.

Here the style and spirit betray Garrick.

Tate, however, may have been telling of his talks
with the manager, and these hints may have been
worked up into an imaginary letter. Foote saw
and heard of these things, and was at last goaded
into doing something, and some grotesque scenes
followed.

Foote was under a very remarkable and eccentric
personage as his manager—viz., Thomas Sheridan,
of whom "Bozzy" gives us a very distinct drawing.
His was an agitated, almost pathetic story of ill-
luck and trouble through a long life. A fine actor
of the turbulent school, he somehow never "caught
on." Misfortunes pursued him in battalions, and
at this very moment he was struggling with his
two colleagues against impending disasters. Here
were three well-inspired tragedians, Mossop, Barry,
Sheridan—Irish all—dogged by miseries and troubles.
Mossop and Sheridan were "inflated" by vanity to an
extraordinary extent; they saw hatred and prejudice
everywhere. Sheridan unluckily attracted Foote's
notice, who, moreover, booked him for his next
"show." One of the most diverting scenes conceivable was the reception of the impudent mimic's
cool proposal to take him off, and so draw money to
the house. Sheridan had been consulting him on
their desperate state.*

---

* "I said: 'My good Mr. Sheridan, I have hit upon the very
thing to establish myself as a favourite with you and the town.'
He seemed all impatience to know what it could be. 'My dear
sir, a thought has just entered my pate, which I think will draw
money, and be of infinite service to myself.' 'What is it? what
is it?' says Sheridan, with the utmost eagerness. 'Why, sir,' says I,
'your rank in the theatre, and a gentleman so well known in
Dublin, on and off the stage, must naturally occasion any striking

So strange was the behaviour of these eminent
Hibernian players that one is inclined to think they
were all a little mad, either with vanity, jealousy, or
other passions.　Thus, when Tate first met the two
protagonists—Macklin and Mossop—who were in the
same company, they were infuriated with him because
he had engaged himself to the other house.　The
reason was plain : they feared he was going to "take
them all off."　Mr. Mossop "breathed hard, rolled
his eyes, and sniffed the air ; spoke not, looked not,
smiled indignant, and with resentment ; put his hand
upon his sword : his eyes looked terror ; all was sunk
in silence."　Macklin was angry and tragic.　The
youth was afraid to go, could not get out of the
house ; and when at last he rushed away, Mossop

---

imitation of yourself to have a wonderful effect.　I have paid great
attention to your whole mode of acting, not only since I have been
in Dublin, but two years before, when you played the whole season
at Covent Garden Theatre, and do actually think I can do a great
deal on your stage with you *alone*, without interfering with any
other actor's manner whatever.'

"Hogarth's pencil could not testify more astonishment.　He
turned pale and red alternately; his lips quivered.　I instantaneously
perceived I was in the wrong box.　It was some time before he
could speak ; he took a candle from off the table, and, showing me
the room door—when at last his words found utterance—said he
never was so insulted.　What ! to be taken off by a buffoon upon
his own stage !　And as to mimicry, what is it ?　Why, a proceeding
which he never could countenance—that he even despised Garrick
and Foote for having introduced so mean an art ; and he then very
politely desired me to walk downstairs. . . .　I was obliged to march,
and really felt petrified with my bright thought, which had turned
out so contrary from what I had ignorantly expected.　Mr. Sheridan
held the candle for me only till I got to the first landing, and then
hastily removed it, grumbling and squeaking to himself, and leaving
me to feel my way in the dark down a pair and a half of steep
stairs, and to guess my road in hopes of finding the street door.'

rose up of a sudden, and said : " Sir, I wish to attend
you." This was alarming. " But, on crossing the
channels, which were remarkably dirty, he offered his
hand very politely, then suddenly walked on for the
space of five or six minutes, and after a tragic ejacula-
tion he stopped, and said : ' Sir, Mr. Wil-kin-son !
How do you dare to live, sir ? You are going to
play in Crow Street with Barry, sir ; and, sir, I will
run you through the bod-y, sir, if you take the liberty
to attempt any manner of mimicry on the stage.
You must promise me, sir, on your honour, you will
not dare attempt it. If you break that promise, sir,
you cannot live : and you, Mr. Wilkinson, must die,
as you must meet me the next day, and I shall kill
you, sir.' Wilkinson made a sort of half-laughing
protest to the madman, who, somewhat taken aback,
broke out : ' You *dare* not take me off, sir, *more than
a little ;* if you do more, sir, you shall die !' He then
instantly departed, as majestic as the ghost of Cæsar."
Wilkinson, however, according to his own account,
was not to be intimidated, and gave some imitations ;
but it appears that Mossop was more or less content,
declaring that the young man had done what he was
directed to do—*i.e.*, had taken him off *a little.*

Foote must have been disgusted to find himself
committed to the disastrous venture. Wilkinson
arrived on the Christmas Day, and tells us how he
had been encouraged by Garrick to make free with
the two deserters. The great man had furnished him
with a letter which secured him an instant engagement. Foote hardly calculated what an annoyance
this fellow was to be to him. The other, however,
showed much duplicity. He reasoned with himself
that he must keep friends with Barry and Woodward,

as they might be useful to him, and so resolved to show mercy. They had sent an emissary deprecating his mimicries, all but imploring, for any ridicule would do them injury. They even offered to engage him.

Foote, however, was fair game for him. He proceeded to seize on all his plays, exhibitions, and business, in the most lawless way, beginning with " Taste," and " The Diversions of the Morning," or " Tea." Foote said roughly : " D—n the pug ! What can he do against me ?" They had rival benefits within a few days of each other, and rival supporters. Wilkinson had, no doubt, plenty of friends among the second or middle classes. Tate spitefully records that his friend had a thin house.

Mossop, broken down and broken-hearted, beset by his creditors—his performers months in arrear and half starving—this strange Mossop, inflated with pride and arrogance, took on him all the airs of state, and haughtily turned applicants away. The melancholy thing was that there was no money among the party—all were " broke "; and yet the insane competition went on.*

---

* Just as the play was beginning one night, an unhappy actress forced her way into his room, and, falling on her knees, implored Mossop : " Oh, sir, for God's sake, assist me ! I have not bread to eat. I am actually starving, and shall be turned out into the streets." " *Mossop* (in state). Wo-man, you have five pounds a week—wo-man ! *Mrs. Barden.* True, sir ; but I have been here six months, and in all that time have received only six pounds. I call every Saturday for my salary, but ' No money' is the answer. *Mossop.* Wo-man, begone ! and, wo-man, if you dare ask me for money again, I will forfeit you ten pounds." This unlucky Mossop was patronized by ladies of fashion, who brought their friends to his theatre, and would invite him to their routs and parties, where high play was in vogue· The manager, with money in his pocket from some well-supported piece, would gamble it all away, leaving his players unpaid.

Meanwhile the pampered players, uncontrolled and unpaid, had grown so careless and so insolent that they fancied they could take any liberties with an audience which, to say the truth, was as licentious as its entertainers.   Any sort of buffooning exhibition seemed to be tolerated.   Such was the show with which the impudent Tate, with his confederate Mrs. Abington, thought they would try the patience of the Dublin audience.   Like all the rest, it is amusingly told by one of the culprits, and is worth recounting here as a specimen of the condition of the stage.

Here is a specimen of this disorderly insolence.   It is all but inconceivable.

" Mrs. Abington had often entertained several genteel parties with some droll stories of a good gentlewoman she named Mrs. Fuz.   I had been on parties with Lord Miltown and Lord Clambrazil, when in high spirits and good humour, and had diverted myself and the company with stories and anecdotes of my dear, favourite old lady, Mrs. White. . . . Mrs. Abington had promised Lord Miltown she would produce herself as Mrs. Fuz, and she would prevail on her friend Wilkinson to do the same, as Mrs. Jenkins (alias Mrs. White) ; which information his lordship made known to all families of distinction in Dublin.   But the peer did not reflect that those stories told by myself or Mrs. Abington over the convivial table gave a kind of explanatory key to the strange characters. . . .   Before the night came, we often entertained ourselves with extempore rehearsals, and conceived ourselves easy, perfect, and entertaining. . . .   It was a crowded house, part of the pit laid into the boxes.   Mrs. Abington had ordered an excellent supper, superbly lighted, etc., and had wrote a little introductory dialogue scene in the street between two gentlemen, giving a description of a party they were that night invited to, and where two extraordinary characters were asked for the entertainment of the lady's guests, at whose house the rendezvous was appointed ; but each person was enjoined to lay their fingers on their lips, and not to laugh on any account whatever, but to pay every mark of attention and approbation, in order that the two ladies might with more unlimited freedom display their different absurdities. After the dialogue was finished, the scene was drawn up, and discovered several well-dressed ladies and gentlemen at supper : Miss Ambrose was sitting at my elbow as the daughter of Mrs. Jenkins, who intended bringing her on the stage ; Mrs. Fuz was seated at one front corner of a long supper-table, and I was at the other ; Mrs. Kelf was at the head as lady of the ceremonies, which was the only good part, for there were the servants with wine, and she displayed on the occasion her being mistress of a good knife and fork. On being discovered, and looking scornfully at each other, our two figures had for some time a fine effect ; loud fits of laughter succeeded, and from these great expectations were formed.

" Mrs. Fuz then desired Mrs. Jenkins to begin, Mrs. Jenkins desired Mrs. Fuz would do the same, and we found ourselves in an awkward situation. But after a few efforts the two ladies entered into a hobbling short conversation, which was received very well from the eager opinion that something better would follow, for the audience were all eyes and ears ; but we soon flagged. Mrs. Fuz asked for a glass of wine ;

says Mrs. Jenkins, '*Upond* my *sould* and I will have a glass of *wind* too.' That did not do, and the Abington began to feel it a service of danger, perplexity, and disgrace. Mrs. Jenkins called to her daughter to act Juliet, and observe her manner, and to stick herself upon the stage as if she was chilled and stabbed *throughout*. But as she kneeled down to act Juliet, the strange old lady, Mrs. Fuz, got up, gave her a kick, ran away, and abandoned Mrs. Jenkins to the mercy of the audience; I was well aware of what might be expected, and therefore lost no time, but arose and ran after her, crying out, ' Mrs. Fuz ! Mrs. Fuz !' The audience began to smoke the joke, and by their tokens of anger gave the necessary hint to the staring ladies and gentlemen on the stage, that a retreat would not be imprudent if they regarded their safety; so they ran away also, which caused a laugh, for it was evident when Mrs. Abington and I had eloped they were ignorant what to do. . . .

" When the curtain dropped, which was with loud marks of censure, the ladies universally arose, and, by way of joke, laughed and curtsied to each other, saying, ' Your servant, Mrs. Jenkins; your servant, Mrs. Fuz.'"

I have gone, perhaps, too minutely into these curious scenes in order to show how contagious is what may be called a tolerated licence, and what abuses it is certain to bring about. For here we have found the managers of the two patent houses—Garrick and Rich—Foote, Sheridan, Mossop, the chief actors of the great houses, all thrown into confusion, set by the ears, by one malicious, venomous creature. These scenes are well worth reflecting upon.

How imperceptibly and yet how rapidly accom-

plished have been the changes in theatrical customs
and arrangements! Who thinks now of the actor's
benefit! Yet the benefit was at one time, to the
general nuisance of the playgoer, an essential element
in the actor's life. At the close of the season came
regularly a round of benefits. It was a form of
licensed begging, degrading on both sides. It was
supposed also to make up deficiencies in the salary ;
but those who had most effrontery, and who were
skilled in the arts of begging, gained more than their
fellows. The more obscure actors got little. What
arts were employed can be seen in Boz's vivid and
truly humorous scenes.

"One night before my benefit happened, Mr.
Foote (who of all men in the world ought not to
have been offended) found himself much hurt and
wounded, and so little master of himself, notwithstanding the unbounded liberties he had taken, not only
with the players, but also often to the disturbance of
the peace of private families, that he actually visited
me in great wrath, attended by Mr. Larry Kennedy,
and in Pistol-like manner protested, 'If I dared take
any more liberties on the stage in future with him,
he was determined the next day to call me to
account.' But I pursued my plan, and was obliged,
amongst other favours to Mr. Foote, that he was not
observant, but let me rest in quiet. We often met
drawn up at noon in different parties in the Trinity
College Gardens as perfect strangers, but never at
any house of visiting ; if we had, his talent or wit
would have forced me to have felt the severity of his
lash. . . .   This made his visit to me a standing joke
against him in the green-room."

CHAPTER XII

1760

" THE MINOR "

WHEN he was in Dublin, Foote had with him a new comedy, or rather the draft of one, for it was quite incomplete; he thought he might try its effect upon an Irish audience. It might give him an opportunity of "paying off" the viper or gadfly that had been harassing him. To this end he had written a special character—a clever but libellous portrait of Wilkinson —calling it "Shift." Its author saw no risk in failure, because he intended it for a larger and more important audience. He wished to see how the characters would tell, and the drama work out on a small area. It was not likely that the Dublin audiences could recognize the originals of Dr. Squintum, Mrs. Cole, and Smirk, though Shift they had among them. Whitefield had but a slender following in Ireland, and the Mrs. Cole type was not very familiar.

Foote, no doubt, told everyone he knew in Dublin who it was intended for—to wit, "the hound" Wilkinson. One must be astonished at the quiet, business-like fashion in which Wilkinson accepted these affronts and the falsehoods as to his birth and rearing, such as his description as a crossing-sweeper or link-boy. The reason was, he perfectly forecasted that Foote might want him later, and would be useful to

him in town.   So it proved ; and the pliant mime
found Mrs. Cole a standing character, which he acted
with much spirit and grotesqueness, while someone
else was performing Shift and describing his degrading
origin and situation !*

We can only understand the prodigious success of
the play when we consider the enormous extent to
which the craze for exaggerated piety had spread.
Whitefield's fanatical utterances at this time were
provoking derision.   His absurd attacks on pastimes
and theatres—couched in almost farcical language—
caused resentment.   But the "conversion" of a repro-
bate woman, whose only change of life seemed to be
the adoption of religious cant, caused general disgust,
and this phase Foote was to deal with, and with
infinite humour.   Yet Whitefield was sincere and
unsparing in his labours, and it might be that the
actor thought that the success of a rival performer
would interfere with his own.   Disagreeable as is the
description of Dr. Squintum, it is as nothing when
compared with the stroke of introducing Mother Cole
—an odious and repulsive satire.†

When the "unfortunate Dr. Dodd," as he was called,
got into trouble through his offer of money to the Lord
Chancellor's wife for a living, an offer which brought
disgrace on the notorious chaplain to the Magdalens,

---

* The wit of this piece is often very brilliant, and much _à la_
Congreve—as when the gay spendthrift said he was setting up an
opera-dancer at 300 guineas, so as to be in the fashion.   "What
a cormorant !" says one of his friends.   "She must be devilish
handsome !"   "_I am told so_," says the other.   "What ! did you
never see her ?"   "No."

† Boz followed the same tactics in " Pickwick," when he showed
the results of the Shepherd's and Deputy Shepherd's teaching
on Mrs. Weller.

Foote was on the watch, and introduced a Mrs. Simony in his piece. The incident was a vulgar piece of roguery unworthy of public notice outside the courts of law ; but Dodd was a notable public character on account of his sensational sermons at the Magdalen Chapel. This was in Foote's line, and much could be made of it. There was certainly something unchivalrous in thus gibbeting those who were already gibbeted. Of course he " made up" the character after the proper dress, manners, and other peculiarities, and this secured laughter and crowded houses.

It would almost seem that he had resolved to win the title of English Aristophanes by satire conceived on a large scale, and directed against a conspicuous and growing abuse — viz., a system of hysterical sanctity, which under Whitefield's guidance was gathering vast crowds of devotees. He would exert all his powers of humour and ridicule, and amuse as well as chastise. Hence the first sketch of his great and best play, " The Minor." He had made regular studies for this purpose, and had attended Whitefield's services.

The little-scrupulous Tate Wilkinson had been at one time an active follower of Whitefield's, and thus, knowing him by heart as it were, could take off all his peculiarities. He, indeed, supplies a portion of a sermon which is really excellent, and probably a genuine specimen. Shuter also used to attend White-field's Tabernacle at Tottenham Court Road, where he was so liberal in his contributions that, when his benefit came on, Whitefield actually invited his con-gregation to support him. Yet this traitor used, with Wilkinson, to regularly attend the services, with

the view, especially in the case of Tate, of taking
their pastor off. Here is the portrait of Tate
as Shift: "*Sir William Wealthy.* Who were
your parents? *Shift.* I was produced, sir, by a left-
handed marriage, in the language of the newspapers,
between an illustrious lamplighter and an eminent
itinerant cat and dog butcher—'Cat's meat and dog's
meat! Hearts, liver, lights, or a good sheep's heart!'
I dare say you have heard my mother, sir? But as
to this happy pair I owe little besides my being,
I shall drop them where they dropped me—in the
streets.* My first knowledge of the world I owe to
a school which has produced many a great man—the
avenues of the playhouse. There, sir, leaning on my
extinguished link, I learned dexterity from pick-
pockets, connivance from constables, politics and
fashions from footmen, and the art of making and
breaking a promise from their masters. 'Here, sirrah!
light me across the kennel.' 'I hope your honour
will remember poor Jack.' 'You ragged rascal, I
have no halfpence—I'll pay you the next time I see
you.' But, lack-a-day, sir, that next time I saw as
seldom as his tradesmen. *Sir William.* Very well."

Foote's associations with Ireland were of the most
agreeable kind. To the jovial natives, as they were
then, he was most acceptable for his wit, humour,
and good spirits, to say nothing of his histrionic gifts.
The actor loved to be what is called "king of his
company," and this sort of sovereignty the Irish
were heartily willing to afford him. English visitors,
indeed, have always assumed an air of haughty superiority to the aborigines, which the latter, owing

---

* This was one of Foote's unscrupulous libels, as Wilkinson's
father was the Chaplain of the Savoy and a respectable cleric.

perhaps to their old servitude, have accepted with complacency. Foote—always rough and domineering, even in his most convivial moments—would tell them rude truths, and when he " set down" some awkward Hibernian the company joined in the ridicule, and enjoyed the treatment their fellow had encountered. There was a young man of fashion then in Dublin—Mr. Coote, later Earl of Bellamont, whose Court portraits of himself and his Countess are among Reynolds's most picturesque works—well noted for his dandified airs and supercilious bearing. The boon company was delighted to have brought him under Foote's eye, and, so soon as he had gone his way, set up a loud laugh, recapitulating his absurdities. But Foote said : " I see nothing absurd about him. In fact, I think this Mr. Coote of yours is the *only* well-bred, sensible person I have met in Dublin." This was insolent enough, but his obsequious followers laughed and applauded. Hard drinking was then the *basis* of all conviviality.* There was a well-known toper, Sparks by name, who had an official title of the " Lord Chief Joker," and whom Foote, no doubt, often sat beside at feasts, being urged: " Now, Misther Fot, ye're not drinking." Our actor must indeed have been a right good companion, so diverse and adaptable, suited to the company of politicians like Fox, of sages like Johnson, of players, topers, Lord Chief Jokers, and the like. It was a pity, as

---

* When the author was a boy, the taste for punch still prevailed, and he recalls being shown or told of certain rosy-tinted men who " could take their ten tumblers at a sitting." There were also the " two- and three-bottle men." Duelling, also, was only beginning to die out, and he recalls a benevolent old lawyer who had " killed his man." The Irish now are almost less convivial than their English and Scotch brethren.

Johnson said of his Bozzy, "that he had not better bottom."

For Foote the portion of the day that was "worth living for" was the supper—the gathering of jolly listeners, the applause; the night drawn out to morning. In such surroundings Foote was king.

After this generation has passed away, will anyone have anything to tell of the personages that figured in festive meetings in our days? I fear there is nothing to record or to celebrate. We have, alas! no Footes, Garricks, Johnsons, Burkes, Goldsmiths— all is mediocrity. There is nothing worth recording. Someone, no doubt, is recording in a diary lunches and dinners at the Savoy and the Hotel Cecil. But nobody has said anything humorous at these places.

Foote to the last showed his attachment to the Irish. He was constantly paying visits to the country. When introducing "The Nabob" to his admirers on November 19, 1773, Foote reminded his audience that it was twenty years since he had last appeared before them. He hardly forecasted that this was to be his last or farewell appearance. He seized that opportunity to offer a happy compliment to those who had always been his hearty admirers:

> " Humour, the foremost of the festive crew,
>   Source of the comic scene, *she gave to you.*
>   Humour, *with arched brow and leering eye,*
>   *Shrewd, solemn, sneering, subtle, slow, and sly—*
>   Serious herself, yet laughter still provoking,
>   By teasing, tickling, jeering, joking:
>   Impartial gift, that owns nor rank nor birth!
>   If aught derived from her adorns my strain,
>   You gave—at least, discovered first—the vein."

Speaking as a native of the pleasant country, I can testify that no happier or more exact description

could be given of the Irish humour—such as the
" slowness," " sneering," " leering eye." These are the
elements, as indeed they were of Foote's own method.
Instead of slowness, however, Foote's stroke was rapid
and overwhelming. At present Irish humour, if not
extinct, is but a debased article ; one would almost
take it to be borrowed from the low artificial type
of music-hall humour. The accompaniments described by Foote are always present—artfully used to
entice a laugh—but the humour is not there. Affectation and desire of applause—this, as in other things,
has spoiled the market.

When he appeared in town after his Dublin
failure, he carried it off at the coffee-houses with
much flourishing and boasting. " Pooh ! hang them!"
(the Dublin people) ; " there was not a shilling in the
country but what the Duke of Bedford and I and
Mr. Rigby have brought away." Murphy heard him
saying this. He then diligently set to work to re-
model, and indeed rewrite, his piece.*

* I recall that clever dramatist Dion Boucicault—by no means a
Foote in his wit, but far superior in dramatic construction—coming
to Dublin to try the first sketch of his " Shaughraun." It was a
great festival. I attended, and was much pleased by the variety
of incidents and characters. Next day I went and told him so,
when to my surprise he said : " My friend, it won't do at all. All
this and that—this scene, this character, this incident—must come
out ; the whole must be recast and reshaped." So it was ; a really
vast mass of amusing things being remorselessly cast overboard.
This the real, well-skilled artist is always prepared to do.

CHAPTER XIII

1760

" THE MINOR "—*continued*

" THE MINOR," enlarged and equipped with new characters, was brought forward at the Haymarket. It was wonderfully successful, not merely owing to its dramatic merits, but from the excited controversies to which it gave rise. This must have been infinitely acceptable to its author. It was said to be scandal that religion should be ridiculed in a playhouse, and in so gross a fashion. The notion of a person of Mrs. Cole's infamous profession becoming a convert of Whitefield's was repulsive, and it was justly urged that a writer who could introduce such a personage was as bad as, or worse than, the people whom he stigmatized. Such exaggeration was beyond credulity.*

The success was extraordinary; though it was performed by an entirely young and unpractised company, it brought full houses for thirty-eight nights, and

---

* Foote's description of Whitefield in the epilogue as Dr. Squintum was due to an accident. He was passing by his Tabernacle, when he turned in and found him "dealing out damnation" in a comfortable, unctuous way. This entertained him hugely, and out of the notes he made is formed this amusing caricature. It is characteristic of our satirist that he should have given him a name drawn from a physical imperfection for which Whitefield was well known.

continued for some years as one of the stock pieces of
the theatre.

"The Minor" must indeed always be considered
Foote's best piece, it is so full of spirit, and so bright
and entertaining are the characters.   But of plot there
is little.   Indeed, Foote always ingeniously contrives
to "fend off" anything like story or plot; he, as it
were, makes mere statements and exhibits figures.
It is, indeed, only by writing down a strict analysis of
Foote's plots that we see how poor all are.   In truth,
they cannot be called " plots " at all.   Nothing takes
place, and nothing is done.   The author introduces
one of his characters, displays him, lets him discuss
with another character—exhibits, it may be, a certain
ephemeral situation, which leads to nothing.   How
different is the growing—and yet more growing—
interest of the true dramatist, character working on
character, the excitement developing as we go on!

In this lively piece there is a brilliantly-touched
character—Loader, a gambler who sees everything in
the light of gaming, and can express himself in gaming
terms only.   Here Foote showed refined art.   It is a
common *truc* of the dramatist to furnish, say, a
"horsey" man with sporting phrases, but Loader's
talk is truly natural; he seems to *think* in cards and
dice :

"*Sir Geo.* You had your share, Mr. Loader.
Loader. Who, I ? Lurch me at four, but I was
marked at the top of your trick, by the Baron."

As before, he introduced his friend-enemy Wilkinson
as Shift.   As Tate had taken him off, he now repaid
him in kind.   Playing Mrs. Cole and Shift, he produced a curious complication, for Shift is disguised as
the auctioneer Smith, and here Foote, after first

mimicking Tate as Shift, now mimicked a certain London auctioneer.*

Again, there is a scene when Wealthy calls on his spendthrift nephew. It would not be quite unworthy of "Goldy." The natural coolness of the youth is quite admirable :

"*R. Weal.* Well, young man, and what do you think will be the end of all this ? Here I have received by the last mail a quire of your draughts from abroad. I see you are determined our neighbours should taste of your magnificence. *Sir Geo.* Yes, I think I did some credit to my country. *R. Weal.* And how are all these to be paid ? *Sir Geo.* That I submit to you, dear nuncle. *R. Weal.* From me !—Not a soul to keep you from the counter. *Sir Geo.* Why then let the scoundrels stay. It is their duty. I have other demands, debts of honour, which must be discharged. *R. Weal.* Here's a diabolical distinction ! Here's a prostitution of words !—Honour ! 'Sdeath, that a rascal, who has picked your pocket, shall have his crime gilded with the most sacred distinction, and his plunder punctually paid, whilst the industrious mechanic, who ministers to your very wants, shall have his debt delay'd, and his demand treated as insolent.† *Sir Geo.* Oh ! a truce to this threadbare trumpery, dear nuncle. . . . *R. Weal.* One commission, however, I can't dispense with myself from executing.—It was agreed between

* One speech shows how "old Sherry" caught the gay tone of "The Minor." The Auctioneer declares : "Oh, many an aigrette and solitaire have I sold to discharge a lady's play debt ! But we must know the parties ; otherwise it might be knocked down to her husband himself. Ha, ha !"

† Might not these words have been spoken by Sir Peter Teazle ?

your father and me, that as he had but one son and I one daughter—— *Sir Geo.* Your gettings should be added to his estate, and my cousin Margery and I squat down together in the comfortable state of matrimony. *R. Weal.* Puppy! ... Your answer, ay or no? *Sir Geo.* Why then, concisely and briefly, without evasion, equivocation, or further circumlocution —No. *R. Weal.* I am glad of it. *Sir Geo.* So am I. *R. Weal.* But pray, if it wou'd not be too great a favour, what objections can you have to my daughter? Not that I want to remove 'em, but merely out of curiosity. What objections? *Sir Geo.* None. I neither know her, have seen her, inquired after her, or ever intend it. *R. Weal.* What! perhaps I am the stumbling-block? *Sir Geo.* You have hit it. *R. Weal.* Ay, now we come to the point. Well, and pray—— *Sir Geo.* Why, it is not so much a dislike to your person, though that is exceptionable enough, but your profession, dear nuncle, is an insuperable obstacle. *R. Weal.* Good lack! And what harm has that done, pray? *Sir Geo.* Done! So stained, polluted, and tainted the whole mass of your blood, thrown such a blot on your 'scutcheon, as ten regular successions can hardly efface. *R. Weal.* The deuce! ... But then I thought her having the honour to partake of the same flesh and blood with yourself might prove in some measure a kind of fuller's-earth, to scour out the dirty spots contracted by commerce. *Sir Geo.* Impossible! ... Why, what apology cou'd I make to my children for giving them such a mother? *R. Weal.* I did not think of that. Then I must despair, I am afraid. *Sir Geo.* I can afford but little hopes. Though, upon recollection—is the grisette pretty? *R. Weal.* A parent may be partial. She is thought

so. *Sir Geo.* Ah la jolie petite bourgeoise ! Poor
girl, I sincerely pity her.   And I suppose, to procure
her emersion from the mercantile mud, no consideration wou'd be spared.   *R. Weal.* Why, to be sure, for
such an honour one wou'd strain a point. . . . *Sir Geo.*
So, nuncle Richard, if you will sell out of the stocks,
shut up your counting-house, and quit St. Mary Ax
for Grosvenor Square—— *R. Weal.* What then ?
Sir Geo. Why, when your rank has had time to rouse
itself, for I think your nobility, nuncle, has had a
pretty long nap, if the girl's person is pleasing, and the
purchase-money is adequate to the honour, I may in
time be prevailed upon to restore her to the right of
her family.   *R. Weal.* Amazing condescension ! *Sir
Geo.* Good-nature is my foible.   But, upon my soul,
I wou'd not have gone so far for anybody else.
R. Weal. I can contain no longer.   Hear me, spendthrift, prodigal : do you know that in ten days your
whole revenue won't purchase you a feather to adorn
your empty head ?—— *Sir Geo.* Hey-dey, what's
the matter now ? *R. Weal.* And that you derive
every acre of your boasted patrimony from your
great-uncle, a soap boiler ! *Sir Geo.* Infamous
aspersion ! *R. Weal.* It was his bags, the fruits of
his honest industry, that preserved your lazy, beggarly
nobility.   His wealth repaired your tottering hall,
from the ruins of which even the rats had run.   *Sir
Geo.* Better our name had perished ! Insupportable !
soap-boiling, uncle !"

This scene is truly admirable, and even more lively
and natural than any in Sheridan's play.

Not unnaturally, it went round that he had offered
to submit his piece to the Archbishop of Canterbury's
perusal.   On the instant it was humorously fore-

casted that Foote would gravely issue an announcement that it had been *revised* by His Grace the
Archbishop, who would thus be accountable for
Mother Cole and other enormities. His Grace was
shrewd enough not to fall into the trap, as it was
considered to be.*

Foote's jest on the Archbishop of Canterbury was
well founded, for he strove hard to prevent the piece
being licensed, and Walpole says that the Chamberlain allowed him to strike out some passages. A
letter of the Chamberlain's to Garrick, however,
shows that this is a mistake, as an offer was actually
made to the Archbishop to erase any passages that
he objected to.

An angry controversy about " The Minor " raged
for a time, no doubt to the satisfaction of the
author. There were quite a number of pamphlets
issued pro and con. He was attacked from all sides.†
Letters on " The Minor," prompted by friends of
Whitefield, appeared, and the adroit author was only
too glad to reply. He gave his pen full range, and
dealt roughly with his antagonists.

An extract from this lively retort will entertain
the reader. It is addressed with mock civility to

---

* I confess that I cannot see the point of Foote's jest of opposing
" Tom Cant " by " Tam Cant." What was " Tam Cant "?

† " Bozzy," then a youth at Edinburgh, was among the assailants
of " The Minor." He issued a sort of slight " skit," of which I
have never seen a copy. So thus early began their antagonism.
Assisted by two friends, " Bozzy " also wrote a skit on Dodsley's
" Cleone "—a rare thing, of which I once possessed a copy ; but,
alas ! not knowing its value, I destroyed it. I have never seen or
heard of it since. I have had, however, several of Boswell's rare tracts,
such as " The Cub at Newmarket," which have found a home in
the Johnson House Library at Lichfield.

" The Reverend Author of the Remarks, *Critical and Christian*, on ' The Minor.' "

" Your next remark, I think, was upon the cruelty and indecency of producing your friend at the theatre on the score only of a mere natural infirmity, an inconsiderable weakness in the optic nerve, which, instead of retaining the eyes in the reciprocal direction they are generally placed in, lets them loose to run rambling about the head. This criticism you sustain by an observation of my own, that provincial dialects are not the proper objects of comedy ; and if not dialects, surely much less natural infirmities. . . .

" But this is a trifle to what occurs in the progress of your poem. You there make a conveyance to your disciples of certain seats, which you pretend to have in the realms above ; and you promise them not only a good neighbourhood of patriarchs, *apostles*, and martyrs, but that the Tottenham teacher himself shall certainly settle among them."

The old converted Mrs. Cole,* acted by Foote himself, is an inimitable character drawn with extra-ordinary power and strokes of humour. I heartily wish I could present some specimens to the reader, but it is too coarsely drawn, and it makes us specu-late how such things could be stomached by a decent audience. After her conversion she calls on two of her old patrons. This follows :

* Foote, ever unscrupulous, has, it seems, borrowed or " con-veyed " this character from another piece which had been entrusted to him by a fellow-dramatist, Reed. This writer protested : " As there is a palpable similarity between Mrs. Cole and Mrs. Snarewell, it may be necessary to declare that the piece was put into Mr. Foote's hands in August 1758, on his promise of playing it at Drury Lane." Here is a very palpable insinuation or charge. But such things never affected him ; he went on his way as before.

" *Mrs. Cole.* Hold, hold, Mr. Loader! Heaven help you, I could as soon swallow the Thames. Only a sip to keep the gout out of my stomach. *Load.* Why, then, here's to thee.—Levant me, but it is supernaculum.—Speak when you have enough. *Mrs. Cole.* I won't trouble you for the glass; my hands do so tremble and shake, I shall but spill the good creature. *Load.* Well pulled. . . . Crop me, but this Squintum has turned her brains. *Sir Geo.* Nay, Mr. Loader, I think the gentleman has wrought a most happy reformation. *Mrs. Cole.* Oh, it was a wonderful work. There had I been tossing in a sea of sin, without rudder or compass. And had not the good gentleman piloted me into the harbour of grace, I must have struck against the rocks of reprobation, and have been quite swallowed up in the whirlpool of despair. He was the precious instrument of my spiritual sprinkling. . . . *Load.* Pillory me, but it has a face. *Mrs. Cole.* Truly, consistently with my conscience, I wou'd do anything for your honour. *Sir Geo.* Right, Mrs. Cole, never lose sight of that monitor. But pray how long has this heavenly change been wrought in you? *Mrs. Cole.* Ever since my last visitation of the gout. Upon my first fit, seven years ago, I began to have my doubts and my waverings; but I was lost in a labyrinth, and nobody to show me the road. One time I thought of dying a Roman, which is truly a comfortable communion enough for one of us; but it wou'd not do. *Sir Geo.* Why not? *Mrs. Cole.* I went one summer over to Boulogne to repent; and, wou'd you believe it, the bare-footed, bald-pate beggars would not give me absolution without I quitted my business! Did you ever hear of such a set of scabby—— Besides,

I cou'd not bear their barbarity. Would you believe it, Mr. Loader, they lock up for their lives, in a nunnery, the prettiest, sweetest, tender young things! —Oh, six of them, for a season, wou'd finish my business here, and then I shou'd have nothing to do after. *Load.* Brand me, what a country! *Sir Geo.* Oh, scandalous! *Mrs. Cole.* Oh no, it would not do. So, in my last illness, I was wished to Mr. Squintum, who stept in with his saving grace, got me with the new birth, and I became as you see, regenerate, and another creature. [*Enter* DICK.] *Dick.* Mr. Transfer, sir, has sent to know if your honour be at home. *Sir Geo.* Mrs. Cole, I am mortified to part with you. But bus'ness, you know—— *Mrs. Cole.* True, Sir George. Mr. Loader, your arm—— Gently, oh, oh! *Sir Geo.* Wou'd you take another thimbleful, Mrs. Cole? *Mrs. Cole.* Not a drop—— I shall see you this evening? *Sir Geo.* Depend upon me. *Mrs. Cole.* To-morrow . . . We are to have at the Tabernacle an occasional hymn, with a thanksgiving sermon for my recovery. After which I shall call at the register office, and see what goods my advertisement has brought in. *Sir Geo.* Extremely obliged to you, Mrs. Cole. . . . *Mrs. Cole.* Softly, have a care, Mr. Loader—— Richard, you may as well give me the bottle into the chair, for fear I should be taken ill on the road. Gently—— so, so!"

Mr. Forster justly admires Foote's retort to an adversary who spoke of this libellous piece being played " under authority." " Under authority. What! do you suppose I play, as you preach, upon my own authority? No, sir, religion turned into a farce is by the constitution of this country the only species of the drama that may be exhibited for money without permission." I doubt if in our time this refined bit of irony would be understood or appreciated.*

Later, Wilkinson so far condoned the libellous portrait of him in "The Minor" that he was content to take a part in the play. Foote, with all his faults, did not bear malice or a grudge. He could be angry, but did not revenge. His sense of his own interest set him above such petty feeling.†

After all his troubles with Foote, and after having received such a lesson, it might have been expected that Garrick would have been cautious. But the younger mimic, who was still in his service, knew how to work on his feeling and prejudices by talking to him on the subject of Foote. Wilkinson had gone to Covent Garden Theatre, where the eccentric

---

* Forster was the last survivor of the old trained, well-schooled literary man. He was deeply studied in all the old writers, never went anywhere without his pocket Shakespeare, knew the old poets by heart, and was an admirable critic of sure judgment. His bosom friend, Elwin, whom I knew well, was of a similar type. Our critics now are not equipped with this solid baggage, for they have no need to be. The public, it is to be feared, are indifferent to this fossil era, and I often think I have been somewhat rash in offering this elaborate account of one whom nobody is much interested in. And yet, some thirty or forty years ago, at Mr. Murray's sale dinner, I can recall a work of such heavy, repelling character as "The Life of Charles the Bold" being sold off to the assembled booksellers.

† "The Minor," however, is further remarkable for the fact that it indirectly supplied us with the imperishable comedy of "The School for Scandal." Sheridan was a dramatist in his art of putting a play together, but for incidents and characters he resorted to other sources. He drew deeply from Foote's wells, not only characters and situations, but wit. The smartly-contrived jests or epigrams were his own, but always seemed inappropriate in the mouth of the person who spoke them. All this I shall show in detail.

Rich, who always called him "Williamskin," was
eager to secure him a long engagement; but the
other preferred a temporary one, as giving him an
opening for his mimicries, and, above all, for worrying Foote afresh.

He joined with an actor at Covent Garden—one
Sparks, whom he had driven to madness by his
mimicries, but who was now his great friend—in a
plot to all but compel the manager to bring out
Foote's "Minor," with all his mimicry pieces. Rich
was not inclined to follow this course, but was at last
persuaded. He was not unwilling to take his share
in plaguing "Mr. Footeseye," as he rechristened him.
There was a sort of race for the first production
between the two theatres, in which Drury Lane
eventually won. Wilkinson, with incredible effrontery,
laid out his plan for performing not only "The Minor,"
but other "shows" by the same author—his prologues,
epilogue, Lady Pentweazle: and this within a stone's-
throw of Drury Lane! Foote, not unnaturally, was
stung to fury by these piracies, and the result was
a scene of extraordinary violence, but one which is
amusing enough. He rushed to Covent Garden and
forced his way in to the manager.

"'Damn it, you old hound!' he furiously exclaimed, 'if you dare to allow Wilkinson, that pug-
nosed son of a ——, to take such a liberty with me
as to mimicry, I will bring yourself, Rich, on the
stage! If you want to engage that pug, black his
face, and let him bring the tea-kettle in a pantomime;
for, damn the fellow, he is as ignorant as a maid!
And if he dares to appear in my characters in "The
Minor," I will,' said he, 'instantly produce your
old and ridiculous self, with your three cats, and that

hound of a mimic, all together, next week at Drury
Lane, for the general diversion of the pit, boxes, and
galleries ; and that will be paying you, you squinting
old Hecate, too great a compliment !' And after a
few sarcasms Foote hastily departed, denouncing
vengeance on him and his cats, and immediately
Mr. Rich appeared with a most woeful countenance,
and said : ' Why, *Muster Sparkish, Muster Footeseye*
has been here, and he says if I let *Muster Williamskin* act his parts on the stage, *Muster Sparkish*, he
will write parts for me, my cats, and *Muster Williamskin*, and bring us all upon the stage ; so we must not
act what we intended.' ' Why, surely, sir,' said
Sparks, ' you cannot be so weak as to let Mr. Foote's
vapouring visit frighten you from your purpose, or
intimidate you from having a piece acted that may
be of service to your theatre, and to the young gentleman. . . .   Now, Mr. Rich,' added Sparks, ' let me interest myself in this matter, I augur success ; therefore
let us of Covent Garden Theatre immediately rally our
forces, take the field, let slip the dogs of war, and act
" The Minor " in defiance of his own guards at Drury
Lane.'   Rich agreed, seemed pleased—but he was
still frightened of Foote, and, I believe, dreaded an
affront on his favourite cat more than on himself.
All was settled to have the performance brought forward as soon as possible, for, as Sparks observed,
' advantage *fed them fat while we delayed.'* Indeed,
' The Minor ' was ready at Drury Lane, and they
meant not to lose time, for Foote entertained not the
least doubt of victory.

" We, from various obstacles, could not get it
decently on the stage in less than a fortnight, as other
pieces were preparing. . . . And on the end of the week

that this matter had been settled, it was advertised on
the Thursday from Drury Lane, and on the Saturday
was pasted on every wall—' THE MINOR'; and that
favourite little comedy had been all the week puffed
and paragraphed in every newspaper by Mr. Foote.
But unforeseen events sometimes do and undo what
our utmost wisdom and wishes cannot, as here was
an extraordinary instance ; for the bills were but a few
hours exhibited to public view, when it so happened
they were as hastily plucked down as they had been
vigilantly put up. It was on Saturday the 25th of October, 1760, when the sudden death of our truly beloved
and lamented monarch, King George II., occasioned,
for three weeks, a suspension of theatrical hostilities
and diversions of all kinds in the great city of London."

The theatres were closed for about a fortnight—a
costly form of mourning for the performers. Here
was a righteous Nemesis, and it served the pirates
right. But they persevered. On November 24 the
rival "Minor" was produced, and, it would appear,
with more success than fell to that of Drury Lane.
Wilkinson literally rioted in Foote, "taking him off"
in many forms. Foote seems to have been quite
helpless. The whole episode well illustrates the
loyalty of these mimics to one another.

Meanwhile the inferior mime was still obsequiously
ingratiating himself with Mr. Garrick, who patronized
and even indulged him. Thus when, on May 14,
Tate had chosen a tragic character for his benefit,
the manager interested himself, went over the part
privately with him, and on the night of the performance carefully "made up"—as it is called—his
face. On the same night he was again allowed to
give his various imitations of Foote. This does not

13—2

seem handsome. There can be no doubt he "fed fat" on these mimicries, and relished them, and the young fellow—only twenty-one—was really clever and entertaining.

The enterprising Foote, who was versatile enough in his schemes, found himself shut out of his little theatre for the summer season of 1761. He complained that a licence had been refused to him on the ground, we may presume, of his rude treatment of the community. He, however, jocosely attributed it to the engagement of some others, who had been beforehand with him at the Chamberlain's office. He proposed to Arthur Murphy—their old dispute had long been forgotten—to enter into alliance and become joint managers of Drury Lane Theatre for the summer months. Now, as we cannot find any instances of Garrick's subletting his great theatre, it is quite easy to conjecture that he did so under Foote's pressure. He felt he dared not refuse. He let it to the pair at a moderate price, and it was arranged that both should write new pieces for the season. They opened in June, 1761. A number of Murphy's comedies formed the staple of the entertainment, and their season proved successful.

CHAPTER XIV

FOOTE, WIT AND HUMORIST

AT the present moment it would seem as though the race of English humorists were extinct. In whatever direction we look, hardly one greets the eye. The one and only comic paper week by week supplies its " word-catches "—small puns and so-called " jests. ' In the social life there is the same dearth. We do not meet " funny " or witty men. Even the late much-vaunted Father Healy was as nothing to the old pattern, but he had the merit of freshness and surprise. Foote might be considered the last professional humorist of the true breed, as distinguished from the carefully prepared concocters of droll things—the Sydney Smiths, Jerrolds, Brothers Smith, etc. He never *prepared* anything. He was always ready. He knew not himself what next was to come. Someone incautiously applied the match, and loud explosion followed. He was inexhaustible ; the operation was automatic.

As we look back to this strange era, what strikes us most is the general reign of laughter. It seemed a time of universal good-humour. That familiar phrase, *laughing it off*, became a scientific process. A difficulty arose, even a tragic affair—it could be turned into ridicule, and so disappear. Foote got out of most of his difficulties in this fashion. And what a contrast to our own sober-grey era, where everyone is so "literal" (Elia's abomination), and where everything fanciful, wit, melodrama, romance, low comedy, has disappeared—I must say, with disastrous result !

The greatest tribute ever paid to Foote's gifts was by Charles Fox. To Rogers he described a dinner at Lord W. Bentinck's, to which he had been invited. Fox looked forward to meeting the trading professional diner-out, the teller of "potted" stories, and expected to be bored. Never was there such a surprise. Foote delighted them all. Whatever subject was started—classical, topical, political—he was ready, and treated it with a lively geniality and wit that amazed and enchanted.

Churchill devoted to him just ten lines, which may be read with enjoyment. He, however, does his chastisement gently—at least, not with the harshness he dealt out to others :

> " By turns transformed into all kinds of shapes,
>   Constant to none, Foote laughs, cries, struts, and scrapes :
>   Now in the centre, now in van or rear,
>   The Proteus shifts, bawd, parson, auctioneer.
>   His strokes of humour, and his bursts of sport,
>   Are all contained in this one word—distort.
>   Doth a man stutter, look asquint, or halt,
>   Mimics draw humour out of Nature's fault,
>   With personal defects their mirth adorn,
>   And hang misfortune out to public scorn."

In this, though severe enough, there is no malice ; he seems to have a secret admiration. The gay swing of the lines is delightful, and the rebuke delicately administered.

It was said that Foote, always quick to resent, prepared a reply written in prose, but presently thought it would be prudent to suppress it. The same reason—awe or dread of Churchill—made him forbear to introduce him on his stage. What must have stung Foote more than anything else was the praise Churchill lavished upon Garrick—praise so cordial and heartfelt and so brilliant in its discrimination that the great actor must have felt a thrill of pride. He was almost the only one in the long gallery of portraits who was so distinguished. He was really treated *heroically*, while Foote was treated with a sort of banter. The introduction of Wilkinson made it the more humiliating:

> *" The first a mere mere mimic's mimic stood."*

In truth—like his friend Garrick—he was an actor not merely on his professional stage, but also on " the boards " of life, where he performed with an energy and a versatility that were astonishing. He was perpetually expending himself in fun and frolic and convivial meetings: broad jokes and witty sayings never ceased to flow from his lips ; he was surrounded by friends, flatterers, and admirers, who cheered him on, and with whom he " heard the chimes at midnight." Yet he found time for all things, and never neglected business. In all directions, even when on his travels, we hear of him as well feasted, as a wit and " good comrade," keeping the tables in a roar, while his health, as his purse, seemed to well stand the strain. He had troops of convivial friends.

Foote was associated with two tumultuous beings—daring, reckless, and ever at war with their fellows. It would be difficult to find in the history of English social life three such specimens of the " stormy " life and brilliancy at the same moment as Wilkes,

Churchill, and Foote. Their wild and combative careers were as extraordinary as they were interesting and dramatic. They were always "in assailment"— Foote from the stage, Churchill from his desk or from the gaol, Wilkes from the House of Commons. The public was being constantly thrown into commotion or expectancy by their acts. All three in their respective lines were men of power and capacity, and dangerous to meddle with. It was a sort of terrorism. All three were debauchees and loose-livers. The moral, however, is, that the end was disastrous for two of the party : Wilkes, indeed, ended his days in peace and comfort, but only by striking his colours and reforming his turbulent life. And how, it will be asked, came the public to tolerate these disturbers so long ? Simply because they found entertainment in the spectacle, which was a most exciting one. In our own day we have nothing analogous. A scurrilous or offensive attack on an individual is promptly brought to the Courts and disposed of.

Between Foote and Churchill there was little intimacy, for Churchill had found a place for him in his pillory, as, indeed, he did for most of the notable persons of his acquaintance. It is said that Foote's last words were about Churchill, the pair dying within a short time of each other—the one at Boulogne, the other at Dover. The meteoric, hectoring Wilkes was more congenial to him. There was, indeed, scarcely time for such intimacy with Churchill to mature, for the famous satire appeared in 1761, and he died three years later. There was this curious similarity between these remarkable men, that one ridiculed the players by mimicking their defects, while the other described their various failings in bitter but amusing language.

One was satirist on the stage, the other off it. Both
were rough, cruel men, and when they hugged it was
a bear's hug. Churchill, reviewing the theatrical
ranks, was not likely to pass by Foote; but, as we
have seen, he did not handle him very severely—he
spoke more of his system than of himself.

No one, as I said, so combined pleasure and a
sort of roaring joviality with business as did the
boisterous Foote. One of his most congenial comrades
was Sir Francis Delaval—half eccentric, half man
of pleasure, but a strange original. He was a fair
specimen of those reckless *viveurs* who allow nothing
to stand in the way of their whims and humours.
With such, money—whether they have it or have it
not—does not count; anything suggested in the name
of enjoyment or amusement had to be carried out.
Foote liked him, was always with him, but was as
regularly faithless to him as he was to all other
" friends."

Long years of disorderly conduct naturally involved
Sir Francis in debts and difficulties, for which he
consulted his friend, who of course could not help
him. Foote happened, however, to know a very plain,
elderly spinster of quality, Lady Harriet Paulet, but
with £90,000 " to her fortune," and it occurred to him
that this might be a suitable match for Sir Francis.
There was a difficulty—that Sir Francis, like Sir
Antony in the play, " would not touch anything old
or ugly to save his life." He contrived that the lady
should visit a conjurer, or fortune-teller, who had
been well primed, and his prophecies so impressed
her that, when Sir Francis appeared, she yielded at
once. So all was arranged happily. Once, growing
suspicious, he asked Foote why he had not " gone in

for" the lady himself, on which Foote pleaded that he was "already married to his washerwoman."*

In the midst of his riotous follies Sir Francis was seized with a fit. He died, without ever recovering from it, on the following morning.

"Foote," says Cooke, "heard of this melancholy event with a sincere sorrow. He loved him with as much constancy of friendship as he could feel towards any man. ... He burst into a flood of tears, retired to his room, and saw no company for three days. On the fourth, Jewel, his treasurer, calling on him for the arrangement of some urgent business, he, with swelled eyes and in faltering words, inquired when Sir Francis was to be buried. 'Not till the latter end of next week, sir,' replied the other, 'as I hear the surgeons intend first to *dissect his head.*' This last expression (as in instances of madness) striking the chord of his ruling passion, he suddenly exclaimed: 'And what will they get *there?* I'm sure I have known poor Frank these five-and-twenty years, and I never could find anything in *it.*'"

It may be conceived that when a party was collected at Seaton-Delaval—Sir Francis's home in the country —these merry men had what are called "high jinks." Practical joking of an almost scientific kind was in favour. Angelo, the fencing-master, and other professionals, contributed their exertions. It was contrived to be all one ceaseless practical joke. No one was spared. When the fencing-master swung himself across a marble basin to show "how easy it was," it was contrived that he should be dropped in the water, the rope being purposely made short. He later

* Horace Walpole, however, states that Foote had been intimately connected with this lady—which would be a more probable story.

wagered that he would creep blindfolded on his knees
for a hundred yards to a wood. They soon found
out that he was guiding himself by a silk thread fixed
by pins to the ground, when the wags artfully diverted
the course of the thread, making it lead to a pond, into
which he fell. There was, however, one first-class jest
for which Foote was entirely responsible. Among the
guests was a solemn Baronet who had been crossed in
love, and whose jeremiads and low spirits annoyed the
party. He also found that his health was affected,
and had a new complaint every day. It was Foote
who thought of a most original device. When the
Baronet was gone to bed, a tailor was brought, who
"took in" his clothes considerably, so that when he
put them on—or tried to do so—he was so terribly
scared by what he thought was a sudden fit of dropsy
that he lay in bed for three days. He was at last
induced to get up, and the clothes being brought back
to their former size, to his joy he supposed the dropsical
attack had passed away. Not less amusing was what
followed on his "recovery," at supper. Foote had
the wax candles painted different colours, a black
one being specially placed beside the hypochondriacal
Baronet. They observed him looking curiously at the
phenomenon. "The candles have different colours,"
he said. "How so?" they said. "What colour but
one should they have?" He said nothing; but when
the servant filled his glass, he asked him what colour
the black candle was. "White, sir, to be sure." On
which he broke out, "This is too much!" and rushed
upstairs, leaving the next morning. These belong to
the *haute école*.

There was a "fumigating" quack named Dominecetti, who cured people by directing steam on the

weak part, and who, it will be recollected, furnished
Johnson with one of his rough speeches, directing
someone—was it Bozzy?—to get the steam turned
on to his head, for that was *his* weak spot.

There was a Dr. Kennedy who was intimate with
Sterne and Garrick, and free of the green-rooms.
Three nights in the week, at the least, was he to be
seen at the theatres, and never for years absent from
a first night's performance. " His friendly hands,"
said Foote, " were as hard with clapping as a cobbler's
lap-stone."*

It will be recalled how Bob Sawyer, to increase his
practice, used to have himself called out of church
during service-time. Dr. Kennedy, however, anticipated him, and on a more elaborate system. A
hired emissary in a hired livery used to go to the
theatre where he was, and, obtaining admission, would
call out between the acts, "Dr. Kennedy!" Another,
going to another theatre where he was seated in
a front row, would also call out, " Dr. Kennedy!"
The doctor would then rise, and, taking his hat and
cane and bowing right and left, would depart. " Bless
me," the people near would say, " that Dr. Kennedy
has half the patients in town!"† The doctor was,
however, soon " smoked," as it was called, by the
galleries, who soon began to call out, " Dr. Kennedy!"
when he appeared in the boxes.

One of Foote's victims whom he was fond of
exhibiting at social meetings, dinners, suppers, etc.,

---

* Part of the machinery of Foote's humour was the suggestion of
some base or earthy element or association, so as to level anything
in the way of creditable sentiment.

† Dickens must have read this in Angelo's " Memoirs"; for his
Bob Sawyer adds, that people in church would say : " Bless me,
what a practice that young man has !"

was Mr. Justice Clive, a lethargic old Judge who had married a young and handsome wife. Foote used to attend in his Court to make notes, which furnished him with these exuberant displays. Mr. Cradock reports that a gentleman, after listening to one of these ebullitions—quite shocked at their libellous extravagance—turned to Johnson, and said : "Why, Dr. Johnson, it is impossible that this impudent fellow can know the truth of half of what he has told us." "Nay, sir," was the reply, "if we venture to come into company with Foote we have no right, I think, to look for truth."

Foote was a member of a theatrical club known as Wright's Coffee-House, in York Street, Covent Garden. Many actors were members of it, including Holland and Powell, with a few writers. One night Mr. Cradock asked Foote's leave to bring Dr. Farmer, the Shakespearian scholar, whom Foote was delighted to see, and welcomed with many compliments on his learning and ability. He also exerted himself to show off all his talents for his guests' entertainment, so as to appear a cultivated, well-read man.

It so chances that two witnesses have left an account of an incident in which Foote figured as chief actor—an incident which was repeated with only a change of characters. It illustrates forcibly his incurable taste for a ridicule that could not spare either host or guest. The occasions were two dinners, at one of which Foote was host, at the other a guest. When he was host he ridiculed his guest; when he was guest, his host. It is worth while bringing these two significant displays of character together; they prove how impossible he found it to restrain the spiteful humours of his nature.

The first : One day Garrick asked Cumberland to bear him company on a visit to Foote down at Parsons Green, expecting to be asked to dine. Foote was kindly, and hospitably insisted that they should stay for the dinner. It is but fair to Foote to quote Cumberland's testimony. It was often repeated, he says, that Garrick always showed himself reserved and uneasy in Foote's company, but now Garrick had never been more at his ease or in a happier flow of spirits. An East Indian Baronet, Sir Robert Fletcher, dropped in just before dinner and made the fourth of the party. Sir Robert appears to have been a dull sort of man, and after a couple of hours he rose to depart. There was a screen at the bottom of the room which concealed the Baronet from view, and Foote, fancying that he was gone, at once began a highly amusing criticism of his late guest, turning him into the utmost ridicule. Of a sudden came a voice from below : " I am *not* gone, Foote ; do please spare me until I am out of hearing." Then, returning, he added : " And now, with your leave, I will stay till these two gentlemen depart, and then *you will amuse me* at their expense, as you have amused them at mine." This was turning the tables indeed ! Foote for once was overwhelmed with shame and confusion ; he knew not what to say. " No wit could furnish an evasion ; no explanation could suffice for an excuse." The offended Baronet was inclined to take it seriously, when Garrick interposed, and with equal skill and good-nature contrived to turn the whole thing into a jest, and to soothe the offended victim. Here was true kindness and a valuable lesson for Foote. The situation was certainly most original—amusing to a degree. " I hope Foote was grateful," says Cumberland ; "but when a man has been completely humbled, he is not very fond of recollecting it."

The second scene, where Foote was guest, is really a bit of legitimate comedy, rich in dramatic character. It is set before us with much vivacity by the faithful Wilkinson, who was present, and supplies what is, perhaps, the best portrait of Foote that we have :

"On the afternoon I called at Sir F. Delaval's ; it so happened that Mr. Foote was there, with whom I had been on distant terms ever since our breach in March 1759. This visit was almost immediately after dinner. Sir Francis, expecting me, had desired I might be shown into another room, knowing his friend Foote's and my antipathy. . . .

"So, under the sanction of being Sir Francis's particular guest, I entered the room where Foote was, and several other gentlemen. Foote seemed hurt at first, but after the introduction, as proposed, he behaved with great politeness.

"As the circling glass went round, Mr. Foote grew more cordial and cheerful, and began speaking of tables in the first style of elegance in Ireland and Scotland—that several noblemen's houses in both places were supported with every luxury that a London table could furnish ; for if London had the superiority in some particular articles, the other places had in greater perfection what London could not so easily purchase, which made the equality of good things more upon a level than the English would readily admit, but to which Sir Francis would not assent. And as a trait I have before observed in Foote's character when his real best friend, Sir Francis Delaval, left the room, where there were not less than eight or ten persons, each of whom he knew

would relate again what he said, he burst out into a
loud laugh, and, turning to me, said : 'Wilkinson,
did you ever hear such a hound giving his sentiments
on good tables and living ?   Since my return from
Ireland,' added Foote, 'I have had the mortification
to dine here six times, and each day a d—— d large
loin of pork on the table, which he calls a dinner !
By G—d ! I'll not dine here again these three months;
for I suppose he means to run his loin of pork against
"The Beggar's Opera !" '—which had been acted a
great number of nights at Covent Garden.

" On this occasion it chanced that the host had not
left the room ; he was at the door, and heard every
word.   But he said good-humouredly : 'What ! still
at my loin of pork !   Well, Foote, I think you might
have waited till I had left the room.'   'No,' said the
incorrigible jester, 'I've not been at your loin of pork,
but your loins of pork have been at *me*.   And if you
don't take them off, in another week I shall be as full
of bristles as Peter the Wild Man.' "

There is one little scene, described by Tom Davies
in a gay, pleasant style, which gives a forcible, telling
picture of that strange miscellany, Foote's character.
Henderson, the young postulant who was anxious to
get forward in London, and had been importuning
Foote, Garrick, and others " to hear him," had been
brought down by some friends to Foote's place in the
suburbs.   They were determined to get his opinion.
This scene followed : " Two friends accompanied him
to North End.   Our modern Aristophanes welcomed
the visitants with great civility ; but such is the
volatility of his genius that it was not possible to
announce the errand immediately : he must be permitted to indulge his peculiar humour, and to let off

a few voluntaries, before he could be induced to hear
of any business whatsoever.　Foote's imagination is so
lively, and his conceptions are so rapid, as well as
exuberant, that his conversation is a cataract or
torrent of wit, humour, pleasantry, and satire.　The
company had scarce unfolded their business, when he
gave them the history of Sir Gregory Grinwell and
Lady Barbary Bramble.　The whimsical situations into
which he put his characters, with his lively and
sarcastic remarks, threw the company into convulsions
of laughter.

"However, Henderson's friends thought it was
now time to stop the current of Mr. Foote's vivacities
by informing him of the reason of their visit.　One
of them took the lead:

"'Sir, our young friend, the Bath Roscius, would
think himself extremely happy to have the opinion of
so acknowledged a judge of theatrical merit as you are;
he wishes you would permit him to rehearse a scene
of a play.'　'Well, sir, what are you for, the sock
or the buskin?　I'll be hanged if you are not quite
enamoured of that bouncing brimstone, Tragedy.'
'Mr. Henderson is not confined, sir, to either.'
'Stick to the sock, young gentleman; the one is all
nature, and the other all art and trick.　Tragedy is
mere theatrical bombast, the very fungus of the
theatre.　Come, sir, give us a taste of your quality.'
Here Henderson began a speech in 'Hamlet,' when
Foote, turning round to one of the company, said:
'Have you not heard in what manner this impudent
little scoundrel has treated me?'　'I protest, sir, I
don't know whom you mean.'　'No; where have you
left your apprehension?　Let me but tell you what
a damned trick he served me lately by lending me a

14

large sum of money.' 'Consider, my dear sir, the time grows late, and we are to dine in town.' 'No, no,' said Foote, 'you shall dine with me upon a stewed rump of beef and a dish of fish.' Now Mr. Henderson begins. Well, once more he endeavoured to open, when, behold, an unlucky joke, a *petite histoire*, some droll thought, or some unaccountable idea, prevented the disconcerted actor from displaying his powers of elocution: his case was now become extremely pitiable.

"However, after hearing this singular genius read an act of his new comedy, take off Lady Betty Bigamy, recite the whole trial of himself and George Faulkner, ridicule the Irish Lord Chief Justice Robinson for condemning his Peter Paragraph for a libel, speak a prologue in the character of Peter, laugh at our most celebrated orators of the Bar, mimic the members of both Houses of Parliament, tell some ludicrous stories of Captain Bodens and the Irish chairman, Henderson was permitted to repeat, without interruption, Mr. Garrick's Prologue, which he spoke on his first appearance, after his arrival from the Continent. This being no caricature, but a genuine and fair representation of the great Roscius's manner, without the least exaggeration, we cannot be surprised that it did not make any impression upon Mr. Foote; however, he paid the speaker a compliment upon the goodness of his ear. Dinner was now announced; everything was princely and in splendid order. Wit flew about the table—I mean Mr. Foote's; for I would advise every man that has any wit of his own, who shall have the honour to dine with this gentleman, to bottle it up for another occasion, for he is himself master of enough and to spare for ten companies. I need not observe that many portraits were drawn, and some of them in a masterly style.

" When Henderson took his leave of him, he whispered one of the company in the ear that ' *he would not do.*' There was a little of his habitual malice in the verdict and in the way of finding it."

Here was Foote all over. He had taken a dislike to the intruder, and showed his malice by " putting him out" in his recitation; more malicious was his carrying it as an obstreperous joke, though it was vital to the poor postulant; and then came his final whispered " won't do."

Of Foote's superior wit, whether written, spoken, retailed, or in action, there can be no question. It is of the first order, though rough and brusque; but was always ready and spontaneous. In fact, his best " good things" were sudden retorts. These were prompted by, and owed their force to, his utter unscrupulousness at the moment, and to his supreme "readiness." This readiness was the motive power. The thought came in a flash, and the discharge followed on the instant. No one of our colloquial humorists can be compared with him, for Theodore Hook and Sydney Smith were of a more refined and artificial class, and they were always under social restraint. Quin's good things had something of the same roughness and point, but only a few are recorded.*

Johnson, who when he chose could show a light touch enough, and be humorous to a degree, has given many accounts of Foote's humour, which he

---

* His best specimen is that broad reply to the lady who asked him, in a sweet, complimentary tone, "if he ever made love." " No, ma'am; I always buy my love ready made."

seems to have thoroughly enjoyed. These descriptions are admirably finished, and remain in the memory. Foote, in his turn, cordially appreciated the Doctor's wit. He took "a wicked pleasure" in circulating one of his lively speeches on the elder Sheridan: "Sheridan, sir, is dull," etc.

Murphy also had the highest opinion of Foote's wit, and was never weary of extolling it. He himself was very grave, and never attempted wit, but he often "carried" the wit of others. Foote was never grave, but always on the watch for something to excite a jest; but as he had no regard for friendship or decency, it is likely that the admiring Murphy must have been his butt with the rest.

Foote's good things are extraordinarily abundant, but they are of a mixed kind—good, bad, or indifferent. They generally provoke a laugh from a sort of surprise and the suggestion of some droll association. Who could resist his speech when someone politely told him that his handkerchief was hanging out of his pocket: "Thank you, sir. You know the company better than I do." There is an ease and simplicity about this that is highly diverting; but it should be recollected that in the case of "good stories," "humorous sayings," and the rest, the whole point depends upon the jest being properly "carried." It is extraordinary in what earthy fashion certain reporters set down a humorous anecdote; where something is forgotten, it is supplied by invention. They feel bound to supply their own humdrum idea of what is comic, and so really destroy the effect. With their heavy touch they destroy the whole. Thus Conversation Cooke, who has collected with really extraordinary diligence a vast number of Foote's

anecdotes and sayings, has imported into the relation
the Cooke idea of what is humorous, which really inter-
feres with, if it does not spoil, the effect of the original.
As I heard the late Mr. Hayward say : " Every good
thing should be *cut down to the bone*." Yet after going
over the three or four hundred specimens of Foote's
wit that he has collected, one can readily distinguish
between the Foote and the foreign elements.

Foote was a sort of *permanent* humorist—a con-
tinuous joker. When in the vein, Foote's thoughts
seemed naturally to assume a humorous shape, and
to fall into the form of smart repartee. But a certain
malice seemed ever to be the motive force, like the
combustible in the tail of a rocket. He was always
ready or on the watch ; he saw the weak place in an
instant, and there was a sort of robust roughness
about his efforts which helped the result. There
was something, too, akin to the French style. I
have mentioned the story of the gentleman who told
him that his handkerchief was hanging out of his
pocket. The incomparable Rivarol also saw an
article hanging out of a gentleman's pocket, and
politely warned him. The owner was a bad writer,
and it was his precious manuscript. Rivarol added :
" Only that you are so well known here, sir, *it might
be stolen*." The wit and malice here are admirable, and
the jest has perhaps more finesse than Foote's.

It is extraordinary how all witnesses testify to
Foote's powers of entertainment as a boon companion. Even the more fastidious judges cannot
refuse their praise. He was unsurpassed. In his
memoirs Wilkinson thus speaks of him :

" Sure, if ever *one* person possessed the talents of
pleasing more than another, Mr. Foote was certainly

the man. I can aver in all my observations that I never met with his equal. Mr. Garrick, whom I have dined and supped with, was far inferior to him in wit or repartee, as, indeed, were persons of rank and degree; for Nature bestows not *all her graces* on the great or the opulent. Mr. Foote was not confined to any particular topic; he was equal in all— religion, law, politics, manners of this or any age, and the stage of course. Indeed, a polished stranger would find it rare to meet with so many agreeable qualities for the conviviality of any company so combined as in a society with Mr. Foote. This is not the tribute of flattery to his memory, but a piece of justice my own impartiality demands; for it would be despicable indeed to point out his foibles, and not be ready to attest his good qualities. As a wit he is too well known."

Cooke gives this description of his colloquial powers, which he acutely distinguishes:

"Foote's conversation was of such a description that 'naught but itself could be its parallel.' Teeming with fancy and various knowledge, fearless of consequences, and privileged in the character of a wit, he took his stand with confidence, and threw his shafts around him with the dexterity of a master, the first and the last of his own school. He was rapid, lucid, and exuberant; and his images of ridicule and portraits of characters were so strong, novel, and whimsical, that he carried the imagination of his hearers insensibly along with him."

The remarkable thing was, the position which Foote asserted for himself among the higher and titled classes of society. It was very different from what we have been accustomed to in our days, where a notable and attractive actor has been favoured with the attentions and invitations of lords and ladies. The fashionable actor was invited as a show lion or as an interesting person. But Foote took his place among the nobles as of right; he wanted no smiles of patronage. Once introduced, he established himself, and required to be on the footing of their other acquaintances.

The low and rather ignoble aim of trying to make the servants laugh at a dinner was a common weakness of Foote's. John Taylor testifies to this, and, as he truly says, the jokes that produce such a result must be highly flavoured. We may have noted in our own experience how such dining-out wits often strive thus to affect the attending menials, since it enlarges the audience and supplies a gallery, as it were. It stimulates the diners to laughter when they see the servants " leaving the room in a roar."*

The secret of Foote's success in society as a humorist was his unabashed effrontery. He did not care what he said, or how he said it, or to whom he said it. Others might be foiled or disabled by the lucky stroke of an adversary, but he took only the quicker rebound from what would have laid them prostrate. This was the form of dramatic praise given by Johnson—viz., his " incompressibility." Foote's nature was so constituted that his impulse was to look for something absurd or ridiculous in

* A few days after the death of his wife, Foote dined out. He at first attempted the "dejected 'haviour of the visage," and actually wept. At last he announced "that he had been all the morning looking for a second-hand coffin to bury her in"! This seems all but incredible, and yet it is somehow in the actor's manner. The servants were convulsed, and for the rest of the meal he was as jovial as ever.

the person before him.   This at once prompted the
delivery of a malicious or venomous speech, with a
personality reflecting on a physical or mental defect—
it did not matter which.   Personality was the very
basis of his wit.   This gave point to what he said.
Other men to whom a personal retort occurred might
be afraid to utter it: Foote feared nobody.   What
an influence, what a power, this gave him!   It forced
everyone to conciliate him, to give way to him.   The
great prompting power of his jest was the weak
place in either the mind or body of the person before
him.   This he never could resist.   Give him this
material, and he was triumphant.   When someone
foolishly joked on his leg, Foote retorted : " Why do
you attack my weakest part ?   Did I say anything
about your head ?"   This, however, as we have seen,
has been credited to Johnson.

The wonder was how this professional lampooner—
who made his living by ridiculing others, and exhibited them on his stage—so long escaped personal
correction.   How was it that in those days of personal
violence and chastisement, when the phrase " knocked
him down " was often heard, no outraged person had
taken him in hand ?   The truth was, Foote could
be as cautious as he could be bold ; when he saw
the matter was growing serious he drew back.   No
one could be more apologetic or more profuse.

Johnson, with his amazingly searching criticism,
supplied the *clou* of Foote's humour as " rude, obstreperous mirth."   Anyone that has been in company with one of these humorous souls—distended as
it were with fun—will understand this.*

* I recall in my youthful days, when dining at one of the Inns
of Court with a jovial and even noisy party, after " the cloth was

Foote's best-known jest, and really of the first class, is his reply to someone asking whether he had ever been in Cork: "No; but I have seen a good many drawings of it." Once, when travelling in a post-chaise with a friend, he met a stuttering Colonel, and, stopping him, asked how he was. The Colonel could get no farther than, " Pretty—pretty—er—we——" Foote, impatient, drew up the window and drove off. His friend remonstrated with him on the rudeness. " Oh, I wanted to save time ; we'll be at Hounslow before he'll be *well* enough to answer us."

To the Duke of Cumberland, who complimented him by saying that he had swallowed all " his good things," Foote could not resist replying that he must be congratulated on his digestion, " as I never knew Your Royal Highness bring up any of them again." This was as coarse as it was rude, but still very good. It was probably only told of the Duke, when, of course, it would have more effect.

Foote has the credit of an oft-quoted piece of advice to a certain bad author who deplored the fact that he had no time to write a poem, " as he had so many irons in the fire": Foote advising him to put his poem where his irons were. The parentage of this jest, however, is not quite certain, though it has always been claimed for him. Still, it is quite in his manner.

A wealthy man from the City, dining one day at North End, was every now and then boasting, with all the insolence of prosperity, of his many thousands

---

drawn," some priggish person told the ancient jest of the ladies' favourite wines : " Isle of Wight," " Port, you gal," and the like— geography jokes which leave one rather sad : whereupon a grave, silent Irishman said slowly, " Bedad, *I'll have man* is much more in their way."

in the funds, his capital in trade, mortgages, annuities, etc., when Foote cut him short by saying "he was very sorry for the circumstance." "What!" exclaimed his guest, "do you envy me my prosperity?" "No, my good sir," said the other; "but you talk so much of your riches that I am afraid the company (who don't know you as well as I do) will think *you are going to break.*"

The following is excellent. A maid came into the room to look for her mistress. "What do you want your mistress for?" asked the master. "Why, indeed, sir, to tell you the truth, she scolds me so from morning to night, I came to give her warning." "What, then, you mean to leave us?" "Certainly, sir," said she, shutting the door after her. "Happy girl!" exclaimed Foote; "I most sincerely wish your poor master *could give warning, too.*"

An artist was eternally complaining of illness, but could never tell what was the matter with him. At last he married, which being told to Foote, he exclaimed: "I heartily wish him joy, for now *he'll readily find out what's the matter with him.*"

Here is the true Foote cynicism dashed with malice. Being asked at what time of life he thought female beauty began to decline, he replied: "Woman is to be counted like a game of piquet: twenty-five, twenty-six, twenty-seven, twenty-eight, twenty-nine —*sixty.*" This is in the French manner.

When someone asked why Garrick did not take the beam out of his own eye before finding fault with the mote in another's, "Because he is not sure of selling the timber," said Foote with instant readiness.

In all such retorts he was incompressible. One night at his theatre Garrick twitted him. "So you have to fall back on one of my farces !" "Why, yes, Davy ; I must have some ventilator in this very hot weather."

A dull dramatic writer, who had often felt the severity of the public, was complaining one day to Foote of the injustice done him by the critics, but added : " I have, however, one way of being even with them, which is by constantly *laughing* at all they say." "You do perfectly right, my friend," said Foote, "for by this method you will not only disappoint your enemies, but lead the *merriest life* of any man in England."

Foote lived in habits of intimacy with Lord Kellie, a very red-faced nobleman. One day his lordship choosing to forget his promise of dining with him, it piqued him so that he called out, loud enough to be heard by the whole coffee-house where they were sitting, " Well, my lord, since you cannot do me the honour of dining with me to-day, will you be so good, as you ride by, as just to *look over* against my south wall, for, as we have had little or no sun for this fortnight past, my peaches will want the assistance of your lordship's *countenance*."

A story of genuine humour is always fresh and novel, and a constant entertainment, such as the Screen Scene in " The School for Scandal," which one can see again and again with the same interest and excitement. Certain choice specimens are a source of renewed entertainment when recalled, and ever seem young and fresh. The reason is that they represent real comic situations, wit in life and action ; whereas verbal pleasantries, such as those of Sydney Smith, appeal to the intellect only. As specimens of the irresistible sort are the French Judge's answer

to the criminal's plea, " Il faut vivre," and the ever
delightful answer of another Judge to Alexandre
Dumas, who, being asked his name as a witness in
a literary case, said with sham modesty, " Were I not
in the city of the great Corneille, I would call myself
an author." " Don't mind that," answered the Judge
reassuringly ; " there are degrees in everything."
Here the situation seems exquisitely comic, the Judge
affecting to take the novelist literally, and consoling
him. It is impossible to resist a smile.

Here is a specimen of Foote's most brutal or
" knock-down " method. Baddeley, the actor, was in
his service, and before taking to the stage had been
a cook. Grumbling one day about his salary and
other grievances, he told Foote " that he did not
treat him like a gentleman." " What !" said Foote,
" when you know that I made a gentleman of you
when I took your spit from the fire and placed it by
your side."

A tailor friend begged of him to furnish a motto
for his carriage just set up. " I've got," said the other,
" what will suit you to a buttonhole. ' List ! list !
O list !' " A doctor consulted him on a similar
matter. " What's your crest ?" asked Foote, " Two
mallards." " There you are : ' Quack ! quack !' " It
is said that when he received his third fortune he
put on his carriage door the motto " Iterum, iterum,
iterumque."*

It is clear, from this little muster of Foote's good

---

* Yet another evidence of his classical taste, which he always
kept alive by use or quotation. This fondness for the ancients
supplied a sort of high tone to his otherwise coarse life, and gave
him a striking advantage over Garrick, who had no University
education, and whom he could always " down " in this way.

things, that they all depended on *the sudden delivery*
and the rough utterance, and on the simple effort to
" hit hard." A well-directed personality is certain to
gain a laugh.

Then there is the oft-quoted criticism on the Irish
beggars, when he said that he never knew till his visit
to that country what the English beggars did with
their cast-off clothes. In this there is true wit. His
rough abuse of the Duke of Leinster's table—where
there was a vast quantity of plate and of made dishes—
was that he did not care to dine in a silversmith's shop
on dishes brought in from the apothecary's. This
was simply abusive, but it "told." Almost his last
jest on his leaving for Dover was addressed to one of
his old actors, who declared that he was not at all
himself that day. Foote answered him gravely:
" Well, then, I wish you joy ; for though I don't know
who you are *now*, anyhow you must be a gainer by
the change." This is in Rivarol's manner. To a conceited young fellow who was anxious as to what he
should say as an excuse for not attending a party the
day before, " Say !" cried Foote, " why, nothing,
for no one missed you." Merely a rude speech.

Many of the recorded, and even admired, jests are
trivial, such as that of the eighteen tailors whom he
addressed : " Gentlemen, I wish you *both* good night."
Still, delivered in his boisterous, *acted* way, the effect
was no doubt droll, for he seemed to argue the matter
out gravely. At a nobleman's table, praise was given
to his claret, which he declared was a return for two
hounds he had sent to a French gentleman. " Excellent it is," said Foote, " and dog cheap." Here
again we must supply the acting and spontaneousness.
I have already quoted the story of a little bust of

Garrick on Foote's bureau. "You are surprised, no doubt," said the latter, "at my letting him be so near my cash, but you will observe he has no hands." The finesse here is admirable, and of the first class, with the sly allusion to Garrick's avarice, etc. Someone was complaining of a red-faced Irish gentleman, declaring that he would pull his nose. "Pull his nose!" said Foote. "Why, you might as well thrust your fingers into a furnace!"

The happy "turn" Foote could give to his bons-mots can be well illustrated by his well-known jest on Mrs. Catherine Macaulay, the female Republican, who had written a pamphlet which she entitled "Loose Thoughts on," etc. This was too obvious for the common jester to miss, but Foote really undertook the author's defence. "I see no objection to that title," he said, "for the sooner the lady gets rid of her loose thoughts, the better."

Foote's temperament was eminently connected with action, just as his dramatic feeling was, and we find this strongly present in all his wit. It is ever wit in action. This is shown in one of his happiest efforts, which is a perfect *scene :*

A gentleman in the country who had just buried a rich relation, who was an attorney, was complaining to Foote of the very great expenses of a country funeral, in respect to carriages, hatbands, scarfs, etc. "Why, do you bury your attorneys here?" asked Foote gravely. "Yes, to be sure we do; how else?" "Oh! we never do that in London." "No!" said the other, much surprised; "how do you manage?" "Why, when the patient happens to die, we lay him out in a room overnight by himself, lock the door, throw open the sash, and in the morning he

is entirely off." " Indeed !" said the other in amazement; "what becomes of him ?" " Why, that we
cannot exactly tell. All that we know is, that there's
a *strong smell of brimstone in the room the next
morning.*"

This is one of Foote's best " things," and is truly
droll.

A pleasant story related of Foote's persiflage shows
us how Garrick and he, the friend-enemy pair, used to
meet at the table of Lord Mansfield, the Chief Justice,
where there were other notables. This was not a
mere occasional compliment, but it is evident that
both were asked, not as being distinguished in their
profession, but because they were brilliant additions
to a dinner-party. On one of these occasions Garrick
solemnly held forth on the subject of thrift and
economy, illustrating the fatal results of waste and
extravagance by Churchill's death. Foote not unnaturally struck in, and saw how to profit by this
sermonizing. He put forward a grave and satirical
argument in favour of debt, which he urged was not
such a mischievous thing as was supposed. Debt
presumed the existence of fortune at some time, or
you would not get credit. Then, by living on credit
you got rid of the trouble of using money or keeping
accounts. It checked avarice, encouraged generosity,
for people were more liberal with other people's money
than with their own. Of his other first-class jests we
most relish these. He described a certain Sir J. D. as
" a good sort of man," and being pressed by a lady to
explain what he called a good sort of man, " Why,
madam," he said, " *one who preserves all the exterior
decencies of ignorance.*" Very happy this. Laughing
at the imbecilities of a common friend one day, some-

body observed: "It was very surprising, as Tom Davies knew him very well, and thought him far from being a fool." "Ah, poor Tom!" said Foote; "he is like one of those people who eat garlic themselves, and therefore can't smell it in a companion." This is another very happy stroke.

"Who is that woman?" he was asked by someone, pointing to a fat, coarse-looking actress. "Mrs. Reddish." "Reddish? What Reddish?" "Don't you see? Horse Reddish, to be sure." This is rather too obvious.

I could give many more specimens, for the collection is enormous, but I have here selected and set before the reader what seem to me to be the choicest.

CHAPTER XV

1763

"THE MAYOR OF GARRATT"—GEORGE FAULKNER

WE have followed the amusing conflict between Foote and his mimic which led to a breach between them, almost irreconcilable in the case of other men. Five years had elapsed, so the hostility seemed likely to be permanent. But this was not Foote's way. His interests now called for a reconciliation. He had a piece ready, full of grotesque character. Tate was a very convenient, useful auxiliary, all but indispensable. Both understood each other, and on the stage, or in company, were always acceptable to audiences.

In 1763 Wilkinson was at the Norwich Theatre, when an emissary named Kennedy arrived from town with the most handsome proposals from Foote. Everything was offered. Foote said that he had begun to think that his audience had grown tired of seeing one person alone upon the stage; Wilkinson should have generous terms. There was a character written for him, which he would "cut out" if Tate did not undertake it. He should have benefits, etc., all as he pleased, with a division of the important characters. And he wished also to have him not merely as an actor, but as his particular friend; his house and his table would be always open to him.

These flattering proposals were joyfully accepted, and Wilkinson set off for town. He tells us what followed: " I paid my devoirs to the manager at the Haymarket Theatre, where I found Mr. Foote earnestly employed in a work of training his militia company to prepare for a summer campaign. He soon espied me in the orchestra, where I had observingly placed myself. The rehearsal was soon finished ; I mounted the stage, and after a most friendly greeting, to the astonishment of everyone, the most amazing coalition of intimacy made its wonderful appearance, and equalled any change politics had ever presented to view. The troop was mute, glad, but more surprised when the carriage was ordered, and Mr. Foote insisted on my dining with him that day, as a large party of the first persons were to be at his table. I did not expect such civility, but it may easily be supposed I could not resist. It also seemed to augur an intention of good-will at least ; and if not, a good dinner, good company, and Mr. Foote at the head of the table, few persons even of rank would have disliked ; besides, it placed me not only on a footing of superiority, but prevented any suspicion in myself as to ill-treatment from Mr. Foote, of which I had not entirely divested my mind. He was then preparing his ' Mayor of Garratt,' in which piece he had wrote a part, he informed me, that was in fact abstracted from the piece, and that he could do with or without it. It was impossible for himself to do it, for with a false belly for his intended Major Sturgeon, and to undress for Matthew Mug, it was not practicable. The part was entitled Peter Primmer, intended as a stroke of satire levelled at Mr. Sheridan senior, who about that time had busied himself much with delivering lectures on oratory, and proposing a plan for the establishment of an academy for the teaching of pupils the true art of public speaking.

"Mr. Foote mentioned our appearing together in the piece of ' The Minor,' for, said he, the public will be better pleased with having both than one, and added, however partial the town might be to him as author and actor combined, yet the same person being perpetually in sight is cloying. . . . It was agreed ' The Minor' should be the opening piece, early in June 1763 : Shift and Squintum, Mr. Wilkinson ; Mrs. Cole and Smirk, Mr. Foote : with the new farce of ' The Mayor of Garratt.' My Shift, with the imitations, was extravagantly well received, and was repeated several nights. ' The Mayor of Garratt ' had great success, and a run of almost every night in the season ; it met with some opposition, which in general only gives a whet to the appetite of those who choose to approve and support."

This new, droll, and truly eccentric piece of foolery, "The Mayor of Garratt," was intended to ridicule the martial airs of volunteer and militia officers, and at the same time divert with its oddity. There was a character intended as a caricature of Sheridan, the actor ; and Wilkinson, knowing Sheridan by heart as it were, was introduced by Foote for the special purpose of " taking him off."

"Peter Primmer I dressed with an old tie-wig, like the barber's in ' The Upholsterer,' a long band neck-cloth, a large rod in my right hand, and a Scotch plaid nightgown, and had six boys with primers and rods, and six girls with horn-books, as my attendants in procession as the candidate for being chosen Mayor of Garratt. My likeness was strong, and it

15—2

was well taken, and as a schoolmaster at Garratt, near Wandsworth, the dress was ridiculous, and not totally improper; but as a resemblance of Mr. Sheridan, who always appeared at his lecture and everywhere as a gentleman, my being *too comical* destroyed the effect; therefore it was judged much better, to answer the purpose intended, to dress it in black and a bag-wig, etc. That alteration gave the people a strong conception of him they knew, whereas the ridiculous wig and gown destroyed every part of the imitation by the absurd appearance."

Colman describes an amusing incident connected with this piece: " Such was the excellence of Foote's inimitable humour that, even to this day, I have a distinct recollection of him in particular scenes; and I can remember the very tone and expression he assumed when, after describing the gallantry of his corps on marching home, he exclaims, ' We were all stopped and robbed by a single highwayman !' The first time that the King attended the Haymarket this farce commenced the evening's performances. When His Majesty arrived at the theatre, Foote, as manager, hobbled to the stage door to receive him, but, as he played in the first piece, instead of wearing the Court dress usual on these occasions, he was equipped in the immense cocked hat, cumbrous boots, and all the other paraphernalia and appurtenances of the most grotesque military uniform imaginable. The moment His Majesty cast his eyes on this extraordinary figure, as he stood bowing, stumping, and wriggling with his wooden leg, the King receded with astonishment, thus addressing his officers:

" ' Look ! what is that man, and to what regiment does he belong ?' "

Colman attributes the speech to George II., but he was dead at the time the play was produced. It was, of course, his successor. This scene shows how well founded was Boz's delicacy when, about a hundred years later, he positively declined to present himself to Her Majesty in his acting clothes.

The strange sensation or craze of the Cock Lane ghost had about this time excited general ridicule ; yet it had been gravely investigated by so judicial a person as Dr. Johnson. Many wondered that he should have taken the business so seriously as to visit the scene of the apparition. Here was grist for Foote's mill, and he found himself irresistibly drawn to present a grotesque portrait of the lexicographer in some ridiculous connection with the " ghost." It seemed an easy matter, and would make a most effective " show." But, as we shall see by-and-by, he reckoned without his host—that is, without thought of the sage's sturdy methods.

As the militia was being " called out " all over the kingdom, the observant Foote began to note the absurdities and oddities of these citizen soldiers, and by-and-by had fashioned these into a roaring farce. Here we may wonder how the licenser tolerated this ridicule of a body of men who were doing their best to protect the kingdom. A most ridiculous figure was made of Major Sturgeon, who described the perils of his campaigning at Brentford and other places. Later, Wilkinson was foolish enough to select this piece for performance in the presence of the York Militia, and was all but mobbed.*

* While this book is passing through the press, the Chamberlain has refused to license a skit under the title of " Territorials," upon the subject of invasion.

The peace of 1762 had led to the disbandment of
the various militia and volunteer corps, on which the
ever-watchful Foote found his opportunity. The
many absurdities of the enrolled butchers and bakers
of the local districts had not escaped his ken. This
piece has supplied a typical figure for mirth and
quotation—Jerry Sneak. The piece was in two acts,
but, as usual, we look in vain for a story. It was
really in the nature of those " sketches " that we see
at music-halls, where comic characters display themselves in grotesque talk ; chatter, sing, describe some
adventure, and pass away to give place to another.
We can see, from Zoffany's admirable picture of
Foote in this character of the fishmonger Major,
exactly how he looked. It was a " stock " piece in my
school-days, with " Midas " and others of the same
pattern, and, acted by low—very low—comedians, produced hearty laughter. Mr. Forster grew enthusiastic
over the farce : " Who has not enjoyed it more than
half the comedians he has seen ?" And very racy and
ebullient it is. Given the topic of militia enthusiasm
in our own day, it would soon be exhausted. A few
pat phrases repeated would illustrate the character.
But Foote illustrated by *action*, not by speech. The
secret of the attraction is the perfect *sincerity* of the
character. The Major is shown to believe firmly in
his campaigns and hardships. It is all quite natural.
Sir Jacob asks him : " Was it not rather late in life to
take to the profession ?" " A little awkward in the
beginning," the Major answers ; " but use reconciles
all them kind of things. Why, after my first
campaign *I no more minded the noise of the guns* than
a flea-bite." Sir Jacob : " No ?" Major : " No.
There is more made of these matters than by
merit." How *natural* this stroke !

But here is a longer specimen of this boisterous piece. Says the Major, describing his exploits :

"In a week I could shoulder, and rest, and poise, and turn to the right, and wheel to the left ; and in less than a month I could fire without winking or blinking." "*Sir Jac.* A perfect Hannibal ! *Major.* Ah, and then I learnt to form lines, and hollows, and squares, and evolutions, and revolutions : let me tell you, Sir Jacob, it was lucky that Monsieur kept his myrmidons at home, or we should have peppered his flat-bottomed boats. *Sir Jac.* Ay, marry, he had a marvellous escape. *Major.* We would 'a' taught him what a Briton can do, who is fighting *pro arvis* and *focus*. *Sir Jac.* Pray now, Major, which do you look upon as the best disciplined troops, the London regiments or the Middlesex militia ? *Major.* Why, Sir Jacob, it does not become me to say ; but, lack-a-day, they have never seen any service —holiday soldiers ! Why, I don't believe, unless indeed upon a Lord Mayor's day, and that mere matter of accident, that they were ever wet to the skin in their lives. *Sir Jac.* Indeed ! *Major.* No ! soldiers for sunshine, Cockneys ; they have not the appearance, the air, the freedom, the *Jenny sequi* that—oh, could you but see me salute ! you have never a spontoon in the house ? *Sir Jac.* No ; but we could get you a shove-pike. . . . *Sir Jac.* No doubt. *Major.* Oh ! such marchings and counter-marchings, from Brentford to Ealing, from Ealing to Acton, from Acton to Uxbridge ; the dust flying, sun scorching, men sweating ! Why, there was our last expedition to Hounslow ; that day's work carried off Major Molossas. Bunhill Fields never saw a braver commander ! He was an irreparable loss to the service. *Sir Jac.* How came that

about ?   *Major.* Why, it was partly the Major's
own fault ; I advised him to pull off his spurs before
he went upon action ; but he was resolute, and would
not be ruled. . . .   At daybreak our regiment formed
at Hounslow town's end, as it might be about here.
The Major made a fine disposition : on we marched,
the men all in high spirits, to attack the gibbet where
Gardel is hanging ; but turning down a narrow lane
to the left, as it might be about there, in order to
possess a pigsty, that we might take the gallows in
flank, and at all events secure a retreat, who should
come by but a drove of fat oxen for Smithfield !   The
drums beat in the front, the dogs barked in the rear, the
oxen set up a gallop ; on they came thundering upon
us, broke through our ranks in an instant, and threw
the whole corps in confusion.   *Sir Jac.* Terrible !
Major. The Major's horse took to his heels ; away
he scoured over the heath.   That gallant commander
stuck both his spurs into the flank, and for some
time held by his mane ; but in crossing a ditch the
horse threw up his head, gave the Major a dowse
in the chops, and plumped him into a gravel-pit,
just by the powder-mills.   *Sir Jac.* Dreadful !
Major. Whether from the fall or the fright, the
Major moved off in a month. . . .   But I got the
Major's commission.   *Sir Jac.* You did !   *Major.*
Oh yes.   I was the only one of the corps that could
ride."

The garrulous Tate has told us how he discharged his
part of the scheme for making ridiculous the worthy
old Sheridan.   But it was found too comical, with too
much of the burlesque, so the dress was changed to
sober black, as more suited to a pedagogue.   One of
the points was the recitation of the familiar ballad

" Nancy Dawson," given with intense seriousness, with the exact tone and manner of the victim.

The late J. S. Le Fanu, a well-known novelist, and a descendant of the gifted Sheridan family,* related to me, I suppose full forty years ago, an odd instance of Foote's malicious enjoyment of annoyance. A daughter of " old Sheridan," the actor, had told him that Foote was very pressing that the family should come and see his new piece at his theatre. He was particularly anxious that the old actor should be of the party, and placed him in the front row. We may conceive his rage, and that of his family, when they recognized his counterpart, the Peter Primmer, with all the peculiarities minutely copied. What are we to think of all these things—this finding entertainment in giving pain and annoyance ? But I really believe that this temper was *constitutional* with Foote, and that he could not restrain it. He might say in defence : " Pity me, but I really *can't* help it—I like it, I enjoy it."

" The Orators," produced in 1762, is the most incoherent of all Foote's pieces, and rambles about in the most extraordinary fashion. There were sixteen characters, and the strong cast included Shuter, Weston, one of the Palmers, Quick, Bannister, and Foote himself as Lecturer. Everything was in the most " free-and-easy " style. It opened with the appearance of two of the performers in a side-box, who have a talk with the candle-snuffer, and finally send for Foote to talk with him. Suds then interrupts from another box, demanding lessons in the

---

* This Mr. Le Fanu was a true Sheridan, overflowing with quaint humour. He lived surrounded by family portraits of rare merit.

art of making a speech, on which Foote begins his lecture, an interminable, all but serious discourse, filling nearly twenty closely printed pages, " dull prosings " one of the characters calls it. The next act is devoted to comic parody of a trial with witnesses, counsel, etc., and here is introduced Peter Paragraph, intended for Faulkner, who is made as ridiculous as possible. It is a perfect mystery how these things could have been endured by a lively up-to-date audience. The fact was, Foote was here reverting to his original methods.

In this wandering piece Foote's indifference to his own dignity and to that of his audiences is shown by his " free-and-easy " exhibition of the mysteries of " Behind the Scenes." He would recklessly show himself in his everyday garb, and talk with the carpenter and prompter. He would make the candle-snuffer fetch out Mr. Foote, who appears and tells them what he is going to do—that is, to give a lecture on Speaking. He begins accordingly, and gives a long discourse of many pages, quite seriously, too, on the principles of Oratory, the Bar, the Church, etc. He then satirizes, or tries to satirize, forensic proceedings, holding a mock trial of the Cock Lane ghost, which had been exciting attention. His pupils, or beginners, took the slighter characters, which are mere cardboard figures, having only a few sentences each. Such was a ranter—ranting being a favourite subject for his gibes—or Peter Paragraph, his late friend George Faulkner, whose lameness, two wives, and Journal were, it cannot be said, ridiculed, but *mentioned*, as though all this were something diverting.

The explanation is, that the jester filled out these

sketches with obstreperous mimicries, face-making, and personalities, evidently filling in his strokes till they produced roars of laughter. The next and last scene was the presentation of the Robin Hood Popular Debating Society, a sort of Cogers' Hall— whither, it will be remembered, Bozzy stole away from his friends. It seems astonishing, by the way, that a person so notorious and so comic in his ways as Boswell should have escaped Foote's " handling."

George Faulkner, the Dublin publisher, is best known from his connection with Swift, most of whose books he issued in handsome and important style, and in various forms. His great edition of the Dean's works—some twenty volumes strong—is a creditable venture for the time. He was also a figure in his own community. If Foote was balked in his attempt on Johnson, he could at least ridicule one of Johnson's friends. It is difficult at this distance to know whether there was anything specially eccentric in this Dublin printer. Cooke tells us that his peculiarities were trifling and his manners inoffensive. Cumberland says that he was ridiculous and farcical in every way ; others make out that he was a noisy swaggerer who boasted of his conquests in spite of every physical disadvantage. Accordingly, Foote prepared a special part—a small character labelled " Peter Paragraph," which he played himself. The piece was brought on in 1762, and caused much amusement. He contrived to rouse a sort of curiosity about the printer.

Incredible to say, Foote, besides mimicking the Alderman's humours and absurdities, actually simulated his wooden leg, and limped and hobbled about

the stage to roars of laughter. Not three years later
he himself was to be hobbling about the stage,
equipped with what he had been laughing at! It is
often found an unlucky thing, as well as indecent,
to scoff at physical infirmities.

The piece called " The Orators " was a rather dull
performance, the first portion being devoted to what
was a sort of oratorical competition, when Foote and
others made long and tiresome speeches—unless,
indeed, he set them off with an unusual amount of
his favourite mimicries. Foote actually makes the
candle-snuffer " a speaking part "—a thing un-
precedented.* Then Peter Paragraph is called, and
tells how his journal makes mention of his departure for England. " I know peers," he says, " and
peers know me." His wife had died, but " I gave
her a prodigious good character in my journal."
Foote also represents Faulkner as getting up a
book on the Cock Lane apparition, and having a
confederate to record the " scratchings," etc. The
third act is devoted to the Robin Hood Society,
—attended by Boswell—altogether a dull performance. The portion devoted to George was, however,
very short and slight. Indeed, there are so many
Irish introduced that there is no contrast. George,
far away in Dublin, no doubt thought it all rather
complimentary. But a friend and patron of his,
Lord Chesterfield, wrote him a letter to prove to him
that he was injured.

" Would you think it! Mr. Foote, who, if I
mistake not, was one of your symposium while you

---

* What a hindrance to the dramatic effect in those days must
have been the entrance of the candle-snuffer, and his trimming of
the long wicks !

were in London, and if so the worse man he, *takes you off*, as it is vulgarly called—that is, acts you in his new farce, called 'The Orators.' As the Government here cannot properly take notice of it, would it be amiss that you should show some spirit upon this occasion, either by way of stricture, contempt, or by bringing an action against him? I do not mean for writing the said farce, but for acting it. The doctrine of *Scribere est agere* was looked upon as too hard in the case of Algernon Sidney, but my Lord Coke in his incomparable notes upon Littleton, my Lord Chief Justice Hales in his Pleas of the Crown, my Lord Vaughan, Salkeld, and, in short, all the greatest men of the law, do with their usual perspicuity and precision lay it down for law, etc."

Mr. Forster, not unnaturally, assumes that this is a specimen of Lord Chesterfield's ill-natured wit. The advice, he holds, is ironical ; that, while encouraging his friend to take action, he is laughing at him in his sleeve. But I think the passage scarcely bears this meaning. Chesterfield's other letters to Faulkner are always kindly and friendly, full of a sincere interest in his affairs. I believe he was quite in earnest in the advice he gave to prosecute Foote, though he accompanies it with a little good-humoured persiflage which also might have a reference to Foote's ridicule of law and law process, which was so profusely treated in " The Orators." This, it was likely enough, was appreciated by George himself ; otherwise we must assume that the cold-hearted peer was sneering at his friend, and seriously pressing him to go to law by foolish jesting and a pretence of quoting influential legal authority, of which he knew nothing.

Faulkner was too shrewd a man to be thus imposed upon.

However this may be, the Alderman did bring his action in the Dublin Courts, where the wit was cast in damages. Lord Chesterfield wrote his congratulations : " You scorned an inglorious victory, and called on justice and the laws of your country to punish the criminal. I take it for granted that some of your tributary wits have already presented you with gratulatory poems, etc., upon this subject. I own I had some thought myself of inscribing a short poem to you upon your triumph ; but, to tell you the truth, when I had *writ* not above two thousand verses of it my muse forsook me, my poetic vein stopped. I threw away my pen and I burned my poem, to the irreparable loss, not only of the present age, but also of latest posterity."

It seems to me that this last passage, conceived in a spirit of ostentatious burlesque, supplies a key to the whole incident. The Earl was " having a little fun " with his friend, " chaffing " him on his victory ; but I can see no sneering.

It is said that the Judge who was to try the case was not favourably disposed to Foote. The actor, later making one of his flying visits, had to undergo the mortification of giving bail. According to the story, he left the country, preferring not to trust to the mercies of the Irish, and it was said that his bail had to make good the sum. He, however, later made good the sum forfeited.

Foote, when he got back to town, sat down and hastily wrote off an amusing parody of the Dublin action, and this he produced before a Haymarket audience. The scene was the interior of a court of

law. Foote first appeared as the prosecuting counsel,
Demur, and then, slipping off his robe, as Foote
himself.

 " My Lord," he began, " I am counsel against this
Mr. Fot, and a pretty sort of a parson this Fot is,
every inch of him (*coughs*). You may say that—
whee, hee, hee (*as a deep cough*), but I should be glad
to know what kind of right now this Fot has to be
anybody at all but himself ; indeed, my Lord, I look
upon it that he may be indicted for forgery—whee,
hee, hee (*coughing*). Everybody knows that it is
forgery to take off a man's hand ; and why not as bad
to take off a man's leg ? besides, my Lord, it concerns
*yourself, yourself ;** for, God willing, I don't despair
in a little time of seeing your Lordship on the stage.
A pretty sort of a business this, that your Lordship
is to be taken off the bench, there where you are
sitting, without your knowing anything *at all, at all,*
of the matter ; and all the while that, to your thinking,
you are passing sentence here in the four Courts, you
may, for what you can tell, be hearing causes in the
Haymarket. So that, gentlemen of the jury, if you
have a mind to keep yourselves to yourselves, and
not to suffer anybody else to be you but yourselves,
and your Lordship does not choose to be in London
whilst you are living in Dublin, you will find the
prisoner Fot guilty." *Judge.* " I agree entirely with
my brother Demur, that this Fot is a most notorious
offender, and ought to be taken measure of, and
taught how dangerous a thing it is for him to tread
upon other people's toes ; and so, as my brother

* A mode of expression peculiar to the Irish, as, " I don't mind
it, faith ! at all, at all."

observes, to prevent his being so free with other people's legs, we will lay him by the heels."

There is nothing very brilliant about this; it seems rather ponderous. No doubt Foote used the brogue plentifully, and took off the Dublin Judge's oddities with good effect. It must have seemed rather flat and pointless, for the victim was almost unknown to the London public, though he may have been considered an eccentric in his own city. Set upon the London stage, he could present little more than the familiar type of the stage Irishman, speaking with a vulgar brogue. Later, ever rash and reckless, Foote came to Dublin, and actually produced his " Orators," with Faulkner as Peter Paragraph.

The season at the little theatre proceeded prosperously enough until the ill-regulated Wilkinson, ever mischief-making, brought about a turbulent scene on the occasion of his benefit. Here we have yet another instance of the lack of propriety, and even decency, that was found among the players. The mime himself shall tell the story: " The Haymarket Theatre then was on a smaller scale, and the dwelling-house in Suffolk Street did not appertain, as now, to the theatre. I supposed he judged it his interest to be on terms with me, and I was superior to any ill-treatment, being in fact the richest man of the two. . . . Mr. Foote now and then got a great deal of money, which was soon expended . . . and he owed many hundreds; nay, even at last, I am afraid I relate a truth when I affirm his funeral was at Mr. Jewel's expense; for notwithstanding his income from Mr. Colman was not less than sixteen hundred a year, besides profits on the nights he acted, yet I have been informed he had not effects by any means equal to the payment of his debts. It shocks me to have related an account of so many stage-struck geniuses of birth and talents that have fallen a sacrifice to grinning poverty, and incurred neglect and ignominy with great incomes. Pray God to allot me a more fortunate finale, be its statement appointed for a longer or a shorter date.

" But to proceed with a more particular account of our Haymarket sessions. I gained ground with the audience weekly ; my benefit was fixed on the 20th of August, on which night I revived the rehearsal and acted Bayes—the house overflowed from every part, no such receipt the whole season. Mr. Garrick was in Italy, and had not acted Bayes for some years. My imitation of Holland had such a sudden effect that Mr. Churchill, who sat in a balcony with the late Lucy Cooper, after laughing to a very violent degree, most vociferously encored the speech, which was echoed by the whole voice of the theatre, and complied with by me, of course, with great pleasure. The whole play went off with universal satisfaction, and I was highly delighted. *Mr. Foote that night was not pleased, but rather chagrined at my good fortune;* these things will happen, and stage minds in general are sooner irritated and hurt than any other set of people.

" Mr. Mendez, a Jew, and an appraiser in Bow Street, was the treasurer that season. On his benefit he requested me to repeat the character of Bayes, which entreaty I granted. He had a full house, and the comedy received additional credit. I had very near been deprived of the play, as Mr. Foote's theatre at that time merely consisted of a few trumpery scenes ; no wardrobe but such as was hired

16

from Mr. Barber's, in Monmouth Street; and as to
stage properties, they were less known there than in
the most distant rustic company that scoured the
country round. It was a custom for the gentleman
and his lady who were proprietors of the Haymarket
Theatre to reserve a box for themselves, of which
they kept the key. I sent a card the week of my
benefit requesting the favour of that box, as all the
others were disposed of. A very rude refusal was
sent back, at which time Mr. Ruspini, now of Pall
Mall, and some gentlemen, were with me, and complaining of not being able to procure any box
whatever. On my receiving an uncivil answer, I
said, 'Damn this Mrs. Proprietor! It would serve
her ill-natured spleen right to break open the door
and fill the box.' The hint was no sooner given than
seriously taken and put into practice, for, as soon as
the doors were opened, a large party paid, and finding
every place was taken except the Proprietor's—which
the box-keeper assured them could not be opened on
any pretext whatever—they unanimously burst the
old lock and filled the whole box, nor had the turnkey
of the recess rhetoric sufficient to have the least effect,
for expostulation did not signify; so they remained
sole masters, and sat in triumph till near seven, when
the play was going to begin; at which instant up
came a limb of the law, no less a personage than
Mr. George Garrick, escorting the Lady Proprietress
with a large party *gratis*, who summoned the garrison
to surrender and be treated as prisoners of war; but
they were as obstinate as Turks, and determined to
defend the citadel sword in hand. The Lady Proprietress was astonished at the rudeness committed,
and insisted on her privileged right; then tried angry

and soothing words ; but neither her persuasive eloquence nor the authority of Mr. George Garrick, aided by John Doe and Richard Roe, of Westminster Hall, with all their united prowess, could by any means avail. The possessors of the inside works defended their entrenchment from any breach, and they only in exultation laughed, and told George Garrick if himself and party would pay a crown per head they should be admitted, not otherwise. It cannot be imagined that it was an easy matter to extract coin from a lawyer's pocket, consequently the lady, George Garrick, and party, finding it ineffectual by staying in the box passage, retreated in disgrace, but denounced vengeance on Wilkinson. . . . Next day the enraged lady waited on Mr. Foote—who loved mischief and despised his landlady—where she gave an ample scope to her anger and repeated her wrongs : but Mr. Foote told her it was impossible to prevent what had happened ; as to the improper conduct respecting the box, he could only say he was sorry for her disappointment; and as to Mr. Wilkinson's rudeness, he wished to excuse it, but he had not sufficient authority to whip him for his fault, and there the matter rested."

Such scenes make the judicious grieve. It is evident that Foote was but a lax manager when he could tolerate such excesses. It looks as though he was in terror of his follower, just as Garrick was in terror of him.

The eccentric Foote, who was always doing what was unexpected, was now to surprise his public by the announcement that he had engaged two of the most tragic performers to play in his little theatre. These were " the silver-tongued " Barry and his wife ! One

might as well imagine the late facetious Toole
engaging his old friend Irving with Miss Terry for
his little "bandbox" theatre in King William Street.
Only the year before, the two great players had
been performing at the Opera House which faced
Foote's theatre, and had drawn large audiences.
Odd to say, the actor's experiment proved successful.
When his friends rallied him on this proceeding, and
wondered how he could pay such high prices—to
tragedians, above all people!—Foote was, as usual,
ready with an obstreperous jest : " Why, to tell you
the truth, I have no great occasion for them ; but they
were *such bad neighbours* last year that I find it
cheaper to give them board and lodging for nothing
than to have them any longer opposite to me." There
was some truth as well as wit in this plea.

CHAPTER XVI

1766

A SERIOUS ACCIDENT—HAYMARKET PATENT

THERE was now to befall our actor what is perhaps the most serious misfortune that a performer can be afflicted with—namely, the loss of a limb, or even the infirmity of lameness. The fierce light that always beats upon the player in his every movement magnifies this form of helplessness; no amount of contrivance or ability will surmount it; and the spectator is likely to associate the infirmity with the character itself. Only good-nature will tolerate it.

Foote, like so many of the fraternity, was somewhat "snobbish" in seeking the society of lords and high-born folk. The fault was theirs, as they were glad to have him at their tables to amuse their company, they themselves taking freedoms with him— which, however, they were made to rue. Early in the year 1766 he had been invited to Lord Mexborough's place, Methley, near Leeds, to meet a distinguished party consisting of the Duke of York (George III.'s brother), Lord Delaval, Sir Francis Delaval, and others. To entertain His Royal Highness, as we may suppose, it was determined to "roast" the professional wag, who was a good deal given to somewhat boastful assertion. They were specially amused by his vauntings about horsemanship; "that he could ride as well as most men he knew, though indeed he preferred a post-chaise." Next morning there was hunting, and a cruel trap was prepared. They mounted him on a too mettlesome steed of the Duchess's, who at the first touch of the spur flung the luckless actor to the ground and fractured his leg in two places. He had a long illness at his host's. The best surgeons attended him. He bore his trial with extraordinary good spirits, " cracking" uproarious jests on himself and his limbs. He hoped to become a *patientee*, etc. When it was found that the leg could not be set, he himself urged amputation, and presently poor Foote was left with but one leg! A one-legged actor! No matter, " he would not change his one good leg with Lord ——'s two drumsticks." If he could not walk, he could hop. These were his jests. But it must have been an awful affliction for the mercurial being.

Colman the younger used to describe the almost ghostly effect of Foote's " full-dress leg," as he saw it behind the scenes, leaning against a chair and waiting to be fitted on, with a black silk stocking and gold buckle. The ordinary leg was of the old Greenwich pensioner pattern, with a peg at the end, which delved deep holes in a field or garden as one walked. Foote himself led off the jests on this famous " foot" or " leg." Certainly he showed a spirit and courage that well might warrant his title " incompressible."

It was a low and heartless practical joke. It is clear that they made the actor their butt, and that, if the jest seemed to involve danger, the guest deserved it in return for his rough tongue and rude sallies. The unfortunate man with his broken limb bid fair to lose his means of support, and had almost starvation

in sight; for audiences are unaccountably offended, as
Elia has pointed out, by the sight of infirmities on
the stage: both play and character suffer when the
performer is limping and shuffling about.

But the jokers who had caused his misfortune were
somewhat ashamed of themselves, and felt that he
had claims on them. The Duke of York exerted his
influence in high quarters, and actually procured for
him the rare favour of a patent which allowed him to
open a theatre in Westminster, with the somewhat
meagre privilege of performing pieces from May 14
to September 14 in each year—a summer season, it
was called. How it could have paid him it is hard to
see. Hitherto he had been renting the little Haymarket Theatre from the executors of Macklin, and
his tenure was precarious. Now he was *rangé*, a
regular manager, to rank with those great " Panjam-
drums "—as he would have called them—Garrick
and Rich.

By a curious fatality, it came to pass that no fewer
than three well-known mimics were to become maimed
or crippled, thus losing the free use of their limbs.
Tate Wilkinson broke his leg and never recovered its
use; the elder Mathews remained a cripple for the
rest of his life; while Foote had to submit to the
loss of his leg. The original of Dr. Squintum would
have called out that here was a clear "judgment of
the Lard."

Among simple country-folk there is a feeling that
mimicking infirmities or natural imperfections is an
" unlucky " thing, and there is a familiar proverb that
" Mocking is catching."

The unlucky actor, cruelly maimed and disfigured,
was still to discover some crumbs of comfort and

compensation in the accident itself. This comfort was, characteristically enough, of a grotesque kind. He would get a good deal that was histrionic out of his false limb. He would call attention to it, act with it, make jokes on it—in short, work it "for all that it was worth." One cannot but admire this rollicking spirit.

And how noble and generous was Garrick! Hitherto foes, as it were, and supposed to be cherishing a permanent vendetta, it was astonishing to find them interchanging the most tender sympathies. Nothing could be more kind or devoted than Garrick's outpourings ; everything was at the service of his friend, and the latter overflowed in expressions of a grateful heart. It was truly wonderful!

Garrick had written a most affectionate, sympathizing letter, assuring him how grieved all his friends were : " If I could convince you of my regard by any other proof than that of mere words, I should be proud and happy to show it upon this occasion. All I shall say at present is that, should you be prevented from pursuing any plan for the theatre, I am wholly at your service, and will labour in your vineyard for you in any capacity till you are able to do much better for yourself." This was kind indeed. The sick actor wrote from his bed quite touched, and in a strain unusual with him. It seemed another Foote altogether. He thanked his friend warmly for his offer as to " my hovel in the Haymarket ; but the stage to me at present is a very distant object, for, notwithstanding all the flattery of appearances, I look upon my hold in life to depend on a very slender tenure ; and, besides, admitting the best that can happen is a mutilated man, a miserable instance of the weakness and frailty of human nature. It has

been my misfortune not to know Mrs. Garrick much,
but from what I have seen, and all that I have heard,
you will have more to regret when either she or you
die than any man in the kingdom.   As to my present
condition, I wish I could meet you with a more
favourable account : *but I am in truth very weak, in
pain, and can procure no sleep but by the aid of opiates.*
Oh, sir, it is incredible all that I have suffered !
And you will believe me when I assure you that the
amputation was the least painful part of the whole."
A sad, pathetic letter.   The roistering humorist
was indeed sobered.   But he was soon to be himself
again, making a jest of his affliction.

Yet it is sad to think that after an interval all
Garrick's affectionate solicitude was forgotten, and
we find Foote at his old game of sneers and abuse—
"that stingy hound," etc.   It is to be feared that he
was incurable, and that nothing could bind him.
But Garrick, with his wonderfully even temperament,
seemed unaffected by these changes of temper ; he
was compassionate because he thought Foote's condition needed all his pity, while to Foote's unkind
return he showed himself indifferent, because he did
not expect him to be otherwise.

In the course of this narrative it has been repeated
that Foote's career was a succession of surprises ; but
it is almost startling to find to what a strange use
he turned his misfortune.   In nearly every case the
sufferer wishes his blemish to be overlooked or forgotten ; he will even think it indelicate to be reminded
of it.   When someone unconsciously let his eyes rest
on Lord Byron's misshaped foot, he presently found
the poet glaring at him with rage and mortification.
Foote, the incompressible, on the contrary, loudly

advertised his deformity, and invited the public to come and laugh with him over his lame leg. He wrote a comedy on lameness; he called it "The Lame Lover," and the leading character Sir Luke Limp, while he himself took the part of the Lame Knight. The audience, though it laughed loudly, must have felt pity and contempt for the poor mime; not content, he did not care, but on every opening made comic allusion to his infirmity.

Here is a specimen of this self-rallying: "*Serj.* I was just telling Charlotte that you was not a whit the worse for the loss. *Sir Luke.* The worse! much the better, my dear. Consider, I can have neither strain, splint, spavin, or gout; have no fear of corns, kibes, or that another man should kick my shins or tread on my toes. *Serj.* Right. *Sir Luke.* What, d'ye think I would change with Bill Spindle for one of his drumsticks, or chop with Lord Lumber for both of his logs? *Serj.* No! *Sir Luke.* No, damn it, I am much better. Look there. Ha! What is there I am not able to do? To be sure, I am a little awkward at running, but then, to make me amends, I'll hop with any man in town for his sum. *Serj.* Ay, and I'll go his halves. *Sir Luke.* Then as to your dancing. I am cut out at Madam Cornellys', I grant, because of the crowd; but as far as a private set of six couple, or moving a chair minuet, match me who can. *Char.* A chair minuet! I don't understand you. *Sir Luke.* Why, child, all grace is confined to the motion of the head, arms, and chest, which may sitting be fully displayed." The allusion to Bill Spindle was one of his sick-bed jests, converted into a speech delivered by himself in this play of "The Lame Lover."

CHAPTER XVII

1767

THE HAYMARKET THEATRE

THE "Little Theatre in the Haymarket," as it used to be called, has always been regarded with interest and indulgence as the home of brilliant and animated acting. We of a later generation—many of us, at least—can look back over some sixty years to the happy "Buckstone" nights, when the first mere chuckle of that mirth-moving creature, heard from behind the scenes, set the audience off into convulsions of anticipatory enjoyment. Happy nights indeed were those; truly bright and exhilarating! All felt a joyous elation. This being liked and loved by an audience is a truly precious thing; it carries one over failures and deficiencies.

Built in 1721 by a common carpenter named Potter,* it was destined to last for a hundred years.

---

* I have a letter of this illiterate carpenter-manager which is characteristic:

"To HIS GRACE THE DUKE OF GRAFTON:

   "*The representation of John Potter, owner of the new Theatre in the Haymarket.*

"MAY IT PLEASE YOUR GRACE,

   "As my Inclination Lead me to my duty to obtain Leave to waite on you and also to aply to the Right Honble. Sir Robt. Walpole in order to prevent what was Intended to Be Represented

251

At this moment it is the most interesting of existing
theatres, and has perhaps the most valuable traditions
of all—as an institution, that is, although the original
Haymarket is not standing. These traditions reach
back for nearly two hundred years—to December 29,
1721—when the original house was built. There are
great names associated with it—Fielding, Macklin,
Foote, the two Colmans. In 1821 the theatre was
pulled down and a new one erected. The cheerful
portico lends a brightness and animation which are
rather unusual in the case of a London theatre, and
suggests the classical treatment of the Paris theatres
on the boulevards. Later managers were but temporary occupants, and passed without leaving any
special mark.

The two great patent theatres were almost irresponsible institutions. They had abundant privileges.
They were all but State theatres, like the Théâtre
Français, for the State protected them. So longingly
were they regarded, that speculators were glad to
obtain so meagre a privilege as the being allowed to
build and open a theatre for a few months in the

---

in my theatre in May last it was your Grace's pleasure to declare I
should meet with a Reward for such dutifull Behaviour and I have
Read the promise of Sir Robt. Walpole to the same purport with
this addition Soe soon as your Grace and Sir Robt. should taulk on
that head I should with the Rest of mankind, find due Incurrage-
ment to bear an honnest mind.

" I therefore Begg Leave to address my self to your Grace that
you would Be pleased to Remember me when you shall see Sir Robt.
and I att the same time begg your Grace to beleive me faithfully
attached to the utmost of my Power against all scandall and
defamation. I am with all due difference your Grace's most devoted
obedient and most humble Servant

" JOHN POTTER.

" 7 Janry. 1737."

summer, when the two great houses were shut up.
It was on these terms that the carpenter built his
Haymarket house, and Odell his in Goodman's Fields.
It is wonderful how the system could have " paid " at
all.   Foote, however, had contrived it very well by a
sort of combined system, acting his own pieces in
the summer, then taking engagements with Garrick
or Rich.

It was called " the Little Theatre in the Hay.," to
distinguish it from the great Opera House opposite,
Sir J. Vanbrugh's work, the ground of which is now
partly covered by His Majesty's Theatre.   It was
opened on December 29, 1721.   Some of Fielding's
pieces were acted here, notably " Pasquin."   The
proposed performance of " The Historical Register,"
and its wanton licence, brought about the famous
Licensing Act of 1737.   It was thus under Foote's
auspices that the reign of licence continued for thirty
years, he receiving only one or two checks.   Macklin
was manager in 1744, and in 1747 it was taken over
by Foote, who, with his own pieces and his own
acting and mimicries, contrived to make it pay very
well indeed, and that for thirty years.   In July 1766,
he was given, as we have seen, a patent as compensation for his lost limb, on condition that he rebuilt.
In the following year he was allowed to add the
term *Royal* to the description.   In the year of his
death the lease was sold to Colman ; to Colman
succeeded George, the son.   In 1820 the present
theatre was built by Nash, and opened on July 4,
1821.   Finally, in 1897, under the Bancroft management, it was completely remodelled.

Here is the original licence under which Foote held
the Haymarket Theatre :

" George the Third, by the grace of God, of Great
Britain, France, and Ireland, King, Defender of the
Faith, etc., to all to whom these present shall come,
greeting: Know ye, that we for divers good causes and
considerations us thereunto moving, of our especial
grace, certain knowledge, and in our motion, have
given and granted, and by these presents, for us, our
heirs, and successors, do give and grant unto our
trusty and well-beloved Samuel Foote, of the parish
of Saint Martin's in the Fields, in the county of
Middlesex, Esq., from the twenty-fifth day of June,
in the year of our Lord Christ one thousand seven
hundred and sixty-six, and to continue for and during
the term of the natural life of the said Samuel Foote,
full power, licence, and authority, to gather together,
form, entertain, govern, privilege, and keep a company
of comedians, for our servant to exercise and act
between the fifteenth day of May and the fifteenth
day of September in every year (except on Sundays,
and at such times as the Chamberlain of our household shall judge it proper and expedient, either on
account of mournings or otherwise, to stop performances on the stage), such tragedies, plays, operas, and
other performances on the stage, only as have already
been or shall hereafter be licensed by the Chamberlain
of our household, within the house commonly called
or known by the name of the Little Theatre in the
Haymarket, or within any other House or Theatre,
built or to be built, where he the said Samuel Foote
can best be fitted for that purpose within the City of
Westminster, or within the liberties thereof; which
said company shall consist of such members as the
said Samuel Foote shall from time to time think
meet. And we do hereby, for us, our heirs, and

successors, grant unto the said Samuel Foote full power, licence, and authority, to permit such persons at and during the pleasure of the said Samuel Foote, from time to time, within the time aforesaid, to act plays and entertainments of the stage of all sorts peaceably and quietly, without the impeachment or impediment of any person or persons whatsoever, for the honest recreation of such as shall desire to see the same. Nevertheless, under the regulations herein-after mentioned, and such other as the said Samuel Foote, from time to time, in his discretion shall find reasonable and necessary for our service. And we do hereby, for us, our heirs, and successors, further grant to him, the said Samuel Foote as aforesaid, that it shall and may be lawful to and for the said Samuel Foote to take and receive of such persons as shall resort to see or hear such tragedies, plays, operas, or other performances on the stage, such sum or sums of money as either have been accustomably given and taken in the like kind, or as shall be thought reasonable, by the said Samuel Foote, in regard of the great expenses of scenes, music, and such new decorations as have not formerly been used. And further for us, our heirs, and successors, we do hereby give and grant unto the said Samuel Foote, full power to make such allowances out of the money which he shall so receive by the acting such tragedies, plays, operas, and other performances on the stage as aforesaid, to the actors and other persons employed in acting, representing, or in any quality whatsoever about the said House or Theatre, as he the said Samuel Foote shall think fit : And that the said company shall be under the sole government and authority of the said Samuel Foote ; and all scandalous and mutinous persons shall, from time to time, be ejected and disabled from playing in the said Theatre. And for the better attaining our royal purposes in this behalf, we have thought fit hereby to declare, that from henceforth no representation be admitted on the stage, by virtue or under colour of these our letters patent, whereby the Christian religion in general, or the Church of England, may in any manner suffer reproach; strictly inhibiting every degree of abuse or misrepresentation of sacred characters tending to expose religion itself, and to bring it into contempt; and that no such character be otherwise introduced, or placed in any other light, than such as may enhance the just esteem of those who truly answer the end of their sacred function. We further enjoin the strictest regard to such representations as any way concern civil policy, or the constitution of our government, that these may contribute to the support of our sacred authority, and the preservation of order and government. And it being our royal will and pleasure, that for the future our Theatre may be instrumental to the promotion of virtue and instruction to human life, we do hereby command and enjoin, that no new play, or any old or revised play, be acted under the authority hereby granted, containing any passages or expressions offensive to piety and good manners, until the same be corrected and purged by the said governor from all such offensive and scandalous passages and expressions. Provided always, nevertheless, that if the said Samuel Foote do or shall sell, assign, transfer, or alienate in any manner, to any person or persons whatsoever, our letters patent granted to the said Samuel Foote, that then these presents are, and shall be to all intents and purposes, from the day of such sale, assignment, transfer, or alienation, altogether void and of none effect, any thing hereinbefore contained to the contrary thereof in anywise notwithstanding. And these our letters patent, or the enrolment or exemplification thereof, shall be in and by all things good, firm, valid, sufficient, and effectual in the law, according to the true intent or meaning thereof, any thing in these presents contained to the contrary thereof in anywise notwithstanding, or any other omission, imperfection, defect, matter, cause, or thing whatsoever to the contrary thereof in anywise notwithstanding. In witness whereof we have caused these our letters to be made patent.

" Witness ourself at Westminster, the fifth day of July, in the sixth year of our reign.

" By Writ of Privy Seal,

" Cocks."

It was significant that the term of this patent was very restricted—for Foote's life only. He enjoyed it but for eleven years, and sold it a year before his death. This of course he could do; yet with his death it would seem the patent was extinguished. We may presume that Colman, then bankrupt and living " within the Rules," appealed *ad misericordiam,* on the ground that he had only enjoyed his bargain for about a year, and so may have obtained a renewal.

The poor maimed Foote now set to his task with infinite spirit. It is often mentioned in the books that he at once rebuilt and beautified his theatre; but this the shrewd and painstaking Genest shows to be a mistake. He quotes Foote's free-and-easy prelude on the opening in May, when he has a talk

with Scaffold, his carpenter, *in propriâ personâ.*
"Consider," the latter says, "what expedition we
have made—all this work here in three months!
A tight job, Master Foote:" which shows that the
house had been merely remodelled.

Foote might be considered the "actor-manager"
in its most typical form. The modern actor-manager
is framed, as it were, in his own theatre; he must
have fine settings and plenty of grouped figures to
throw out the central one. Garrick is often considered
an actor-manager; but this is a mistake, as he had a
complete company, with an abundance of well-mounted
pieces. He only *managed* his theatre, occasionally
"starring it" in his own company. But Foote was
all in all—manager, actor, and author. Unflagging
in his exertions, and indomitable, he carried on his
enterprise on this one-man principle for many years.
After he became a writer of comedies, to be produced at a theatre of his own, he found that he had
need of a large and yet larger canvas; his treatment
expanded, and required a large cast of characters.

He equipped it with a large and efficient corps.
All his pieces were supported by some distinguished
players; while some had a long and expensive cast of
characters. He was, however, careless as to his
scenery and dresses. He kept no regular wardrobe,
and usually hired costumes, or bought at old-clothes
shops anything that suited his purpose. Coats too
large or too small, sleeves too long, were often
noticed, and the manager himself, when making one
of his rambling orations, would detect these incon-
gruities and make humorous allusion to "the gentleman in the sleeves." The truth was, he relied almost
entirely on his own talent and stock of humour; *there*

was his true wardrobe and his scenery. It was, perhaps, more "legitimate," and showed better knowledge of the dramatic principle than our moderns do.

The characters of most leading actors during the Garrick period were marked with a certain eccentricity and brilliant oddity. One of Foote's most valuable supporters was Shuter, whose name was probably Shooter. He pursued the usual rambling course of instruction that was open to the strolling player—and a valuable sort of instruction it was—and was engaged so early as the year 1747 at the Haymarket, under Foote, with whom for the rest of his life he maintained a rather intermittent connection, though Foote generally contrived a second humorous character written specially for him. He was indeed a valuable *aide*. His training was found at the two patent theatres, where he performed a vast round of characters which furnished him with a variety and experience which, with his own exuberant humour, helped him to his great reputation. Garrick was said to have considered him the greatest comic genius he had ever seen. He had the art of working the muscles of his face in a peculiar fashion, even of changing its expression. He was not, however, to be depended on. Like his colleague Weston, he was addicted to the bottle—was, in fact, a drunkard. He would leave out portions of his part, and put as much into it, justifying Churchill's pleasant stroke that he "never cared a pin what he left out or what put in." He was, moreover, a gambler, and also a sort of "revivalist" and a follower of Whitefield's. This combination must have furnished his manager with many hints for Mother Cole's character. He could say good things, and was reputed a wit. His remarks

17—2

on darns and holes in stockings had as much philosophy
as wit : " A hole is the accident of a day, but a darn
is premeditated poverty."

Through his long course at the Haymarket, Foote
could always rely on two faithful and efficient followers, who gave admirable point to his humorous
creations. He wrote the parts specially for them.
They were of the foremost rank, and stamped, as it
were, with the Garrick hall-mark. These were
Weston and *Shuter*, whom I have just outlined.

Shuter's great coadjutor Weston seems to have left
the deepest impression on his contemporaries. North-
cote was almost extravagant in his praises of Weston.
" You could not imagine," he said, " that he was
acting at all. You would suppose that they had
gone out and found the actual character that they
wanted, and brought him on the stage without his
knowledge. Even when they interrupted him with
peals of laughter, he looked about him as if he was
not at all conscious of having anything to do with it,
and then went on as before." An admirable description, and words happily chosen ; for nothing is more
difficult to define than true acting, or how acting has
affected us.

This clever eccentric began by an apprenticeship to
cooking, his father being in the royal kitchen as head-
cook. He ran away, not unnaturally, from his duty
as turnspit, was put into the navy, deserted, and
turned stroller. Foote, who had seen him play, was
struck by his talent, and, thinking he would suit his
theatre, gave him a small part; but the actor's vagabond
taste led him to wander to Ireland and other places.
When, however, Foote was preparing his " Mayor of
Garratt," he selected Weston for Jerry, and deputed

Wilkinson to find him and engage him. His performance of the henpecked husband, Sneak, made
him all but famous, and created a type.

Cooke tells us, " He was different from any that
was seen long before or since his time ; and yet this
general excellence may be comprehended in one article
—namely, a plain and palpable simplicity of nature.
Shuter had a richness of colouring in his comic characters that was pleasant, but often wrong. Yates
was generally chaste and correct, but he often carried
this quality to a degree of coldness which threw a
damp on the performance ; but Weston united taste
and humour in so eminent a degree that when he
raised his audience seemingly to the highest pitch of
laughter, his features became the graver and steadier.
. . . His *by-play*, too, was in the most capital style
excellent. Who that remembers his surprise at
breaking the phial in ' Abel Drugger '; his returning
for his shoes, after his medical examination in ' Doctor
Last '; or his hurrying up his wife's night-clothes, on
the well-known sound of ' Jerry, Jerry, where are you,
Jerry ?' in ' The Mayor of Garratt,' but must have a
picture before them of such superior excellence that
they may well despair of ever ' seeing its like again ' !"

After a course of new pieces, which were successful
enough, Foote bethought him of a holiday in his
favourite Dublin. Of this expedition, which was in
1768, there are some odd incidents recorded, illustrating Foote's utter recklessness and extravagance.
With pockets full of cash, he determined to enjoy
himself on the road, and journeyed by way of the
gay city of Bath, where he halted. At the moment he
had some £1,200 at his banker's (he had made some
thousands by his last piece), and in his pocket was some

£500. Never had he been in such good case. Those were palmy days for managerial profit; for the expenses of mounting a piece, salaries, etc., were very trifling in a small "bandbox of a theatre" like the Haymarket. The monstrous, devouring cost of modern days was not then dreamed of. Cooke tells what followed: "He fell in with a nest of gamblers (the usual attendants on this fashionable place of resort), who, finding him with full pockets and high spirits, availed themselves of their superior dexterity with considerable success. At last his friend Rigby, then Paymaster of the Forces, who happened just then to be at Bath, took an opportunity to tell him how grossly he was plundered; and further remarked, 'that from his careless manner of playing and betting, and his habit of telling stories when he should be minding his game, he must in the long-run be ruined, let him play with whom he would.'

"Foote, who perhaps by this time had partly seen his error, but was too proud to take a lesson in the character of *a dupe*, very ridiculously and ungratefully resented this advice. He told his friend, with an unbecoming sharpness, 'that although he was no politician by profession, he could see as soon as another into any sinister designs laid against him; that he was too old to be schooled; and that as to any distinction of rank between them to warrant this liberty, he saw none; they were both the King's servants, with this difference in *his* favour—that he could always draw upon his talents for independence, when perhaps a courtier could not find the King's treasury always open to him for support.'

"On this Mr. Rigby made his bow and walked off; while *the dupe* went on, and not only lost the five hundred pounds which he had about him, but the twelve hundred at his banker's; and thus, stripped of his last guinea, was obliged to borrow a hundred pounds to carry him to Ireland!

"Fortune, however, who was constantly at his heels (though he so often turned her out of doors), veered about once more in his favour on his arrival in Dublin; for his new comedy of 'The Devil upon Two Sticks' did nearly as much for him there as on the boards of the Haymarket. It brought crowded houses every night to the end of the season, the treasury books constantly reporting from one hundred and fifty to two hundred pounds per night; which, as the expenses of the house were small, and he himself played also upon shares, made his profits very considerable."

We have also just a glimpse of Foote in Paris at the end of the year 1765. "At the moment," Walpole says, "there were three English humorists in the city—Wilkes, Sterne, and Foote—and yet he could find nothing to laugh at. For the first 'does not make me laugh,' the second never could, and for the third I pay five shillings when I have a mind that he should divert me."

At this place we shall pause to make a rather detailed review of Foote's large amount of literary baggage—his clever, even brilliant comedies, which have been too long overlooked.

CHAPTER XVIII

FOOTE'S COMEDIES

FOOTE was a diligent dramatist, and wrote about a score of pieces, not all of equal merit; but, with the exception of three or four, all may be considered good, while at least two—"The Minor" and "The Cozeners"—stand out from the productions of the time. They might be called great plays, from their subjects and treatment, from the living characters introduced, the abuses that were mercilessly gibbeted or lashed, and the wholesome reform that followed. Here Foote might place his claim to the title of "English Aristophanes" on fair foundation; and his work seems akin to that of Charles Dickens when reforming social abuses.

Character is true drama, and it is followed in real life as well as in the theatre with an absorbing interest. The author himself claimed to have furnished no fewer than eighteen *original* characters to English drama, and there is much foundation for the claim. The worthy Genest is unbounded in his admiration. "Though having no plot," he says, "his dialogue is superior to most other writers'; it abounds in wit, humour, and satire, and is peculiarly terse and well adapted to the stage. Seldom is there a superfluous word, or one that could be changed. They contain a history of the follies, customs, and corruptions of his age. He cared not whether the objects of his satire were in high or low life, provided the peculiarities were prominent enough and the persons well known. By his death was lost a great check on fashionable vice."*

Foote lived at an age when talent, and even genius, abounded in all departments. The stage was specially distinguished. Actors, managers, dramatists, politicians, poets, writers of all kinds—all were brilliant. Each actor seemed to have a distinct and marked character of his own, in most cases found interesting enough to furnish forth memoirs and other records. Garrick's life has been written at least six times. The lover of the stage is never tired of hearing about him and Quin and Woffington, Barry, Macklin, Mossop, Woodward, Delane, Sheridan, and dozens more. All their lives are interesting and dramatic; they are living personages, and each a "character." They all got forward in the world and made their mark, because they had talent and originality. The world was their oyster, and they knew how to open it.

In contrast to this happy era, we may look round

* Foote could boast a great deal of "literary baggage." In 1747 appeared his treatise on "The Passions," in which he dealt with the merits and defects of the leading performers—Garrick, Quin, Barry, and others; and though he gives some praise to the great actor's Lear, he points out many blemishes. Later he issued some pamphlets on comedy and tragedy, which show evidences of study and knowledge. Still later he took his share in the controversy about his "Minor." When roused, he could write letters of singularly incisive power. Witness his reply to the Duchess of Kingston, which was admired by his contemporaries and has been praised by succeeding critics. On the whole, Foote's literary work is more than respectable in its quality, and on the ground of his comedies he may fairly be ranked as a man of letters.

on our own society to discover that we are living in
a time of general mediocrity. In every direction there
is a depressing level. If we survey all the professions
—law, the Church, medicine, soldiery, political life,
authorship—all is second-rate and inferior. There is
no one standing at the top—no brilliant figures, as in
the day of Dickens and Thackeray. The most distressing extinction of all is that of humour and states-
manship. In a crisis there is no one to turn to.

Foote's work as a dramatist has been much overlooked, if not undervalued. It is really classical.
Intended equally for untheatrical as well as for
theatrical audiences—for they were sold largely in
book form—his pieces seem always to have been
heartily appreciated. Yet in the published form all
the elements of movement and colour—that is, of
mimicry and other illustration—had to be omitted;
we can conceive, therefore, when presented with
the rich living forces of Foote himself, kindled by
the spirit of the persons taken off, what an overpowering exhibition was the result! Foote became
the actual personage, while he superadded brilliant
illustrative dialogue, eccentric gestures, and other
elements. We may assume that the author was
not prompted by ill-nature or malice when he
" brought on" his victim, but simply found that the
presence of such a model kindled his imagination and
added force. This vital element, however, being now
wanting, it becomes impossible ever to revive pieces
of Foote's. And how brilliant and how amusing
they must have been! What vivacity, what broad
humour, were present, and how original and entertaining! Some of his more notable characters, such as
Hartop, Sir Gregory Gazette, the two Cadwalladers,

the two Aircastles, Mrs. Cole, and others, may be
fairly set beside those of Goldsmith, though lacking
Goldsmith's dramatic power and treatment. But so
entirely local are the allusions, and so completely
based on the spirit and manners of the time, that it
would be hopeless to think of reviving them. They
would be unintelligible as well as tedious. Foote's
pieces, therefore, must remain in the cabinets of the
curious, though at the same time the student will
find them worthy of his attention, notably those
who supply pieces to our stage—which, it must be
said without offence, is in a state of destitution as
regards dramatists. The consideration of Foote's
system is very apropos at this moment, when the
Censor question is being submitted to a searching
discussion. At every step of Foote's progress we
feel that the powers of this official should have been
exercised, and why they were not it is difficult to say,
unless it be that he, like the rest, trembled before
Foote's power. The Lord Chamberlain, however,
exercised the duty himself—he was, as it were, the
King's deputy; whereas in the present day the
licenser seems sometimes to be an independent
functionary who does not consult his Chamberlain.

Nowadays no one studies character or human
nature, or plausible incident, or, indeed, any of the
elements that go to amuse or excite. Any such
characters have a sort of stiff, machine-made air; they
repeat forms of words supposed to represent character.
Everything depends on recited passages; no one
thinks of the canon, "We must do it in action."
Who thinks, too, of "the double intention," described
by Johnson in a sentence which conveys the whole
art of stage action? Garrick, disguised as a footman,

did not act the part properly, for " he did not let the
gentleman break through the footman."

At the present moment the English drama shows
signs of exhaustion. The stale devices, the " problem
play," the conversational play of genteel life, are worn
out. Who is not tired of "the woman with a past,"
and the wretched, uninteresting contentions for the
possession of such a creature ? What is wanting for
the resuscitation of interest is the development of
character. Character either on or off the stage is
eternally interesting and diverting, and the play and
contest of character is a drama in itself. In this view
we turn to Foote's long-forgotten pieces, and find
characters of the broadest, boldest kind. But, then,
characters need character-actors to interpret them,
and where are they ?

As Genest says, a valuable element in Foote's
plays is the striking, vivid pictures they present of the
depraved society of his time, as well as of the various
types of character that move through it. We are
shown a whole gallery of rakes, " fast " men—reckless,
gay, and not without spirit and frolic—who are put
forward, not to point any moral, but to amuse. Most
of the allusions in their talk refer to loose life. Those
who are undistinguished by vice are shown as strange
eccentrics and oddities. The women are for the most
part correct in their manners, but mainly without
character, simply because there was no occasion
for losing or defending it ; as in the case of Mrs.
Cadwallader, the tradesman's wife, who seems to
accept a lover's proposal as an ordinary matter. To
introduce such a personage as " Mother Cole "—a
" procuress "—on a British stage might seem going too
far, but she was received without protest or repulsion,

even with infinite relish. Such an apparition was common enough in the days of the Merry Monarch.

Certain abuses he succeeded in making perfectly ridiculous to the community : affectation, or love of china and curios, attended by ignorance ; pretence of religion and inspiration without real feeling—that is to say, hypocrisy ; absurd craze for antiquities ; blatant arrogance of wealth ; pretence of foreign travel ; the vulgarity of tax-gatherers, or " commissaries," who plunder the nation ; scheming women, who were agents of dissolute men—in short, he dealt with an endless gallery of beings who preyed on the weaknesses of the community.*

How strange, by the way, is it that, in our time, we see none of this satirical chastisement of foolish types of character ! Can the reason be that all is uniform and of one decent pattern—that no one is odd or absurd or affected ? Or is the reason the hopeless mediocrity of talent that now reigns in all departments ? Not one, it seems to me nowadays, is a true *dramatist*, though there are many writers of plays and of smart dialogue. No one *observes* or studies life or produces a true, real, full-blooded, natural character— a character which will engender the action.†

---

* Boz by his powers of sarcasm succeeded in abolishing a long list of abuses, which he made to appear perfectly odious ; but Foote had no such lofty aims in view. If he set a corrupt character before his audiences, it was only to entertain them and make them laugh. No one turns in disgust from Mrs. Cole as one does in the case of Stiggins. Dickens had the one stern purpose in view of destroying such monsters. Foote cared little whether they were destroyed or not ; he had no ill-feeling to them.

† Sir Arthur Pinero is a clever man, but his dramas are a little machine-made, and have not much intrinsic life or movement. Mr. Henry A. Jones is nearer to the true model, and knows more of character.

And as we read Foote's scenes we must feel astonished at the power of observation displayed. The author seems to have been familiar with every phase of society. Nothing escaped him; club life, trading life, religious life, licentious life, coffee-house life, gambling life, dandyism, every folly of society was dealt with, and with complete familiarity.*

What a terror this man must have been in every society, whether at the dinner-table, or behind the scenes, or on the stage! As his eye roved round the groups before him, and fell now on this one and now on that, each must have quaked in his shoes, thinking that his turn was at hand. The jester is compelled to keep himself afloat, as it were, by recurring efforts; with him, every movement, the slightest naïve or thoughtless utterance, was an opening. On the instant, the victim was roughly "butchered to make a Roman holiday." He spared no one, particularly those to whom he was under obligation. He would have sympathized with the man who said to certain folk who were lamenting a friend to whom they owed many obligations: "At least you are now free from the burden of gratitude." Foote in such a case not only dispensed with gratitude, but contrived to turn the table by making the benefactor thankful to him for being indulgent.

And yet, on reading Foote's comedies, we are almost surprised to find how little they depend on that

---

* Here was one touch. A club servant tells a friend: "It was but last night Sir Ralph moved that every man in the club should give the waiter two guineas apiece, *just by way of surprising the rascal,* and it was carried *nem. con.* And when surprise was expressed the servant said, 'Oh! the members never flinch at a frolic.'" Here was no exaggeration. Frolics just as reckless and unmeaning were carried on every day by the fashionable "bloods."

element of personality which yet seemed to have been the secret of their success. He could fill them out lavishly with rich and original strokes, all strict developments of the characters. In this the author was a true artist, for he knew that this adoption of a special model really limited the effect, and was quite transitory; and he sought, beneath the peculiarities and eccentricities of the individual, something large and general which could be applied to the many. Thus Dickens, when setting out his fantastic sketch of Leigh Hunt, broadened all the elements, and formed the general type of an airy, selfish creature who lived in dreams of his personality, which people who had never seen the original could recognize. I have little doubt but that, in the case of Mrs. Gamp, her creator had been first attracted by some stray phrase or perversion, such as "the anworks package," and this supplied his ready fancy with a whole language. Thence he went deeper down, and came on the confused, muddling character which prompted these utterances, and which jumbled thoughts as it did words. In the same fashion Foote, struck by the amusing incoherence of Cadwallader, devised all sorts of odd situations for his hero, in which he made him behave exactly as he would have done in real life, and then supplied the *particular* likeness by his vivid histrionic exertions. This, of course, is now lost to the general reader.

As to Foote's acting, it is rather difficult to arrive at an accurate opinion. John Taylor, a pleasant reminiscent, as it is called, whom the older ones of our generation have known—notably the old Mr. Fladgate of the Garrick—had often seen Foote play. He recalled that he acted best the characters that were written by himself, though his voice was harsh and untuned; but the public grew accustomed to him and liked him; and he adds: "His confidence and speech were powerfully effective." He was not suited to the regular drama, though his good sense and broad humour made him very entertaining. He always tried to keep in the front on the stage—which, as manager, he was privileged to do. Taylor speaks genuinely when he says he could not appreciate the *mots* of Foote that were circulated with applause. It must be said that this view is supported by Cooke's collection of "good things" given at the end of his latter Life. Most of these were supplied to him by Taylor, who had but a poor opinion of the humorist.

"I have a full recollection," he used to say, "of his manner. He performed his characters, written by and for himself, with admirable humour and effect, and far beyond any of his successors, though some of these used to take *him* off with great success, notably Bannister the elder. His voice was harsh and unequal; it would be difficult to believe that it ever could have been endured on the stage; but the public had been used to it, and his intrepid confidence and spirit were powerfully effective"—a very happy criticism. Taylor noted that Foote's manner was by no means suited to the regular drama: meaning, no doubt, that his methods were too disorderly and too dependent on the inspiration of the moment. But his "good sense and broad humour" carried him over this and made him very effective.

Who that has written upon the stage but must recall with deep gratitude the faithful, ever reliable, but little recognized authority, that genuine

Dryasdust — PARSON GENEST ? Who has not appealed to him in "a tight place," and been promptly relieved ? This guide has led many an uncertain and perhaps ignorant explorer safely through all the bogs and quagmires of the dramatic chronicles.

This clergyman had been chaplain to the Duke of Ancaster, but fell into ill-health, which compelled him to retire from his profession. He settled at Bath, where for nine years he solaced his sufferings by writing his great encyclopædia in ten volumes octavo: "Some Account of the English Stage," it was called, "from the Restoration in 1660 to 1830." Joseph Knight gives it this generous praise : " A work of great labour and research, which forms the basis of most exact knowledge of the stage. Few books of reference are equally trustworthy, constant investigation having brought to light few errors, and none of grave importance."

It is impossible not to admire and sympathize with him in his drudging pursuit ; he is so keen, and, above all, so much to be depended upon. From the first origins of the stage he plodded on downwards, year by year, theatre by theatre, to about the 'thirties of last century. There he stopped. Studying his bills, he could track the actor from one house to another, and discover, Heaven knows how, that a theatre was closed on a particular night, for some special reason.

I have mentioned "Joe" Knight, whose spirit was congenial to the parson's, and who had the heartiest faith in him. Indeed, it was believed that this admirable and searching critic might one day undertake to bring the monumental work down to the present era. But it would have been a work of appalling labour, and might have sealed his fate. The good, honest "Joe" Knight was himself a sort of Genest. He had the same drudging accuracy, the same love of dates and details, the same profound knowledge of theatrical history—writing, working with energy, serving three or four papers, and, alas! "burning the candle at both ends," until there was no more candle to burn. There was too much of the recuperative supper, too much, perhaps, of the small-hours. "Joe's" great task was the preparation of the dramatic biographies in the "Dictionary of National Biography." I really believe that he described every actor, actress, and theatrical person, with infinite accuracy and pains; dates, places, incidents, all might be accepted as on oath, so scrupulous and laborious was he in his researches.*

And what a force he was—how overpowering and "Falstaffian!" He could say amusing, overpowering things. At a theatre, on a first night, how entertaining to listen to his jocose comments all through the piece! The Garrick Club knew him well. On a "first night" he would come there after the play, take his place at the long supper-table, and "keep it up," as it is called, with unabated animation till the dawn.

---

* And yet of good, honest "Joe" it must be said that his work is a little soulless—a series of catalogues, dated entries, etc., without poetry or imagination, with a sort of legal flavour about the whole. This was shown particularly in his account of Garrick, which he expanded into a formal Life in succession to mine, printed some forty years before. It is an admirable consultative work, but dry and uninteresting, and difficult to read. He had no idea of realizing the actors' characters. I speak merely as a critic of his curious style and methods; for I liked him exceedingly, and he made me many affectionate apologies for trespassing, as he called it.

Poor Joe ! He must have had a difficult time. He was a great bookworm : he collected old French works of a Rabelaisian cast, and made a vast library, but having, as he told me, no shelves or room, had to *stack* his treasures on the stairs.

Considering the long list of friends, acquaintances, and familiar public characters, who are framed and glazed, as it were, in Foote's pieces, we may wonder how the eccentricities of the amiable " Goldy" escaped being brought upon the Haymarket stage. One reason may have been that he was a dangerous person to meddle with, and, like Johnson, might have bought a cudgel. As it was, he had beaten, or rather tried to beat, a bookseller.

But now comes a surprise, for Goldsmith was to pay Foote the admiring compliment of studying his pieces and helping himself from the dish. He carefully studied his methods and his special treatment of character. He was too well equipped to think of borrowing or copying ; but Foote's images, as well as his humorous conceptions and treatment, remained with him. It will be interesting to consider for a moment what his two great comedies owe to Foote. From him Goldsmith certainly took the idea of Tony, the loutish son of a foolish mother. In Foote's case it was a foolish father. In both cases the parents had settled a suitable match for their offspring, but their designs were frustrated by their son's marrying a buxom country girl—Mally Pengrouse in Foote's play. In both pieces—"The Knights" and "She Stoops to Conquer"—each heroine is courted by a young spark from town, and each young lady has been selected for two uncouth sons. The young Timothy extols his Mally Pengrouse, just as Tony does his Bet. Goldsmith's piece begins with Mrs. Hardcastle's complaints of the stupidity of country life—" Here we live in an old rambling castle, seeing nobody," etc. Her husband makes growling, sarcastic comments on his wife's complaints. Mrs. Aircastle grumbles in the same way : " Folks that travelled barefoot to London roll down in their coaches, but still we stick." When the mother, who dotes on her Tony, says, " He coughs sometimes," old Hardcastle growls out, " Yes, when his liquor goes the wrong way." Mrs. Aircastle says to her Timothy, " Shoulders back !" on which Aircastle, " His breastbone sticks out like a turkey's," and adds, " Grace ! he has neither grace nor grease."

That Tony Lumpkin was suggested to " Goldy " by Foote's " Knights " will be clear to anyone who reads this passage between Timothy and Hartop. It is exactly Hastings patronizing Tony :

" *Hart.* But have you left in Cornwall nothing that you regret the loss of more than hurling and wrestling ? *Tim.* Nan ? what ? *Hart.* No favourite she ? *Tim.* Arra, I coupled Favourite and Jowler together, and sure they tugged it all the way up. Part with Favourite ! no, I thank you for nothing : you must know I nursed Favourite myself; uncle's huntsman was going to mill-pond to drown all Music's puppies ; so I saved she : but, fath, I'll tell you a comical story : At Lanston they both broke loose and eat a whole loin-o'-veal and a leg of beef : Crist ! how landlord sweared ! fath, the poor fellow was almost mazed ; it made me die wi' laughing : but how came you to know about our Favourite ? *Hart.* A circumstance so material to his son could not escape the knowledge of Sir Gregory Gazette's friends. But

here you mistook me a little, Squire Tim ; I meant
whether your affections were not settled upon some
pretty girl; has not some Cornish lass caught your
heart? *Tim.* Hush! God, the old man will hear; jog
a tiny bit this way;—won't a' tell father? *Hart.*
Upon my honour! *Tim.* Why, then I'll tell you the
whole story, more or less. Do you know Mally
Pengrouse? *Hart.* I am not so happy. *Tim.* She's
uncle's milkmaid; she's as handsome, Lord! her face
all red and white, like the inside of a shoulder of
mutton: so I made love to our Mally; and just, fath,
as I had got her good will to run away to Exeter and
be married, uncle found it out and sent word to father,
and father sent for me home; but I don't love her a
bit the worser for that : but, 'icod, if you tell father,
he'll knock my brains out, for he says I'll disparage
the family, and mother's as mad as a March hare
about it; so father and mother ha' brought me to be
married to some young body in these parts. *Hart.*
What, is my lady here? *Tim.* No, sure ; Dame
Winifred, as father calls her, could not come along."

Then there is an interview between Timothy and
the lady, neither wishing for the marriage. She
tells him : " Suppose I won't be married to you ?"
Tim answers her : " Nay, miss, such I can't help it,
faith and soul ! But father and mother bid me come
a-courting, and if you won't ha' me I'll tell father so."
Tony and Miss Neville have the same sort of con-
fidences in " Goldy's " comedy. It turns out that
Timothy has gone and married Mally Pengrouse.
Hartop then listens to Timothy, and encourages him
on the score of this Mally Pengrouse, he himself
wishing to secure the young lady who was intended
for Timothy, just as Hastings does. But there is

quite a convincing point, though it is but a trifling
one. Sir Luke, in "The Lame Lover," bids his
servant go with his excuses to Sir *Gregory Goose*—
certainly an odd, unusual name. And we find, in
"The Good-Natured Man," Lofty, who corresponds
to Sir Luke, quoting a Sir *Gilbert Goose*.

Another character certainly inspired "Goldy" for
his capital one of Lofty in "The Good-Natured Man."
Foote supplied the name Lofty in his "Patron," and
the character also, which is unmistakably original, of
"Goldy's" Lofty, in "The Lame Lover." Here is one
admirable scene, quite as good as, if not better than,
Goldsmith's. Sir Luke is a boasting tuft-hunter like
Lofty, and has engaged himself to dine with an
Alderman. A servant delivers a card to him : "Sir
Gregory Goose desires the honour of Sir Luke Limp's
company to dinner." "Gad, so ! a little unlucky ! I
have been engaged for these three weeks." The
Sergeant then mentions that Sir Gregory has been
returned to Parliament. Sir Luke : "Is he so ?
Oh, oh ! that alters the case. George, give my compliments to Sir Gregory, and I'll certainly come and
dine there. Order Joe to run to Alderman Inkles—
sorry can't wait upon him, but confined to bed two
days with the new influenza."

After declaring "that these letter-writers are as
persecuting as a beggar who attacks your coach at the
mounting of a hill : there is no getting rid of them
without a penny to one and a promise to t'other," a
servant brings him a letter from the Earl of Brentford,
and an answer is required. "Answer !" cries Sir
Luke. "Another invitation : dinner at five—taste
for music. Gad, so ! I hope Sir Gregory's servant
'an't gone. Run after him as fast as you can ; tell

him, Quite in despair—recollect an engagement that can't in nature be missed ; and return in an instant."

The servant runs off, but could not overtake the man. Some further talk follows. Sir Luke is taking his leave, when another servant rushes in with a letter :

"*Serv.* Sir, His Grace the Duke of —— *Sir Luke.* His Grace ? Where is he ? Where ? *Serv.* In his coach at the door. If you aren't better engaged, he would be glad of your company to go into the city with him and take a dinner at Dolly's. *Sir Luke.* In his own coach, did you say ? *Serv.* Yes, sir, with the coronets—or I believe so. *Sir Luke.* There's no resisting of that. Bid Joe run to Sir Gregory Goose. *Serv.* He is already gone to Alderman Inkles. *Sir Luke.* Then do you step to the Knight's—hey no ! you must go to my Lord's—hold, hold !—no, I have it : step first to Sir Gregory's ; then pop in at Lord Brentford's just as the company are going to dinner. *Serv.* What shall I say to Sir Gregory ? *Sir Luke.* Anything—what I told you before. *Serv.* And what to my Lord ? *Sir Luke.* What ?—why, tell him that my uncle from Epsom—no ! that won't do, for he knows I don't care a farthing for him. Why, tell him—hold, I have it : tell him, just as I was going to my chair to obey his commands, I was arrested by a couple of bailiffs and carried to the Pied Bull at the Borough. I beg ten thousand pardons for making His Grace wait, but His Grace knows my misfor——"

But Sheridan, as we might expect from our knowledge of his ways, was the most unscrupulous of the depredators. It is not too much to say that the whole conception of Charles Surface and his impecunious association was imported wholesale from

Foote's "Minor." All the devices for raising money—the shark-like Jews and the rest—are there. Charles, with his pleasant, gay indifference to debt and difficulty, is a copy of the young Wealthy.

The latter is impecunious, reckless, and engaging, in spite of all his follies. His father comes from India with a friendly uncle to rescue him from his creditors, and enters into a confederacy with a number of "rooks," he assuming the guise of a foreign Baron, just as Sir Oliver disguises himself as Moses. The young fellow shows signs of grace and nobility, which win his father's heart.

What is most convincing, however, is that we can trace Little Premium back to Little Transfer in "The Minor," both useful brokers or go-betweens. Like the former, Little Transfer has no money himself, but has to get it, in the form of paving-stones or Witney blankets; these can be converted into ready money for the borrower's benefit.

There is a scene in the second act of "The Minor" so reminiscent of "The School for Scandal" that we almost rub our eyes and seem to think it must be a passage in that immortal comedy that we had some-how overlooked. We hear Charles and Little Premium consulting together.

"*Trans.* And what sum does your honour lack at present? *Sir Geo.* Lack! How much have you brought? *Trans.* Who, I? Dear me! none. *Sir Geo.* Zounds, none! *Trans.* Lack-a-day! none to be had, I think. All the morning have I been upon the hunt. There, Ephraim Barebones, the tallow-chandler in Thames Street, used to be a never-failing chap; not a guinea to be got there. Then I trotted away to Nebuchadnezzar Zebulon, in the Old

Jewry, but it happened to be Saturday; and they
never touch on the Sabbath, you know. *Sir Geo.*
Why, what the devil can I do? . . . *Trans.* Well,
well, now, I declare, I am quite sorry to see your
honour in such a taking. *Sir Geo.* Damn your
sorrow! *Trans.* But come, don't be cast down.
Though money is not to be had, money's worth may,
and that's the same thing. *Sir Geo.* How, dear
Transfer? *Trans.* Why, I have, at my warehouse
in the city, ten casks of whale-blubber, a large cargo
of Dantzick dowlas, with a curious sortment of Birmingham hafts, and Witney blankets for exporta-
tion. *Sir Geo.* Hey! *Trans.* And stay, stay! then,
again, at my country-house, the bottom of Gray's Inn
Lane, there's a hundred ton of fine old hay, only
damaged a little last winter, for want of thatching;
with forty load of flint stones. *Sir Geo.* Well?
Trans. Your honour may have all these for a reasonable profit, and convert them into cash. *Sir Geo.*
Blubber and blankets? Why, you old rascal, do you
banter me? *Trans.* Who, I? Oh law, marry, heaven
forbid. *Sir Geo.* Get out of my—you fluttering
scoundrel! . . . [*Enter* Loader.] So, sir, you have
recommended me to a fine fellow. *Load.* What's
the matter? *Sir Geo.* He can't supply me with a
shilling! and wants, besides, to make me a dealer in
dowlas. *Load.* Ay, and a very good commodity,
too. People that are upon ways and means must not
be nice, knight. A pretty piece of work you have
made here! Thrown up the cards, with the game in
your hands. *Sir Geo.* Why, pr'ythee, of what use
would his—— *Load.* Use! of every use. Procure
you the spankers, my boy. I have a broker that
in a twinkling shall take off your bargain. *Sir*

Geo. Indeed! *Load.* Indeed! Ay, indeed. You sit down to hazard and not know the chances! I'll call him back. Holo, Transfer! [*Enter* Transfer.] ... Come hither, little Transfer. What, man, our Minor was a little too hasty; he did not understand trap: knows nothing of the game, my dear. *Trans.* What I said, was to serve Sir George; as he seemed—— *Load.* I told him so; well, well, we will take thy commodities, were they as many more. But try, pr'ythee, if thou couldst not procure us some of the ready for present spending. *Trans.* Let me consider. *Load.* Ay, do, come: shuffle thy brains; never fear the Baronet. To let a lord of lands want shiners—'tis a shame. *Trans.* I do recollect, in this quarter of the town, an old friend that used to do things in this way. *Load.* Who? *Trans.* Statute, the scrivener. *Load.* Slam me, but he has nicked the chance. *Trans.* A hard man, Master Loader! *Sir Geo.* No matter. *Trans.* His demands are exorbitant. *Sir Geo.* That is no fault of ours. *Load.* Well said, knight! *Trans.* But, to save time, I had better mention his terms. *Load.* Unnecessary. *Trans.* Five per cent. legal interest. *Sir Geo.* He shall have it. *Trans.* Ten, the premium. *Sir Geo.* No more words. *Trans.* Then, as you are not of age, five more for insuring your life. *Load.* We will give it. *Trans.* As for what he will demand for the risque—— *Sir Geo.* He shall be satisfied. *Trans.* You pay the attorney. *Sir Geo.* Amply, amply. Loader, despatch him. *Load.* There, there, little Transfer; now everything is settled. All terms shall be complied with, reasonable or unreasonable. What, our principal is a man of honour. [*Exit* Transfer.] Hey, my knight, this is doing business. This pinch

is a sure card. [*Re-enter* Transfer.] *Trans.* I had
forgot one thing. I am not the principal; you pay
the brokerage. *Load.* Ay, ay; and a handsome
present into the bargain, never fear. *Trans.* Enough,
enough. *Load.* Hark'e, Transfer: we'll take the
Birmingham hafts and Witney wares. *Trans.* They
shall be forthcoming. You would not have the hay
with the flints? *Load.* Every pebble of 'em. The
magistrates of the Baronet's borough are infirm and
gouty. He shall deal them as new pavement. [*Exit*
Transfer.] So that's settled."

In " The Knights " we find Miss Penelope Trifle, a
spinster aunt, who is a sort of duenna to Miss Sukey,
and who talks in a stiff, pedantic strain, with high-
sounding words, quite as Mrs. Malaprop does in " The
Rivals," though without any " derangement of epi-
taphs." She lectures in the same fashion her niece,
who is destined for Timothy, as Lydia was for Captain
Absolute. But the young lady has in view another
lover. Sukey asks for a glass of ale at the inn.
Miss Pen. " Fie, fie, niece! Is that liquor for a
young lady? *Don't disparage your family and breeding.* The person is to be born that ever saw me
touch anything stronger than water," etc. Then the
girl answers her; on which the duenna: " Now, Miss
Flirt, none of your sneers." Later she says: " It is
indeed, Sir Gregory Gazette, a most *critical con-
juncture, and requires the most mature consideration.*"
Sir Gregory says: " Lack-a-day, ma'am! while we deliberate the boy may be lost." *Miss Pen*: " Why, Sir
Gregory Gazette, *what operations* can we determine
on?" " Lack-a-day, ma'am! I know but one." *Miss
Pen:* " *Administer your propositions*, Sir Gregory
Gazette; you *will have my concurrence, sir, in anything*

that does not derogate from the regulations of conduct, for it would be most preposterous in one of my character *to deviate from the strictest attention.*" She then goes on to talk of "*the previous preliminaries*" and "the accelerations of the nuptials." Then she asks: "Can you unravel this perplexity, untwine this mystery, Sir Gregory Gazette?" Later she asks: "How, Mr. Jenkins, *would you participate* of a plot, too?"

A favourite character with Foote was a certain Puff, a sort of verbose expounder of things, an auctioneer or charlatan. We find him also in "The Critic," name and all. One of Foote's pieces opens with the visit of two men-about-town to the stage, about rehearsal time. To them appears Foote, who answers their criticisms and questions, and explains to them his theatrical systems. This machinery was transferred to "The Critic."

The staple of Foote's show, "The Diversions of the Morning," was a mock-tragedy called "Tragedy à la Mode," in which all the devices of such pieces are burlesqued. It is curious how ingeniously Sheridan has disguised the hints he "conveyed." Fustian, the author, explains and comments exactly as Puff does. We have, "Enter the King's guards, two on each side, who seize them both; both are forced off on opposite sides." Lindemira is the heroine, and raves like Tilburina. "*Fustian.* Here ends the act. *Townly.* The act is short, Mr. Fustian. *Manly.* But everything is here that the dramatic laws require. *Fust.* Now enters the Prince in the presence chamber in deep reflection. [*Enter* Prince.] *Prince.* How frail is man—perplex! Surely the gods—— [*A trumpet blows.*] But hark! the sprightly trumpet speaks the

King's approach. Down, down, my heart! [*Enter
the* King.] O Royal Sir! if e'er your suppliant
slave—— [*Exit* King.]" All this is quite as lively
as "The Critic."

There were other writers who helped themselves
to Foote's wares, such as his friend Murphy, who
seized on Sir Gregory Gazette, that devourer of newspapers, and introduced him with little variation into
his "Upholsterer." *

* Mr. Forster has furnished a carefully-compiled list of Foote's
pieces, with their dates of production. It runs : " The Diversions,"
etc., 1747 ; " Auction," etc., 1748 ; " The Knights," 1748 ; " Taste,"
1752 ; "The Englishman in Paris," 1753 ; "The Englishman returned
from Paris," 1756 ; "The Author," 1757 ; "Diversions," etc., as a farce,
1758 ; " The Minor," 1760 ; " The Lyar," 1761 ; " The Orators,"
1762 ; " The Mayor of Garratt," 1763 ; " The Patron," 1764 ;
"The Commissary," 1765 ; " The Devil upon Two Sticks," 1768 ;
"The Lame Lover," 1770 ; " The Maid of Bath," 1771 ; " The
Nabob," 1772 ; " Piety in Pattens," 1773 ; " The Bankrupt," 1773 ;
"The Cozeners," 1774 ; " The Capucin," 1776.

Joseph Knight speaks of some other pieces in manuscript which
have been attributed to Foote.

CHAPTER XIX

FOOTE'S COMEDIES—*continued*

FOOTE's important comedies, in which he dealt with notable abuses on a large, Aristophanic scale, distilling all his acid, venom, and fury, simulated or real, I have dealt with in their proper places, as being formal *acts* of his life. His other comedies, which are of far slighter texture, I shall deal with here in collective fashion, briefly sketching their plots and characters.

"The Nabob," produced in 1772, was one of Foote's pictures of the shifting manners of his day. The country at the time was filled with returned Indian functionaries and traders who had "shaken the tree," as it was called—who had gone out with some small appointment, and contrived to amass a huge fortune, which they returned to spend in England. They presently acquired the nickname of Nabobs, and Macaulay has presented a lively sketch of their odious methods, their attempts to secure everything—place in society, seats in Parliament, etc. They were all odiously purse-proud, and delighted in outbidding or ousting the impoverished country gentleman. In "Sir Matthew Mite" Foote has given a most unpleasant portrait of this class, which is also exceedingly spirited and amusing. Witness his talk with Mrs. Match'em, one of the most unsavoury types of female agents, which Foote presented rather too often.   The wit here was certainly imitated by Sheridan: "*Mite.* Perhaps I shall be confined a little at first; for when you take or bury a wife, decency requires that you should keep your house for a week : after that time you will find me, dear Match'em, all that you can wish. *Match.* Ah! that is more than your honour can tell.   I have known some of my gentlemen before marriage make as firm and good resolutions not to have the least love or regard for their wives; but they have been seduced after all, and turned out the poorest tame family fools! *Mite.* Indeed!"   This is " Sherry " all over.

The piece is written with much spirit, and the character of the rapacious Mite cleverly detailed. But of a sudden the author indulges in a sort of *freak*, and seems to disregard all the dramatic proprieties.   He represents him as joining the Society of Antiquaries, being initiated by mystic rites, and then reading a burlesque paper on the subject of Whittington and his Cat, in which he gravely discusses the legend—very much in the spirit of Mr. Pickwick when treating of the Cobham Stone. It seems that some such topic had actually been before the society, and been gravely debated, and it was much laughed at in consequence.   Foote could not resist the " actuality " of the thing.   At the same time, none knew so well as he what would " go down " with his audience, and his own tremendous spirit and rollicking humour was certain to smooth

over every intrusive element of the kind, and make
it seem probable.

Jekyll told Moore that the origin of Sir Matthew
Mite in the play was a certain Nabob, one General
Smith, whose father was a cheesemonger. He must
have been an absurd personage enough. He once
put off some invited friends with the excuse: "I
find my damn fellow of a steward has in the meantime sold the estate." He spoilt his hand, he said,
by shooting peacocks with the Great Mogul. Someone brought Foote to visit this original, I fancy at
his request. He was pressed to stay, and hospitably
treated. Having just left the house, Foote said:
"I think I can't possibly miss him now, having had
such a good sitting."

This General Smith had "stood" for the corrupt
borough of Hendon in the early part of the year
1776, but was committed to the King's Bench Prison
by Lord Mansfield on a charge of bribery. Being
excluded from Almack's, he wished to draw the
young men of fashion into his net, and built a new
and splendid club in St. James's Street. Here he
was ready to furnish expectant heirs with moneys
up to the amount of £40,000, this bait bringing ruin
on many opulent heirs.

The name Mite, with the profession or calling
of cheesemonger, must have pointed out the original
to the audience. On this occasion, as in the case
of Cadwallader, the actor was nigh getting into
serious trouble owing to the unusual spectacle of
the victim's resenting his treatment.

There was a good story retailed of a deputation
of indignant Nabobs repairing to Foote's house in
Suffolk Street to call him to account for his ridicule

of their order. The satirist was clever enough to know how to deal with these gentlemen. He is said to have welcomed them with effusive cordiality, but whenever they approached the dangerous subject he adroitly turned it aside with humorous tales—in short, put them in such a good humour that they consented to stay and dine with him! Certainly, he was a wonderful creature. It no doubt furnished him with a capital story for his "show," and he probably mimicked his two visitors in a diverting way. But who could respect such a being? Nor can we respect the two visitors who allowed themselves to be bamboozled by their lively host, who can have said or done nothing that could alter his caricature. Could it be that the visitors saw that nothing was to be got by intimidating Foote, and that it might be better policy to conciliate him?

"The Lame Lover," produced in 1770, was apparently written to nullify in a grotesque way the consequences of the author's unfortunate accident. The title, the leading character, called Sir Luke Limp, and the many allusions to lameness, were all devised with this view—to carry off his infirmity as a jest. The wise warn us never to laugh at ourselves, though we may at other folk, by way of deprecation. It is a complete mistake, and only produces contempt. Sir Luke jocosely tells of a wager he had with a German, a challenge to drive a corking-pin into the calves of their legs: "Mine, you may imagine, was easily done, but when it came to the Baron," etc. And, again, Charlotte says: "A pretty thing for a girl to be tied to a man with one foot in the grave!" "One foot in the grave," is the witty reply; "the rest of his body is

19

not a whit nearer for that. But I hear his stump on the stairs." When Sir Luke appears, he protests that he is all the better for his loss. "Consider, I have neither strain, splint, spavin, or gout; no fear of corns, or that another man should tread on my toes. What, d'ye think I would change with Bill Spindle for one of his spindles?" He then admits he is a little awkward at running, "but as far as a *chair minuet*, match me who can. That is, as all grace is confined to the motions of the head, arms, and chest, which may sitting be as fully displayed as if one had as many legs as a polypus." He thus illustrates it: "A leg—a redundancy, a mere nothing. Man is from nature an extravagant creature. In my opinion, we might all be full as well as we are without half the things we have." It is impossible to resist the wit and buoyancy of these sallies. But the plot is incoherent; rather, there is no plot. One scene is truly far-fetched, when Mrs. Circuit enacts a counsel at the Bar, and recites a long speech on the action of Nobson and Hobson. It is quite unmeaning.

There was a well-known man-about-town— "Charles Skrymisher Boothby Clopton, Esquire"— who bore among his friends the more convenient nickname of "Prince Boothby." The Boothby family was well known to Johnson, who had a particular affection for Miss Boothby, an interesting woman. This Prince Boothby, being of ancient family, might naturally command a distinguished round of acquaintances, but was well known to be what is called a "tuft-hunter," carrying out his chase with a ludicrous eagerness. Hence "*Prince* Boothby." Foote heard of, or more probably met, this personage

—saw his capabilities, and introduced him into his "Lame Lover," adding the lameness from his own experience. It is an odious character—hollow, vapid, chattering, unfeeling, and selfish—but decidedly amusing. The author brings out the tuft-hunting weakness in a rather original fashion. This unhappy being committed suicide, having left a declaration that "he was tired of dressing and undressing."

The scene between the Serjeant and his daughter, where he presses her to marry, may have suggested that between Sir Anthony Absolute and his son the Captain in Sheridan's play: "*Charlotte.* A sweet object to excite tender desires! *Serj.* And why not, hussy! *Char.* First as to his years—— *Serj.* What then? *Char.* A pretty thing, truly, for a girl at my time of life to be tied to a man with one foot in the grave. *Serj.* The rest of his body is not a whit the nearer for that. There is only an execution issued against part of his personal; his real estate is unencumbered and free. *Char.* Sir, I know how proud Sir Luke is of his leg, and have often heard him declare that he would not change his bit of timber for the best flesh and bone in the kingdom."

Here we have yet another of Foote's unbecoming references to his infirmity. But the Serjeant's epigrammatic reference to the "one leg in the grave" is exactly in the spirit of Sheridan, whom it must have inspired. "I would have law merchant for them also," etc. "The Nabob" must be classed with "The Commissary," another corrupt type which he held up to scorn and ridicule. This had been brought out in the year 1765. These officials had become wealthy through contracts during the wars, and, like the Nabobs, tried by all manner of arts to get into society.   The brothers Fungus are shown taking regular lessons from Professors, the author here copying wholesale from Molière, even to the fencing scene in "Le Bourgeois Gentilhomme," made as farcical as Foote could contrive it.   Thus he introduced a sort of mechanical horse that rocked by machinery.   "The Commissary" has much more "bustle" than any of the preceding pieces.   It would seem that Foote was gradually acquiring his art and learning to marshal his plots.   It turns on the adventures of a couple of Commissaries, who were engaged in learning to be men of fashion under hired instructors who preyed upon them.   As may be conceived, the author went to Molière's comedy for this notion, and even borrowed some scenes. Fungus was the name of the two brother Commissaries.

Foote nourished some unaccountable prejudices against various societies, such as the College of Physicians and the Society of Antiquaries, whom he never tired of ridiculing in a rather heavy and clumsy fashion.   This burlesque of pundits and medicos is never difficult.   Scott's "Antiquary" is supreme. Mr. Pickwick's discovery of the incised Cobham stone is happier burlesque than Foote's.

The Nabob is introduced to the Society of Antiquaries, whose investigations as to Whittington and his cat were exciting uproarious laughter.   And physicians, whether as individuals or as corporations, he never spared.

"The Liar," or "Lyar," was produced in 1761. Foote had no part.   It was virtually an adaptation of Corneille's play, and though animated enough— the two Palmers, Jack and Robert, performed in it—

it is artificial and rather uninteresting; but with a "rattling" player, such as the late Charles Mathews, who at one time played it, it was effective. The adaptation is done with great freedom and animation.

In 1764 he brought out his "Patron," dedicated very obsequiously to the Chamberlain, Lord Gower, to whom he acknowledged many obligations, "which let me boast I have had the happiness to receive untainted by the insolence of domestics, the delays of office, or the chilling superiority of rank—mortifications which have been too often experienced by much greater writers than myself, from much less men than your Lordship." This seems like an allusion to Johnson's treatment by Lord Chesterfield. With the various Chamberlains he appears to have been on intimate footing, and, as they protected him as far as they could, it is no wonder he was grateful. There was, however, a lack of tact in dedicating his pieces to these functionaries.

It has been almost accepted as a truth that Bubb Dodington—Lord Melcombe—was intended in this comedy. This nobleman was no doubt almost the last of the official patrons. He has written a play which he wishes to be brought out on the cheap and convenient terms that a dependent shall take all the failure on his shoulders, while in case of success the real author's name is to leak out. This does not exactly fit with what is known of Lord Melcombe, and is merely a perversion of a story concerning his patronage of a friend. It seems that there was an amateur drama played for which Foote lent his theatre. This was called "The Wishes," and was written by a dilettante, Mr. Bentley. A sort of mystery was associated with it. A rehearsal was given under the patronage of Bubb Dodington, at his villa on the Thames. It was later "produced" by Foote. Some distinguished folk were present, and there was a prologue full of obsequious compliments to the young King and his favourite, who was present. Foote was heard to say, "This is too strong," and he declined to repeat it. The producer went about *more suo*, sneering and laughing at the performance.

But though he did not actually glance at Lord Melcombe's dramatic ventures, he no doubt found him effective as a character. But how like Foote it was to introduce and ridicule his own client, the writer whose play he had undertaken to produce! Walpole wrote of Bentley, the author: "He would have died to be supposed an author, and writing for gain." This clearly refers to Bentley, and not to Lord Melcombe, as is generally stated in the biographies. Walpole, indeed, found Lord Melcombe reading the piece to a select circle. Foote was also summoned to hear it read, and adopted it for his stage, but objected to the Prologue.

In this piece he makes merry with a returned Indian, Sir Peter Pepperpot, whose account of his turtles is really amusing: "*Bever.* You seem moved; what has been the matter, Sir Peter? *Sir P.* Matter! why, I am invited to dinner on a barbicu, and the villains have forgot my bottle of chian. *Younger.* Unpardonable. *Sir P.* Ay, this country has spoiled them. . . . Well, dear Bever, rare news, boy: our fleet is arrived from the West. *Bever.* It is? *Sir P.* Ay, lad; and a glorious cargo of turtle. It was lucky I went to Brighthelmstone; I nicked the time to a hair: thin as a lath, and a stomach as sharp as a shark's : never was in finer condition for feeding. *Bever.* Have you a large importation, Sir Peter ? *Sir P.* Nine ; but seven in excellent order : the captain assures me they greatly gained ground on the voyage. *Bever.* How do you dispose of them ? *Sir P.* Four to Cornhill, three to Almack's, and the two sickly ones I shall send to my borough in Yorkshire. *Younger.* Ay ! what, have the provincials a relish for turtle ? *Sir P.* Sir, it is amazing how this country improves in turtle and turnpikes : to which (give me leave to say) we, from our part of the world, have not a little contributed. Why, formerly, sir, a brace of bucks on the Mayor's annual day was thought a pretty moderate blessing. But we, sir, have polished their palates. Why, sir, not the meanest member of my corporation but can distinguish the pash from the pee.

" The Bankrupt " is one of the most perplexing and, it must be said, unmeaning of Foote's pieces. The chief character's name is quite far-fetched—Sir John Riscounter. A lady of title has a paragraph inserted in the papers reflecting on the character of her stepdaughter, with a view to securing the wealthy suitor for her own daughter. Her husband is on the verge of bankruptcy, but at the close is saved ; the newspaper plot is discovered, and the lady and her daughter turned out. A truly singular plot ! The author has combined with it an attack on all the abuses and tricks of bankruptcy, taking a high moral tone which must have amused his friends ; for the censor was himself ever in pecuniary shifts and difficulties and in want of cash, being a gamester and a borrower. It is hard to conceive how the plot was tolerated. It is said there was a friend of Foote's—a financier named Fordyce—who was figured in the piece, but he lost his fortune in some great crash; so Foote thought it would be scarcely decent to bring on the boards.

Someone casually mentioned Le Sage's famous story of " Le Diable Boiteux" to Foote, as a subject suitable for dramatic treatment. Foote loudly scoffed at the suggestion; it was quite unsuited, he said. Within a short time he had prepared a piece on this subject, entitled " The Devil upon Two Sticks." The subject has been treated in our own time, very much upon the same lines. In both cases the Evil One goes about visiting various scenes, and making pungent and sarcastic comments as he goes. There is a prodigious amount of talk and speechings of inordinate length, and with wonder we learn that it was completely successful and brought the author abundance of cash. Here is a specimen:

" *Hel.* But now, Dr. Last, to proceed in due form : are you qualified to administer remedies to such diseases as belong to the head? *Last.* I believe I may. *Hel.* Name some to the College. *Last.* The toothache. *Hel.* What do you hold the best method to treat it? *Last.* I pulls 'em up by the roots. *Hel.* Well replied, brothers! that, without doubt, is a radical cure. *All.* Without doubt. *Hel.* Thus far as to the head : proceed we next to the middle! When, Dr. Last, you are called in to a patient with a pain in his bowels, what then is your method of practice? *Last.* I claps a trencher hot to the part. *Hel.* Embrocation; very well! But if this application should fail, what is the next step that you take? *Last.* I gi's a vomit and a purge. *Hel.* Well replied! for it is plain there is a disagreeable guest in the house; he has opened both doors; if he will go out at neither, it is none of his fault. *All.* Oh no—by no means. *Hel.* We have now despatched the middle and head : come we finally to the other extremity—the feet ! Are you equally skilful in the disorders incidental to them ? *Last.* I believe I may. *Hel.* Name some. *Last.* I have a great vogue all our way for curing of corns. *Hel.* What are the means that you use ? *Last.* I cuts them out. *Hel.* Well replied ! extirpation : no better method of curing can be. Well, brethren, I think we may now, after this strict and impartial inquiry, safely certify that Dr. Last, from top to toe, is an able physician. *All.* Very able, very able indeed. *Hel.* And every way qualified to proceed in his practice. *All.* Every way qualified. *Hel.* You may descend, Dr. Last. [Last *takes his seat among them.*] "

To see what a terror Foote must have been to any respectable oddity, we have only to call up a certain old knight named Browne, who might be described as a sort of physician-antiquary, who was pursuing his researches in a retired fashion. He wrote many learned disquisitions in the Latin tongue, and got into hot controversies with his medical brethren. There was a certain droll eccentricity about his dress and manner. Foote soon " marked him down." It is difficult to conceive how a person utterly unknown to the public should be at all acceptable if they did not know the original. For the essence of the pleasure derived from mimicry is the comparison of the original with the copy. Foote's cleverness, therefore, must have been extraordinary, as he was able to make the mere *copy* or imitation suffice. I fancy he made this so vividly entertaining that the auditors began to think that the original would be

more enjoyable still. All these things contribute
to the conclusion that Foote must have possessed
a special power which held and stimulated his hearers
without any reference to his models.

Sir William Browne, just referred to, was President
of the College of Physicians—an eccentric being, and
therefore one offering himself as the ready prey of
Foote. His dispute with the Licentiates was attract-
ing attention, and his odd figure was reproduced by
the actor after the most minute study. He copied
his wig, the glass fixed in his eye, and his stiff figure.
The physician took it good-humouredly, sending him
his compliments on having succeeded so well. As
he had forgotten one item—the muff—he sent him
his own. This pleasant behaviour is said to have
propitiated Foote.

He could not spare even his old friend and boon
companion Dr. Kennedy, a quaint personage enough,
and well fitted for a show, besides being a friend of
his own. Accordingly, when the time was ripe, he
proceeded to fit him into a satirical piece—no doubt
among his conclave of doctors—when the sitter was
fortunate enough to meet with a severe accident.
Following Mr. Garrick's sedan-chair in his own, on
his way to a supper at Dr. Goldsmith's, the chairman,
trying to get out of the way of some falling tiles,
gave the sedan such a jerk that the doctor's head
was dashed against the roof. He sustained a con-
cussion of the brain, and his life was in danger.
Foote was good-natured, and forbore his purpose.
Some others whom he had intended for his pieces
he let off, having learned that they were in
affliction.

Foote's sarcastic humour was shown in his answer

to his old friend Wilkinson's free-and-easy announcement that he had surreptitiously got a copy of "The
Devil upon Two Sticks," and was playing it all round
the country. "After having committed the fault,"
he says, "and well knowing he would quickly hear
of my offence, I, by way of preventing his anger,
informed him of my invasion on his property, thinking he would construe it as a very good joke; but
on the contrary he was really irritated, and by return
of post favoured me with the few following whimsical
lines":

Foote to Wilkinson.

"MY DEAR SIR,

"Your favour brought me the first account
of 'The Devil upon Two Sticks' having been played
upon your stage. Your letter has delivered me from
every difficulty, and will procure me the pleasure
of soon seeing you in town, as I shall most certainly
move the Court of King's Bench against you on the
first day of term," etc.

This mixture of threat and pleasant good-humour
was in his happiest vein.

Another doctor introduced by Foote into his play
was Dr. Fordyce, the eccentric Quaker physician.
He figures in "The Devil on Two Sticks" as
Dr. Melchisedech Broadbrim. He used to prescribe
with his hat on (and it was a hat of the most tremendous size ever seen), and was a tall, stiff personage,
always using the dialect of his sect. His conversation
consisted of a number of sentences spoken with an
almost solemn conciseness and importance.

Having completed this review of these gay,
buoyant, and truly witty pieces, which supplied

" laughter holding both his sides," we turn despond-
ingly to the present general dearth of talent, humour,
fun, knowledge of character, and power of entertainment.   The stage is now the last place where you
can look for wit or humour ; indeed, the ear may be
turned in any direction, and fail to catch a single lively
utterance.   Humour, frolic, fun, are at the lowest
standard.   It has come to such a pass that *genuine
humour is hardly understood.*   Irony is taken literally ; a double meaning is too much ; and were Judge
Maule to give his immortal homily to a bigamist
nowadays, he would be set down as mad.   The great
defect of our dramatists is their profound ignorance
of character and of human nature.   Writing plays
now consists in writing dialogues for recitation, but no
one considers, or is capable of considering, whether
these show appropriateness or fitness for the situation
and character.   People only talk, in short.   Could
any dramatic author of our day write, for instance,
such a set of speeches as are uttered by John Thorpe
in Jane Austen's " Northanger Abbey "?   And this
is because they have not learnt to play on those
difficult instruments, human characters and feelings.

CHAPTER XX

1769

THE STRATFORD JUBILEE—"THE MAID OF BATH"

THE great event of the year 1769 was the rather childish festival of "the Jubilee," held at Stratford-on-Avon.

The fitful animosity of Foote towards Garrick was now to be exhibited with more than his usual ill-nature. The pompous celebration at Stratford in honour of the bard was really intended as a glorification of Garrick. The Mayor and Corporation approached him with their apocryphal mulberry-tree, and with many flatteries persuaded him to undertake all the trouble and risks of the business. All his personal friends were invited down to hear him speak, but did not attend. A few, however, came, and the weather was deplorable. Foote took the trouble of attending. He cared little for the bard; he came simply with the one motive—that of plaguing Garrick. He could not conceal his disgust at all the vanity and self-advertisement displayed in the business.

How characteristic it was of his fitful feelings towards Garrick, that he should have come down, *not* to help, but to *annoy!* His companion was Murphy, and the ill-natured pair went about prying into everything, laughing at everything, and disheartening poor Garrick as much as they could. Garrick at the time

was suffering from all the mortifications of failure ; for
everything had gone wrong. The great company
expected did not attend, the weather was bad, and
on the important night an inundation broke in and
deluged the theatre. But Foote did not succeed in
ruffling the actor's sweet temper, or in making him
depart from his rule of restraint. Here, indeed, he
showed that he well deserved " Goldy's " exquisite
compliment—" an abridgment of all that was pleasant
in man."

In pursuance of his laudable intention, Foote went
about talking to everyone and cracking jokes on the
patron. Taking a walk by the Avon, he was recognized by the crowd, whom he regaled with jokes and
remarks, producing peals of laughter. A great stout
man was passing by—an important personage covered
with gold lace—who paid his court to Foote, wishing
to be seen with so famous a wit. The latter at once,
as it used to be said, " smoked him." He accordingly
chaffed him good-humouredly, and finally asked him
jeeringly : " Had the county of Warwick the honour
of giving birth to him as well as to Shakespeare ?"
"No, sir," said the other; " I come from Essex."
" And, pray, who *drove you* ?" said Foote. There was
a roar from the crowd. No flattering attention or
compliment could bind Foote. He " wiped his shoes "
on friends and foes indiscriminately.

Foote did not wait to see the close of the festivities,
and returned to town well primed with all the absurdities he had seen. The flatteries—which were indeed
abject enough—disgusted him. Garrick had to pay
all expenses, so he was in high favour with the town ;
but he had shrewdly arranged a plan for recouping
his outlay, which was to reproduce the whole show
at his theatre on the grandest possible scale—a scheme

which aggravated Foote even more than the rest.
" A Jubilee," he would say wittily enough, but ill-
naturedly, " as it has lately appeared, is a public
invitation circulated and arranged by puffing ; to go
posting without horses to an obscure borough without representatives, governed by a Mayor and Alder-
men who are no magistrates ; to celebrate a great
poet whose works have made him immortal by *an ode*
without poetry, music without melody, dinners without victuals, and lodgings without bed ; a masquerade
when half the people appeared barefaced, a horse-race
up to the knees in water, fireworks extinguished as soon
as they were lighted, and a gingerbread amphitheatre
which tumbled to pieces as soon as it was finished."

Garrick, however, managed to bring matters to a
successful close. It was " bold advertisement " for himself, for reports were given in all the newspapers.
It was said, as Cooke tells us, that Foote's jealousy
was roused afresh at this result, which he set to
work to impair by his ridicule.

The irrepressible Bozzy, however, was there.
One of his most fantastic performances was his
appearance and his various pranks. At the time his
head was overflowing with Paoli and Corsica, and
he did not pause to reflect that both the man and
his country had nothing to do with Shakespeare.
He went about dressed up as " an armed Corsican
carrying a musket." He had actually written a
prologue to be spoken at the opening of his
masquerade, " but was prevented by the crowd."*

---

* They began :

> " From the rude banks of Golo's rapid flood,
>   Alas ! too deeply tinged with patriot blood."

I have seen a copy printed in quarto size by the famous Baskerville.

" The celebrated friend of Paoli," as he called himself,
had to be content with distributed copies of his verses
to all who would accept them.   Writing an account
of his own doings for the *Scots Magazine,* he seems to
have quite lost his head : " My bosom glowed with
joy when I beheld so numerous and brilliant a
company of nobility and gentry—the rich, the brave,
the witty, and the fair—assembled . . . but I could
have wished *that prayers had been read or a short
sermon preached.*   It would have consecrated our
Jubilee, and begun it while gratefully addressing the
supreme Father of all spirits, from whom cometh
every good and perfect gift."   He believed that, if
there had been any interruption when the ode was
being sung, the person " would have been in danger
of his life.   I had a serene and solemn satisfaction
in contemplating the scene."

Garrick's " show " at Drury Lane was an immense
and profitable success ; all his leading performers had
to walk in the procession, even though they had
nothing to say.   Several, like Mrs. Siddons, strongly
objected.   It " ran " for nearly a hundred nights.
Foote, thus further inflamed, continued his attacks.
He now began to circulate a story that he intended
to produce at his theatre a rival show in which the
characters should all be puppets.   At suppers and
convivial gatherings he threw out hints of what he
intended to do with Garrick, who was to be made a
specially ridiculous figure—all which was torture to
that amiable man.   " Will your puppets be the size
of life, Mr. Foote ?" he was then asked.   " No, only
the size of Garrick," was the reply.   This persecution
and animosity, tempered by good-humour, seemed
unique.   In time it became a sort of " phobia," which

he could only lull to rest by making some gross attack
on his friend.

"His jealousy," says Cooke, "became so strong
that he intended to bring out a mock procession in
imitation of it, and introduce Garrick himself on the
stage as the principal figure.   In this procession, a
man was to be dressed out so as to resemble Garrick
as much as possible, in the character of Steward of
the Jubilee, with his wand, white-topped gloves, and
the mulberry-tree medallion of Shakespeare hanging
at his breast ; while some ragamuffin in the procession
should address him in the well-known lines of the
Jubilee poet-laureate :

> " ' A nation's taste depends on you,
> Perhaps a nation's virtue too ; '

to which he was to make no other answer, but clap
his arms, like the wings of a cock, and crow out,

> " ' Cock-a-doodle-doo ! '

Garrick had early intelligence of the scheme, which
gave him the most serious uneasiness, and even
torture of mind."   Here was a comic notion indeed !
" A masque was made that bore as near a resemblance
as possible to the countenance of Mr. Garrick, and
this he showed to all his visitors.   A pasteboard
figure of a body was prepared, to be joined to the
head ; a man was to be concealed under this strange
shell, who was every now and then to utter something which the author was to convey to him.   But
so fond was Foote of his favourite Cock-a-doodle-do !
that, as soon as the figure was introduced on the
stage, he was ordered to clap his sides and crow as
loud as the cock in 'Hamlet.'   This mock representation of Mr. Garrick was talked of for a long time,

20

though not announced in the newspapers. He laboured to raise his fears and apprehensions, and at the same time to create an appetite in the public for so extraordinary a dish. That this project was afterwards laid aside, it was generally supposed, was owing to a sum of money which was borrowed, never to be repaid, or perhaps to a gratification, the accepting of which was still more dishonourable. However, this is only conjecture. . . .

" Mr. Garrick returned all the ungenerous behaviour of this eccentric genius towards him by a very different conduct. When there was some talk of suppressing his puppet-show, on various pretences, he exerted all his interest in the author's favour ; and still more, when he laboured under the worst of all accusations, he did not desert him ; he considered the whole as others did, and as the Judge and jury afterwards determined it, an infamous falsehood, and a base conspiracy to ruin him."

"Foote's necessities," Davies tells us, "were brought on by a ridiculous parade of splendid living, by keeping a number of useless servants, and by treating with magnificent dinners those who laughed at his satire and won his money at cards ; for he was a great dupe at play, which reduced him to the humiliating situation of borrowing money of the man whom he intended to expose to public ridicule. . . . He was at no pains to conceal his design of bringing his 'friend' on his stage in some burlesque shape. Garrick, however, had early intelligence of the whole scheme. The uneasiness he felt upon the occasion could not be dissembled ; he dreaded public ridicule as the worst of all misfortunes, and apprehended the ruin of that great reputation which he had been raising so many years. To resent an affront personally to a man with a wooden leg would only have exposed him to laughter.

" It was pleasant enough, during the suspension of hostilities, to see them meet on a visit at a nobleman's door, alighting from their chariots. Significant looks were exchanged before they spoke. Mr. Garrick broke silence first : ' What is it, war or peace ?' ' Oh, peace, by all means,' said the other, with much apparent glee ; and the day was spent in great seeming cordiality.

" What put an end to this project I could never learn, whether a well-timed gratification or Garrick's threats of serving him in kind. But of this last I never heard the least hint, though I am well persuaded that such a menace might probably have had its effect ; for no man was so great a bully as Foote, nor was any man more timorous. At the time when he was dealing out his scandal at the Haymarket, and levelling all characters for his private emolument, he was heard to declare, in a kind of agony, that he was afraid to take a newspaper in his hand, for fear of reading some outrageous abuse against himself or his friends. . . . Still, the thought of ridiculing Garrick on the stage was a morsel too delicious to resign. At the very time when the mind of Mr. Garrick was disturbed by a scandalous and false insinuation, which the author of it publicly and solemnly afterwards disavowed, Mr. Foote made a ridiculous pretence that Mr. Garrick kept his playhouse open purposely to distress him, by acting several of his most favourite characters, and by these means drawing all the playgoing people to Drury Lane."

Foote was loud and free with these semi-jocose

menaces of exhibiting his friend, talking everywhere
of the puppet he was having prepared. Thus ingeniously tortured, agonized, and "perplex'd in th'
extreme," it was not surprising that the great actor
gave way, and said one day publicly that it was not
very handsome to treat him in this way, considering
that not long before he had lent Mr. Foote some £500.
This was presently reported to Foote, who was stung
to fury. He disdained to be under any such obligation, and, going among his friends, succeeded in
borrowing the sum, which he triumphantly repaid.
This transaction, which must have inconvenienced
him, further inflamed their relations. Davies describes
this state of armed neutrality vivaciously enough.

Foote was faithless to his friend. When later
on he came to set forth his puppet-show, he could
not resist the temptation. It has been said that he
exhibited him as a manager in treaty with Punch's
wife, giving the actor's exact manner and peculiar
tones, so that all could recognize him in an instant.
This was as disloyal as it was impolitic, for Garrick,
with his high reputation, was on a pinnacle, and
respected by all.

About this time Foote went once more to Dublin,
where he was assiduously patronized by the Viceroy,
Lord Townshend, who attended his theatre and constantly invited him, treating him as an intimate
friend. He was now immensely popular among the
Irish nobility and gentry, was asked everywhere, and
kept the tables in a roar by his never-flagging humour
and boisterous spirits. The Irish always relished his
brusque, even coarse, personalities, while to the last
he always enjoyed himself among them.

" His Excellency not only commanded his comedy

several times during the winter, but invited the
facetious author to Court, where by his wit and
sprightly conversation he ingratiated himself so much
with the Irish nobility and gentry (those legitimate
sons of gaiety and good-humour), that he soon became
as great an attraction at the Castle as at the theatre."
No wonder that Johnson called him incompressible!

" Thus recovered in his finances, and further established in his reputation, on his return to London in
the spring of 1769 he gave his muse a *fallow* season.
One new piece, however, was produced at his theatre
in this year (written by the late Isaac Bickerstaff),
called ' Doctor Last in his Chariot,' as a kind of
sequel to ' The Devil upon Two Sticks.' . . . This
little entertainment, though it owned the same father
as ' Love in a Village,' and was ushered in by a very
humorous prologue, written by Garrick and spoken
by Foote, was very nearly damned the first night;
but by alterations and the support of friends it
dragged on its feeble existence to the ninth, ' and
then was heard no more.' The general business of
the theatre, however, succeeded, and as the manager
had more time than usual upon his hands, he enjoyed
the *otium cum dignitate* at North End upon an
enlarged scale, holding out the strongest excitements
to good society, entertainment for both mind and
body."

From Dublin he wrote to his now old friend one of
the most buoyant and brilliant of his letters, describing
his escape from a terrible death by burning. Anyone
unacquainted with Foote's life and character, and
coming upon this paper, would exclaim, " Here
indeed is a man of lively parts !"

Foote to Garrick.

" MY DEAR SIR,

Had it not been for the coolness and resolution of my old friend, and your great admirer, Jewel, your humble servant would last night have been reduced to ashes by reading in bed, that cursed custom! The candles set fire to the curtains, and the bed was instantly set in a blaze. He rushed in, hauled me out of the room, tore down and trampled the paper and curtains, and so extinguished the flames. The bed was burnt, and poor Jewel's hands most miserably scorched. So you see, my dear sir, no man can foresee the great ends for which he was born. Macklin, though a blockhead in his manhood and youth, turns out a wit and a writer on the brink of the grave; and Foote, never very remarkable for his personal graces, in the decline of his life was very near becoming a toast.

" I never saw the *Monitor* you allude to. It is a paper stigmatized here for its virulence. However, it has had no apparent effect upon the public, as it would have been impossible for them to have paid more attention to the nights I have played.

" Little Jephson, who owes his establishment on this side the water to me, is (by being smuggled into Parliament) become in his own idea a man of importance. He has been delivered, in a senate frequent and full, of a false conception or two, and is unanimously declared by his colleagues incapable of either facundity or fecundity.

" The first time I met with my gentleman was about a month after my landing, at the Parliament House. He had fixed himself on the lowest bench next the floor, his arms folded and legs across, the right eye covered by his hat, and the left occasionally thrown on me with an unmarking transitory glance. However, the very polite attention paid to me by the Speaker, the Duke of Leinster, Mr. Conolly, and, indeed, all the men of consequence there, roused the Captain's recollection. He approached with a cold compliment, and dropped a scarce audible apology for not having called at my door ; but public—a—a— affairs had—a—so entirely engrossed him, that he had really no leisure to—a—a—a—— I own I was ready to laugh in his face ; but, recollecting a gravity equal to his own, I applauded his zeal for the commonwealth : begged that no consideration of me should for the future divert his thoughts one moment from the cause of his country : was afraid I had already taken up too much of his time : made him a most profound bow. And the Copper Captain in politics with great gravity retired to his seat. I find he has been left by Lord Townshend as a kind of incumbrance upon his successors ; but I have some reason to believe that they would be glad to get rid of the mortgage. He has since the interview been very frequent and free with my knocker, but the servants have received proper instructions.

"I have often met here a Mr. Vesey, who tells me that he belongs to a club with you and some other gentlemen of eminent talents. I could not conceive upon what motive *he* had procured admittance ; but I find he is the Accomptant-General here, so I suppose you have him to cast up the reckoning.

"I have not seen Alderman Fawkener. I thought myself obliged to take some little notice of him in an occasional prologue. The following is an original letter of his :

" ' *To — Tickell, Esq.*

" ' MY MOST DEAR AND ESTEEMED FRIEND,

" ' Your concurring in opinion with me the last day we spent so agreeably together, that it would be prudent in me forthwith to call in my *debits*, hath induced me to advertise you that I have commissioned our common friend, Mr. Thomas Croaker, attorney-at-law, to sue you to an outlawry for one hundred pounds, as per bond, with all possible speed. The steady and firm friendship we have ever maintained, and the great esteem and respect I entertain for the valuable memory of your very worthy deceased and ingenious father, Mr. Secretary Tickell, compels me to send you this notice, being, my dearest friend,

" ' Your most faithful, affectionate, and obedient

" ' Humble servant till death,

" ' GEORGE FAWKENER.'

" I sincerely rejoice in your success, and feel no compassion for Macklin, Kenrick, Covent Garden, nor that little *Dot*, its dirty director. At this season the winds are so variable that I may possibly see you before you can acquaint me with this reaching your hands. You may assure Mrs. Garrick that flattering is not one of my failings, and that she has the merit of making me constant and uniform in perhaps the only part of my life—my esteem and veneration for her. Adieu, my dear sir. A good night, and God bless you. Take care of the candle.

" SAMUEL FOOTE."

The faithful Jewel clearly saved his life and ran great risk; but the thoughtless Foote took it all as a matter of course, nor did "he take care of him" in his will. Yet it is tribute to Foote that his honest dependent was faithful to the last, brought his remains to London and set up a memorial to him.

Foote to Tate Wilkinson.

"DEAR SIR,

"I am much obliged to you for the offer of your assistance in the town of Newcastle, but the newspapers have laid out a plan for me that never occurred to myself.

"Your old friend D——e has not only lost his situation with me and Colman, but is on the brink of losing his nose; so that his head and his tail have brought him into a pretty condition.

"I hope the Northern crown sits lightly on your brow, and that your immediate subjects are not only dutiful and observant, but that your whole wide-extended empire pay their taxes largely and cheerfully. I have this summer entertained the veteran Sheridan, who is dwindled to a mere cock-and-bottle Chelsea pensioner. He has enlisted some new recruits, unfit for service, and such as might be expected to issue from his discipline.

"I should be glad to chop upon you in my way to Edinburgh, for which place I shall set out about the middle of October.

"Ross is with me, ill and indolent; but, however, thanks to my own industry, the campaign has been happy enough.

"Believe me, most sincerely yours,
"SAM. FOOTE.

"NORTH END,
"*August 16.*"

One of Foote's most daring efforts in personality was to be exhibited in his play "The Maid of Bath," produced in 1771.   All know the romantic story of the young and brilliant Sheridan, and his pursuit of the attractive Miss Linley—how she was all but driven into marriage with an ancient admirer named Long, how she eloped to France with her lover and was happily married.   Moore told the tale in a rather confused fashion, and fell into some serious mistakes.*

As may be imagined, in such a place as Bath the adventure became a subject of absorbing interest. Every lady was on the side of the enchanting songster and her lover.   Foote, who was often in that gay city, seems also to have become a partisan ; but the family could scarcely have anticipated that their whole story should be transferred with literal accuracy to his stage in a farcical comedy.

There was exhibited the Bear Inn, Miss Linnet— that is, Miss Linley—old Flint—Mr. Long (played by Foote himself)—and Major Rackett, a loose admirer of Miss Linley's, obviously intended for Major Matthews.   He ushered in the piece with a gross attack on old Mr. Long :

> "Tally-ho ! a rank old fox we now pursue,
> So strong the scent you'll run him full in view.
> *If we can kill such brutes in human shape,*
> *Let's fright 'em, that your chickens may escape."*

Foote describes a plot contrived by friends of the young girl in order to frighten the old man out of his design.   They warn him of various dangers that he will be made a victim of.   The marriage was fixed for the

* See the author's " Lives of the Sheridans," where the whole story is told at length.

morrow.   He flies to the young woman, and declares
that he will not complete his contract unless she comes
at once with him to his lodging, and takes up her abode
with him for that night ; but on the next morning he
solemnly engaged to go to the Abbey with her.
This amazing proposition seems to have been suggested
by his terror that the family would *not* release him,
but after such a proposal he felt certain they must do
so.   It seems likely that something of the kind may
have occurred ; otherwise Foote would not have dared
to make so libellous an imputation.   He is at last
frightened off, and all ends happily.

Moore's tenderly romantic account is truly absurd
when set beside the real story.   He wished to put
everything in a poet's point of view, so as to make
it agreeable to all parties.   His story is that the
ancient Mr. Long proved the reality of his attachment to her in a way which few young lovers would
be romantic enough to imitate.   On her secretly
representing to him that she could never be happy as
his wife, he generously took upon himself the whole
blame of breaking off the engagement, even to
the indemnifying the father, who was proceeding
to bring him into court, by settling £3,000 upon
his daughter.   He also tells us that " Sheridan
spoke invariably of Mr. Long, who lived to a very
advanced age, with all the kindness and respect which
such a disinterested character merited."*

The comedy was produced at the little Haymarket
in June 1771, and, to add point to his ridicule of
the unhappy Bath gentleman, Foote himself under-

* I recall Mr. Carlyle, at a dinner-party, chuckling contemp-
tuously when Moore was talked of.   " Ah, the puir little Tammy
Moore !" he repeated several times.

took the character, and, we may be sure, made him a perfect picture of a miser.   And when they are trying to make old Flint behave handsomely to the young lady, using threats of law, the Scotch lady at last tells him : " Gad's wull, it sha' cam to the proof. Ye mun ken, guid folk, at Edinburgh laist winter I got acquainted with Maister Foote, the play-actor.   I wull get him to bring the filthy loon on the stage." " And expose him to the contempt of the world," says another.   But old Flint is unmoved.   " Ay, he may write, you may rail, and the people may hiss, and what care I ?"

It will be noted that he introduced the notorious Major Matthews as a jovial *viveur*, treating him in quite a friendly spirit.   He shows him as a gay dog, asking after " my little flame, la belle Rossignole," though at the close he makes Miss Linnet decline his offer of marriage.   At this time, however, Matthews had not begun his violent persecution of the lady.

In his epilogue he boasts that all was true and drawn from life, notably the Knight, the Scotch Lady, the Captain, and the Monster, as he calls Flint.   We may wonder how he could have found anything dramatic in such an incident, and how the Linley family could have relished their daughter and her story being put upon the stage.   But they were professionals, and, of course, well accustomed to the boards.   And they were practical people.   They were all on the boards, as it were—Miss Linley at the concert, her father a public musician, conductor, composer, etc. Bath itself was a huge stage.   So we may fairly conclude that they were not altogether displeased at being brought so conspicuously before the London public. So Miss Linnet prattled away, and sang her songs.

Old Flint had brought down a special parson to marry him, who was a politician and a flaming patriot. This was meant for Horne Tooke. Mr. Forster, who, through Rogers and others, was in touch with men of those days, says most truly that on the face of it Moore's complimentary account of old Long was simply ridiculous, and that it was well known that it was Foote's satire that brought the old curmudgeon to terms. At the same time, as some of the Linley family were alive at the time, Moore might have expected that there would be a contradiction.

CHAPTER XXI

PUPPET-SHOWS

THE years that followed were almost uneventful, and offered scarcely anything of that obstreperous adventure which distinguished the early portion of Foote's life. He was now *rangé*, growing older, and not only manager, actor, and actor-manager, but proprietor. He could take his stand beside Garrick and the patent theatres. He was assured of an independence for the future. And yet it seemed as though now his troubles were about to begin. The sense of struggle was over. Yet he was comparatively young —about forty-six. Perhaps the town, as it so often does, was beginning to tire of him and of his mimicries. Thirty years makes a long theatrical career, and many prudent performers of the first rank have withdrawn before the public has withdrawn from them.* The one who lags inglorious on the stage after the fitting moment for departure has come will in due course receive many a rude hint that he had best be gone. Foote, too, had been for long years literally piling up animosities and enmities

* The most piteous instance was that of the gifted, always interesting Irving, who was *compelled*, as it were, to go on drudging, though in failing health, to the very end, and at the close found he had his fortune still to make.

with which he would have to reckon sooner or later.
Again, there can be no doubt that the disability of
his lost limb was a serious impediment. The many-
headed crowd looks on such deficiency as a sort of
tacit offence, akin to that of the vulgar dislike of a
stranger (" Let's 'eave 'arf a brick at 'im!"). To find
a person, whom you have paid your money to see,
hobbling about the stage, excited a sort of pitying
contempt. They wanted something new in the way
of mimicries, not the old " business," which they
knew by heart, brought out over and over again.*
The only thing left for him was to " pepper" still
higher, for if he did so he was surest to please; and
this was his ruin.

Foote made a great deal of money, but spent it
lavishly. As was said of him, a " paying and a
receiving pocket" was his notion of accounts. He
had a handsome house in the country at North End,
another in Suffolk Street, kept his carriage and
entertained in the best style, drank and gambled.
With all this he was a hard worker, and constantly
wrote, acted, travelled. There came seasons, therefore, when he was completely *au sec*, and had not
a penny left. The stage fashions the most improvident creatures in the world, for there is always the
fairy-tale notion of an Aladdin's lamp waiting only
to be rubbed at the mystic seven or eight o'clock,
when gold cash comes pouring into the purse.

* Here again we think of poor Irving, who felt that he had
exhausted the old stock of attractions, and strove hard to find
something fresh and new. The experiments he made in this direction were all to prove disastrous. It is a curious thing in stage life
that such shifts and changes cannot be made. The actor must be
as he is—*Sint ut sunt aut non sint.*

Foote to Tate Wilkinson (undated).

" DEAR SIR,—If I had not a pretty shrewd knack at guessing, it would not be quite so easy a matter to answer your favour from Hull.

" You desire to know if I had commissioned Giordini to give a particular sum (but whether to a horse, a man, or a woman does not appear) for this or the next summer.

" Your old friend Shuter is locked up in the play-house, and is soliciting a letter of licence from his creditors, in which number I find Jewel is included for ten guineas borrowed during the last season. Fie upon him! I am glad to hear that your affairs prosper. I have a piece of three acts, not my own, which I shall give in the month of May, called ' The Tailors.' The subject is a rich one—the dispute between the masters and the journeymen of that respectable profession—and I think the author has done it exquisite justice. It is a parody of the best passages in the most favourite plays conveyed with great gravity in blank-verse. I think you will appear in it to advantage, and I shall be glad of your assistance. I cannot say I am quite so well as I had reason to expect : I thought myself obliged to give Barry a lift two critical nights, which injured me extremely ; but I am now better, and, except the trifle of a leg, as much yours as ever,

                              " SAM. FOOTE.

" *November 3.*"

About this time an Italian show, known as the *fantoccini*, or puppets, was brought to London, and exhibited at a house in Panton Street. Everyone

knows Boswell's story of Goldsmith's amusing jealousy
of these figures. His friend Cradock, who was with
him, gives a more sober account, and tells how the
poet's admiration was excited by the clever mechanism
displayed. At the best it is always a monotonous
sort of exhibition after the first surprise; though we
cannot forget Boz's delight and wonder at the performance, when he saw it for the first time in Italy.

Panton Street is close behind the little Haymarket
Theatre, and Foote, ever " up-to-date," was struck
by the capabilities of the show and the curious
intelligence of the figures. What if he were to
superadd to his living personalities a complete copy
of the actual faces and figures of the persons ridiculed !
The general stiffness and absurd gravity of the puppets
would be an additional comic element. Besides, as
no amount of stage resource or " making-up " of a
human face could secure a perfect likeness, say of
Garrick, these puppet faces, as he fancied it, could
be made to resemble the originals in the most exact
way. But this may be doubted. With his usual
impulsiveness, he lost no time, and seriously set
about having a puppet-show himself, writing a
piece specially.

And this mania beset him for a long time. It is
difficult to know exactly what was the mechanism
of these puppets. Davies, as we have seen, speaks
of a hollow shell with a mask, an actor being concealed within, or the figure might have been with
strings. It seems clear, however, that they were of
life size, to give the satirist better opportunity for
his mimicries. There can, however, be no doubt that
the whole scheme was suggested by the exhibition
at the Jubilee, some three or four years before, and

21

that he had now a sort of restless craving to ridicule
two men of great note and importance, and so cause
a prodigious sensation. These were his old friend
Garrick and the great Caliban of letters, Dr. Johnson.
Accordingly, he now prepared a special piece, in
which was to be set forth these new devices. The
entertainment was described as "The Primitive
Puppet-Show," and the play was named "The Handsome Housemaid, or Piety in Pattens."

But this trivial "show" was to have a sort of
interest, and Johnsonian admirers—of whom there
are now growing legions—were to owe to it one of
the most admirable and dramatic exhibitions of their
grand hero. We have followed the Doctor's curious
mixture of feeling as to Foote—of contempt and
admiration commingled—which he made no effort
to conceal. His loud-voiced condemnation was no
doubt repeated to Foote, whom it was calculated to
mortify and inflame ; but I have little doubt that the
causa causans of his new project was an incident of
the most irritating kind which had occurred not long
before, and which rankled. We find it in a scene drawn
by "Bozzy" in his finest vein of comedy, showing
admirable touchings of character. Into this scene,
to add a flavour, the writer imported his own petty
malice. It is presented with a Zoffany-like brilliancy.
The story, to a certainty, was told everywhere.

"When Mr. Foote was in Edinburgh," Boswell
tells us—which appears to have been about 1770—
"he thought fit to entertain a numerous company
with a great deal of coarse jocularity at the expense
of Mr. Johnson, imagining it would be acceptable. I
felt this as not civil to me, but sat very patiently till
he had exhausted his merriment on that subject ; and

then observed that surely Johnson must be allowed
to have some sterling wit, and that I had heard him
say a very good thing of Mr. Foote himself. 'Ah,
my old friend Sam!' cried Foote; 'no man says better
things; do let us have it.' Upon which I told the
story, which produced a long, loud laugh from the
company." Here was a shrewd, clever trap. But
how admirably has Bozzy brought the scene before
us! And what was the story he repeated to the
Scotch company?

"Pray, sir," asked Boswell, "is not Foote an
infidel?" "*Johnson.* I do not know that the fellow
is an infidel; but if he be an infidel, he is an infidel
as a dog is an infidel—that is to say, he has never
thought upon the subject. *Boswell.* I suppose, sir,
he has thought superficially, and seized the first notions
that occurred to his mind. *Johnson.* Why then, sir,
he is still like a dog, that snatches the piece next
him." The company roared. The overthrow of the
mimic was complete. "But I never saw Foote
so disconcerted. He looked grave and angry, *and
entered into a serious refutation* of the justice of the
remark. 'What, sir!' said he, 'talk thus of a man
of liberal education—a man who for years was at the
University of Oxford—a man who has added sixteen
new characters to the English drama of his country.'"
And how amusing is this sudden sensitiveness in one
who spared nobody, and who would have scoffed at
the plea of someone having been years at a University
or of having written important plays! He never *could*
have forgiven Bozzy for this exposure. One cannot
but admire the spiteful cleverness with which Bozzy
treated his friend, and also the dramatic fashion in
which he tells the story.

Foote had vast plans on hand, and meditated flying at high game to add to the attraction. There can be little doubt but that after the scene at Edinburgh the idea of bringing Johnson on the stage occurred to him. He was not likely to forget or forgive this quasi-public mortification. Even much more likely was he to " pay off Master Boswell," who had caused the mischief. Johnson would of course be shown attended by his faithful henchman, and be arrayed grotesquely but faithfully. The effect would have been highly diverting, for the intimacy between the pair was well known. He was tempted also to cast longing eyes on the Doctor's odd, eccentric figure and grotesque ways. Who was known so well to the public ? Whose sayings so circulated ? Of whom were told such quaint stories ? And yet he long hesitated, for he had an instinct that " my old friend Sam " was a dangerous person to play such tricks with. He was not likely to suffer tortures and wince in silence. Still, Foote had tried it on with many who were quite as doughty, and without ill results. Long tempted, he at last made up his mind. His show was flagging ; he had exhausted his existing models ; the Doctor would be a great draw.

He proposed to introduce a wooden figure fashioned like Johnson, while he himself, behind, was to provide an imitation of his talk. It is not so well known that another wooden figure was to represent Goldsmith, who was very nervous about the matter. The news soon travelled to Johnson. He explained later that on the night he would take his seat in the boxes, and, on the first personality being uttered, would leap down on the stage and thrash the actor. This everyone knew he would have done. The wary Davies took

care to have the news sent round, and the actor dis-
creetly dropped the whole project. The gallant old
fellow never behaved with finer spirit. And, indeed,
if the helpless creatures who were Foote's victims had
stood up to him in the same fashion, the popular
exhibits would have collapsed, and Foote and his
" show " have been extinguished

Yet for this attempt the sage bore the actor no
malice. He dismissed the whole good-humouredly,
and continued to praise Foote as before. He could
afford to be indulgent, and was too dignified to resent.
Still, admirers of this great man may secretly lament
that the incident did not come off. What a scene it
would have been !

The first night was fixed for June 11, 1777. There
was what is called " a full bill." The solid attraction
was " The Merchant of Venice," with a rising actor,
Henderson, as Shylock, and Miss Barsanti, an
intimate of the Burneys, and whom they had no
doubt come to see, as Portia. Henderson had some
time before been brought to Foote with a view to
showing off his powers, but Foote had received him
rather cavalierly. Though he had his jest, he still
engaged him.

The piece was specially written for Mrs. Jewel,
wife of the treasurer. Foote was the Squire ; the
Butler, Weston. The piece was announced as
" Morning Theatricals " — an early instance of the
matinée.

It so happened that there was a pleasant theatrical
party of that delightful family the Burneys present.
Garrick was also there, and in his highest spirits,
making jokes, etc. Someone, who had climbed over
the box partition to reach him, asked his opinion of

" this imitation of Shylock." " Oh, sir," he answered,
" I am no judge." There was a dance of twelve
children, etc., on which he proposed to one of the
young ladies that they should go down and join them.
The good-natured Garrick, however, seemed to enjoy
the play, and laughed " as much as he could have
done at the most excellent piece in the world. Indeed,
as Fanny said on another occasion, " it was bad enough
to be good." His brother George and his family
were also present, and David introduced them to the
Burneys.*

The story was comical enough, and a rather happy
satire on the sentimental crazes of the day. There
was a handsome maid, who is pursued by her master,
much like Pamela in Richardson's story. Thomas,
the good butler, who loves her honourably, warns
her solemnly that, " if she once loses her virtue, she
will have no pretensions to chastity." The master,
struck with her nobility, then seriously offers to marry
her. The heroine desires that the good Thomas be
called in to hear her decision. The good Thomas
appears, when she announces that she had decided to
marry *him*, because he had given her such excellent
advice ! The master, now completely overpowered,
gives his consent. It might have been expected that
all would now end happily, but we have still to
reckon with the high-minded heroine. Affected by
her master's behaviour, she now announces that her
determination is to marry *neither*—that out of
gratitude for such condescension she will remain

* It does seem, though it is not very distinctly stated, that a
sort of " adumbration " of Garrick was actually attempted on this
occasion. If so, Garrick's presence would have lent a piquancy to
the situation.

single for ever, giving as her reason "that *she loves them both*." As a bit of burlesque this is not at all bad.

The piece was actually played with puppets of large size, "with the usual contrivances for the speeches," and they were well-dressed puppets. What these "contrivances for the speeches" were we can only speculate.

In the February number of the *London Magazine* for 1773, we find another account of the performance: "It was a comedy written in the modern taste without a smile or laugh from beginning to end. He almost kept his word. It was a keen satire on the drowsy scenes of the modern comedies, with the insipid dialogue which Kelly, Cumberland, Griffiths, Bicker-staff, and the rest of the sentiment-mongers, have written." The entertainment was in three grand divisions—the oration, the comedy, and the scene with Punch. The opening was a sort of discourse by Foote himself, in which he traced the course of this form of show. In the second portion, the Handsome Housemaid was a parody on the favourite plays of the day. It is impossible to conceive of a so-called burlesque starting with a long homily, like a sermon, protracted, as it must have been, for half an hour, Mr. Foote standing in the middle and talking on after his fashion.

An audience would not discover much wit or humour in "The Handsome Housemaid," for his brother critics had all agreed it was highly improper, and beneath the dignity of a mixed assembly, to show any signs of a joyful satisfaction; creating a laugh was forcing the higher order of an audience to a vulgar and mean use of their faculties. There

is wit and satire here, and the critic must be struck
with the rather refined choice of words and pleasantry
of the style.

A more minute account of the plot—such as it was
—may be interesting. The curtain rose, and a figure,
admirably well made and dressed, was discovered
bowing profoundly to the audience. After a prologue
the story begins, the characters all being sustained by
the puppets. A constable then arrests all the puppets,
who are brought before a magistrate. As usual,
counsel are introduced, to be made ridiculous by
making absurd arguments. It was argued that the
puppets could not be whipped or imprisoned. What,
then, was to be done with Foote? Counsel urged
that he should be sent to the House of Correction, as
he is surely no puppet. This was disputed, as there
was certainly a fourth part of him puppet, his left
leg being composed of the same material as his
figures. If he committed any crime, the puppet
portion might bring an action for damages; or if he
be committed as a puppet, the body may sue for false
imprisonment. It is then decided to wait till they
either catch his leg without his body, or his body
without his leg. All which is amusing if undignified
fooling. There was also a good deal of ridicule of
sentiment, but this was received coldly. The audience
gradually grew displeased; the whole was too short.
Apologies were made and accepted, but the galleries
tore up a bench or two, and the pit broke into the
orchestra. A great dispute and clamour arose as to
the announcement of the repetition of the piece; it
was settled by a show of hands, three to one being in
its favour. Punch and his Wife and Ben the Sailor
were also in the bill, but they were not exhibited.

The figures were nearly as large as life, and constructed with admirable skill, all exceedingly well
dressed, their actions managed with great adroitness,
and their features made striking and expressive. For
the next performance, on March 6, many alterations
were made. Two new songs were introduced. Punch
attacked Foote: "He was too fond of a fee himself
to give me one."

In one of his occasional monologues, Foote speaks
of reversing the whole process by making living
actors play the puppets—that is, we may suppose,
imitate their jerky motions. This, however, may
have been merely a sarcastic stroke at the expense of
the performers.

A puppet was sent on shaped to imitate that
admirable actress, Mrs. Yates. She was supposed to
regret that, if *wooden* actresses were once admitted,
there would be no call for her services, on which
Foote tells her that, as she can put on a melancholy
face now and then, she would do well at Whitefield's
Tabernacle. Cradock and Cumberland had just
supplied her with new pieces, and this Foote took
care to allude to, mentioning the gentlemen by their
names, as persons whose aid she might require. Later
on, they were indignant. As it happened, Foote came
full on Cradock next morning. He did not seem
daunted by the failure, though he looked disconcerted
at the meeting. He carried it off as usual. "You
are not affronted that I hinted at you last night?"
"Not in such good company, Mr. Foote; but I hear
you rather burned your fingers." "Singed them a
little, perhaps; but if we don't take liberties with our
friends, with whom can we take them?"

Kelly, the popular singer, was also introduced, when

a storm arose, and the piece was not allowed to go on.
Mr. Cradock, a fashionable amateur, with Cumberland and others, were treated in ridiculous fashion.

Foote was now to furnish forth the last of his
most buoyant and entertaining pieces, written with
all his old vigour. This was called "The Cozeners,"
produced in 1774, full of a mordant satire, ridiculing
some gross abuses of the society of the time. It is
really Aristophanic in tone, and conceived in deadly
earnest. Some of Dickens's great stories have this
flavour and bitter power of chastisement. But apart
from this didactic element, the piece has two characters
at least full of an unbounded humour and originality.

Aircastle is a perfectly delightful character from its
buoyancy and original humour. When discussing
anything with his lady, he is certain to ramble off by
one step after the other, until he has strayed away
altogether from the topic—a most difficult thing to
present without monotony. Foote, however, manages
the topics with extraordinary spirit and overflowing
humour. Witness the following display: "Did I
not tell you what Parson Prunello said? I remember
Mrs. Lightfoot was by; she had been brought to
bed, that day was a month, of a very fine boy—*a
bad birth:* for Dr. Seeton, who served his time with
Luke Lancet of Guise's, there was a talk about him
and Nancy, the daughter; she afterwards married
Whitlow, another acquaintance, who had great expectations from an old uncle in the Grenadiers, but
he left all to a distant relation, a midshipman on the
Torbay—she was lost coming home, in the Channel;
the captain was taken up by a coaster from Rye,
laden with cheese," and so on. Mrs. Aircastle calls out:
"Mercy on us, Mr. Aircastle! at what a rate you run!

What has this to do with our coming to London?"
Aircastle: " Why, I was going to tell you——"

How natural is all this—the suggested topics
carrying him away with them in the most plausible
fashion! We of course recall Mrs. Nickleby and
Miss Bates ; but her straggling talk is rather of the
author's own conception, not of the character's.*

" The Cozeners" was produced shortly after his
Irish tour. It was extraordinary how many topics,
abuses, etc., he contrived to deal with. He, as it
were, lashed out right and left—Dr. Dodd, who had
offered a bribe for a living, Charles Fox's match-
making, with some ridicule of Lord Chesterfield's
letters, which had recently appeared. The exciting
causes célèbres of Mrs. Rudd and the Perreaus was
also absorbing the town, the lady's adventures
particularly. All these things represented certain
corrupt spots on the body politic, and Foote dealt
with them in masterly style.

The Aircastles are eager to marry their loutish son
to an heiress, and engage the services of an agent,
who undertakes to find for them a West Indian lady
of vast wealth. She has a black girl in her house,
who, she says, favours dark admirers, so the family
colour their boy's face. He is then introduced to a
darkened chamber where the girl is in bed, and can
only answer his questions with the monosyllable
" is "—*i.e.*, yes. All this was flat enough, yet the
house roared, and came again and again to see it,
applying every touch to Charles Fox.

Sir Walter Scott in 1828 heard from a lady, whom

---

* Boz was partial to catchwords — *e.g.*, "not to put too fine a
point upon it "—but he did not make them a note of his character ;
he simply repeated them.

he considered well informed in the matter, a curious story relating to Fox's association with Foote's play. A Mrs. Phipps set up in a fashionable quarter, and contrived to make it known that she had a mysterious influence in securing offices and situations from the great. One of her devices for spreading this belief was by having the carriages of Lord North and other important personages seen at her door. This was effected by bribing the drivers. But a gentleman who had watched actually saw Charles Fox go in. When the imposture was discovered, Fox was asked at Brooks's was the story true, and frankly told his friends the whole. The woman held out hopes of a great heiress, who, however, was never forthcoming. When he pressed the matter, fresh excuses were made. She at last confessed that her heiress was *jet black.* The town, it seems, came to know the story, and crowds went to the theatre to see this incident alone.*

Perhaps the most wanton of Foote's many personalities was his introduction into this piece, in most odious fashion, of a worthy and much-respected Professor of Music. This was the celebrated composer and genius, Dr. Arne, author of several famous operas, and a most accomplished musician. Foote represented him as a degraded client of the procuress. His reputation was quite unsullied. But his oddities had attracted Foote, with the strange

> " Nose and chin to shame a knocker,
> Wrinkles that would puzzle Cocker."

---

* Foote's minuteness in these exhibitions is extraordinary. He brings in the incident of the carriages seen at the woman's door. " Have you prevailed on the coachman?" she asks. " He has promised to parade before your house for an hour after his master is set down at the cockpit."

When he was planning this scheme, he one day saw in the street a common fellow who was the image of the victim. He at once secured his aid, and sent him on the stage "made up" exactly like the doctor. He was mean enough to buy from the doctor's valet an old cast-off suit of clothes. These painstaking efforts show a sort of impish malevolence. The poor Professor had no protection from these outrages, and had to submit.

The Aircastles were shown as striving to mould their Lumpkin boy on the Chesterfield model. Foote's original design was to bring on the stage a father who had tutored his son after this model, to show the educated son as honest to all the world, but cheating his own father. Dr. Johnson, criticizing this project, highly praised it, but would have preferred that the father alone should suffer. Foote's design certainly seems more subtle and dramatic. One may wonder whether, if satire of this kind were to-day set before the crowd, it would understand it. Even irony nowadays is dangerous to use, as it is likely to be taken seriously.

At the time there was much talk about the fashionable Dr. Dodd—not yet dubbed "the unfortunate"—who, pressed by his wants, offered to purchase a living through the Lord Chancellor's wife. It would appear that this was done through the agency of Mrs. Dodd. It was not a very criminal matter, and the doctor had received his punishment. Foote, however, must needs "gibbet," not him, but his unhappy lady, who is accordingly brought on as Mrs. Simony, trafficking for a living with Mrs. Fleecem. "The doctor knows nothing about it," she insists again and again. "He believes in the whole Thirty-nine Articles, and so he would if there were nine times as many." To Foote, therefore—not to Theodore Hook—must be given the credit of this capital and oft-quoted jest.

Again, it must be said that the effect of these squalid pictures as drawn by Foote is that of profound amazement, that such repulsive details should be accepted with enjoyment and applause. It is quite clear that here were the manners and general complexion of the time. The standard seems of the lowest. It may be, however, that Foote's "show" was for a special audience, and that decent folk were not among his supporters.

This was to be the last of Foote's successful pieces, for "The Capuchin," which came later, was a mere piece of patchwork, and intended as a caricature of a personal enemy.

CHAPTER XXII

1776

THE "TRIP TO CALAIS"

THE closing scenes of Foote's jovial, obstreperous life make sad reading. It might be said that the adventurer's later days too often become clouded by decay of fortune, failing strength and spirit, and the coming of new men and new tastes. He has to "hang like a rusty mail quite out of fashion." Old friends that once appreciated have gone, and the new do not understand. With the failure of popularity comes the failure of cash ; there is debt long accumulated and nothing put by. Then follows broken health and disease—inevitable consequence of that "hearing the chimes at midnight." What could be more disastrous or tragic than the last days of the most popular, the most admired player of our time, the amiable, lovable, brilliant Irving, who did not deserve so cruel a fate, and who on the eve of the catastrophe was practically a ruined man! The stage is indeed strewn with ruins. The jovial "children of Momus" seem specially marked out for disaster. The curtain too often descends on darkness and in gloom.

Further, heartlessness is the note of all convivial friendship and admiring joviality. With repeated failures, the "Pommery-Greno friends" fall away.

How sad the end of the noble Dickens or the still
nobler Scott! We think of the amiable "Goldy"
dying when on the brink of ruin—of Bozzy, with his
immortal book, who perished a sot. And now we are
to see our poor joker Foote, the man of a thousand
capital jests and stories, destroyed, discredited, and
doomed to die at a Dover inn!

What a life is that of the player—how precarious,
how full of sudden turns, of "ups and downs"! And
never was it so precarious as at the present moment,
when the day's board cannot be reckoned on. Such
is the case of thousands, of hundreds of thousands.
With the affluent all is taken as a matter of course.
Providence, it is assumed, supplies food and lodging,
without trouble on their part. But think what it
must be to furnish wit, fun, and entertainment,
to please and attract everyone so effectually that
they must supply you with food, raiment, and employ-
ment! Woe to you if you do *not* attract! If once
entertainment fails, you receive nothing! Foote, in
short, had to buffoon, act, libel, ridicule, without
respite, if he would. If he failed to draw laughter
and enjoyment, he could, literally, not pay his rent,
or even pay for his dinner, though this last he could
probably secure from admiring friends. The wonder
is, how a man could be gay and uproarious under such
circumstances—how he could leave his debts, creditors,
miseries, bailiffs, outside the dining-room door!
Much allowance must therefore be made for poor
precarious creatures who have literally to "live by
their wits."

And who cannot but admire, if they pity, the talent
and energy of those poor but plucky folk who have
nothing but their wits to live on? We must confess

it is impossible not to feel some admiration for Sam Foote, the regular *condottiere*, now taking to the road now bullying and intimidating, now "holding up" some timorous being, but always reviving with sufficient spirit. And yet he lived in almost luxury. It seems that the fortunate actors seem to imbibe a sort of elixir of life, which secures them against decay and all maladies. How Foote racked his body with dissipation, fatigues, rioting, and work, is scarcely conceivable. Yet we never hear of his performance being interrupted or of his being ill. Nay, in this time of ours, with the vast legion of London players, it is the rarest thing to hear of one having to strike work from sickness. "Understudies" are spoken of, but rarely called for. Still, Foote was but fifty-six when he died, and, though he held on to the last, he was practically worn out. He was now in a helpless position, literally bound hand and foot to his own libelling system. He *must* go on ; to "draw," he *must* find objects to ridicule. And then, beyond all question, his attraction had begun to decay. After twenty years of personalities, had the public begun to tire of the "English Aristophanes"? In this view, who will forget the bard's thrilling and almost despairing lines on the decay of a reputation?

About this time, too, other troubles began to accumulate about him. Fickle fortune was changing. His hold on the public seemed to relax. He had trampled down many, but was now of a sudden to be defied by an intended victim, more unscrupulous than he was, and more deadly ; for, not content with hindering his purpose, she was to pursue him with revengeful purpose, and finally destroy him and his fortunes. This was the notorious Miss Chudleigh,

22

soi-disant Duchess of Kingston.   It was an evil day for
him when the thought came to him that the scandals
associated with her would serve his dramatic purposes.
The adventuress at the moment was actually waiting
her trial for bigamy, and it must have occurred to
anyone of reasonable sense that neither the public
nor the authorities would tolerate a woman in so
critical a position being gibbeted on the stage.
Neither did the common feelings of generosity and
delicacy, if any remnant of such were in Foote's
breast, restrain him.

This notorious lady had the same unscrupulous
recklessness as her opponent, and never allowed the
restraints of decency or propriety to stand in her
way.   Her life had been an uninterrupted series of
startling proceedings.   She had contrived to extri-
cate herself with success from the results, but at the
moment she was in the most serious of all her
scrapes.

Though sprung from a good Dorsetshire family,
and niece of a Baronet, there seemed to be a low,
vagabond strain in her nature, with a curious and
reckless unscrupulousness.   As it was, she had very
nearly successfully carried through all her schemes.
With a little more prudence and restraint she might
have scored, or even won her game.

A very beautiful girl at fifteen, she began her
adventures at once.   She was poor, and had many
lovers.   Mr. Pulteney, who met her when he was
out shooting, was much interested in her, and tried
to forward her interests, and when she was about
twenty-three obtained for her the place of Maid of
Honour to the Princess Augusta of Wales.   Presently the Duke of Hamilton fell deeply in love

with her. He was only nineteen, but his relations contrived to frustrate his advances. That he would have married Miss Chudleigh is likely, as he presently, with much precipitation, married one of the Gunnings. With her usual good fortune, she now met Mr. Augustus Hervey, one of the Bristol family, and the second son. Him she married privately. They were very poor, and resolved to keep the marriage a dead secret. A child was born and put out to nurse secretly, and soon died. Her husband and she quarrelled, and he went away to sea, being in the navy. His brother became Earl of Bristol, thus making him heir-presumptive, and later there was a serious prospect of his succeeding to the title.

Later appeared on the scene an elderly admirer, the Duke of Kingston, who became perfectly infatuated with her, and, being kept in ignorance of her marriage, offered himself. Now began a series of extraordinary, tortuous schemes and devices for carrying out her plot in the most elaborate way.

It has been said that the husband brought an action for divorce, but it is clear that he was unable to do so, as she had secured all the proofs of her marriage, or had perhaps destroyed them. But the unscrupulous woman, who was now sure of her Duke, impudently brought an action against Hervey for "jactitation of marriage," as it is called—that is, for falsely giving himself out as her husband, and in the court she without scruple took the necessary oath that she was not married to him. Accordingly, the Court decreed that he was not to trouble her, and "enjoined him to silence." Meanwhile, her conduct had become disorderly and quite disreputable.

The fashion in which she conducted the complicated issues of the secret marriage which she wished
to annul, and her aspirations for a public one with
the Duke, while her husband was eager to be rid of her,
yet afraid to take any step, was infinitely daring and
resolute. Hervey's position as heir to a peerage and
the estate was a very critical one, hers very dangerous.
She no doubt feared to let the question of the marriage
be brought forward under any circumstances. If the
Duke came to know of it, it would of course destroy
all chance of her marriage with him ; while if she
consented to a divorce there was the chance of failure,
and the further chance of "frightening off" the
Duke. Hervey's position was almost as embarrassing.
He would shortly become Earl of Bristol, and it was
desirable for him, from every point of view, that he
should be freed from his reckless lady. The open
connection with the Duke, and other scandals,
seemed to furnish sufficient grounds. But he found
it impossible to prove his marriage, as it had been
so secretly contracted and at a period so long before,
and his unscrupulous lady had so contrived it as to
secure or make away with all the necessary evidences
of a ceremony.

Within two or three weeks after the Courts had
decided in her favour, when she had taken the oath
that she was single, she married the Duke. For
five years she enjoyed her state—was even received
at Court. But in 1773 her now *de jure* husband
Hervey presented a petition for a new trial of his
case, shortly after which the Duke died, leaving her
almost the whole of his property, but with the stipu-
lation that she must remain a widow—a clause that
was likely to complicate her truly singular position.

But this bequest put all the Duke's family in motion ;
a strict investigation was set on foot. A maid of
hers was gained over, and evidence secured to prosecute her for bigamy. In March 1775, her real
husband succeeded to the title, so this extraordinary
woman was now legally Countess of Bristol. In
May 1775, she had to appear before Lord Mansfield,
who bound her over to take her trial before the peers.
The matter was thus out of her husband's hands, who
was content to wait the issue of this serious charge,
when he would, of course, secure his divorce. But,
strange to say, so complicated were things that he
was unable to bring the matter to an issue, and he
died in 1779 in this awkward situation. The rest
of her story is well known—how she was brought to
trial in April 1776, and found guilty on the clearest
testimony. The bold woman fled from England on
the very day when a fresh writ had been issued
against her.

As I said, it seems hardly credible that Foote,
a seasoned man of the world—a " hard-bitten " old
stager and experienced reader of character and events
—should in his folly have lightly thought of meddling
with this adventuress. There was nothing in her
record to invite ridicule ; it was a mere vulgar tale
of imposture. But some fate drew him on, and led
him to his destruction. How strange that he should
not have recognized her general success, her cleverness in surmounting all her difficulties ! She was not
a person likely to yield to *him*. But in his thoughtless, reckless way he took up the business with a
light heart.

He accordingly made her the central figure of his
new piece, " writing it round her " as it were, and

placing her at Calais among a crowd of "riff-raff"
figures. (Calais was then a sort of refuge for the
disreputable English.) There are shown swindling
landlords like Tromfort, servants, begging monks,
Abbesses, nuns, with Cockney tradesmen who have
come over on an excursion. It is all lively and full of
strange characters. Lady Kitty Crocodile is introduced
when the play is more than half over. She is shown
quarrelling with her servants and dependents, and is
really not much in the way of a character. It was a
curious coincidence that Foote should have fixed on
Calais as the locale and also title of his piece—a town
which was presently to become the place of refuge
and protection for the pseudo-Duchess herself, and
where she was later to die. Scattered through the
part are allusions to well-known passages in the
Duchess's history, as when Lady Kitty says : " There
are two men, my dear, who solicit your hand—one
found by you, the other whom your father approves.
Supposing then, by way of reconciling all parties, you
were to marry them both." And again : " Besides,
miss, you know I never durst carry you to any of
the conferences I had with the Pope "—an allusion
to the attentions paid to the Duchess in Rome. It
was well known that on the Duke's demise the
widow contrived a sort of display of excessive grief,
shutting herself up, wearing mourning habiliments of
an extravagant kind, all which is happily ridiculed
by the author. Sometimes in an innocent allusion he
will call up the memory of an old scandal—witness
her dress or no dress at a masquerade. She also
alludes to this affected and theatrical display of grief
on the death of the Duke.

The Duchess had two clerical swashbucklers in

her service—invaluable agents, both connected with
the Press and utterly unscrupulous. These were the
Rev. Dr. Jackson and the Rev. Mr. Foster. Jackson
directed a paper or papers, and knew how to threaten
and extract blackmail. They were the Duchess's
obsequious jackals, and did much business for her. It
was they who now undertook the management of her
affair with Foote. I am persuaded that the lady's
hands were far too full at the moment for her to care
much about Foote's proceedings, and I fancy that the
two clergymen were trying to get money from him or
to make some arrangement profitable to themselves.
It was Jackson that wrote the Duchess's scurrilous
and provocative letter to Foote, and the whole bitter
contest was later carried on between Foote and
Jackson.

As this Jackson was the redoubtable champion that
overthrew the hitherto unconquered Foote—so long
the terror of weak and foolish persons—some detailed
account of his singular career will be interesting. He
was certainly a very remarkable person, who played
many parts in a highly adventurous course, during
which his proceedings were reckless and extravagant,
as though he had no regard for consequences. Indeed,
many of these strange beings at the time seem to
have been partially mad or maddened, or driven to
odd freaks by love of excitement. Thus Jackson was
parson, tutor, and a preacher of some reputation at a
chapel in Drury Lane. He proved to be a bold,
capable, versatile, and utterly unscrupulous being—a
vehement, determined patriot or rebel, according as
he is viewed. His principles and his unflinching
devotion to his country were genuine and remarkable.
Turning journalist, he wrote in a violent strain,

always indulging in coarse personalities, with threats, calumnies, and all the weapons of the newspaper highwayman. He presently became editor of a daily paper called *The Public Ledger*, which had its columns filled with short little paragraphs of three or four lines, each containing some malicious or false rumour or statement. He was privileged to write a Radical reply to no less a person than Dr. Johnson when he published his pamphlet " Taxation no Tyranny." It was a strange thing that the fate of this Jackson should have some likeness to that of Foote himself. Both had made their living by the holding up to ridicule the follies of innocent, harmless persons, real or supposed. Jackson libelled grossly in the papers ; Foote ridiculed upon his stage. These practices led both to a disastrous end, Foote having to fly his profession and his country, Jackson committing suicide in the dock when being sentenced to a felon's end.

It was unfortunate that Jackson took up this rôle of lampooner, for he was undoubtedly clever, and mustered many friends, such as Oglethorpe, Horne Tooke, Hargrave the lawyer, Dr. Schomberg, and many others. How, then, a man of such a type could have been drawn into the grossly disgraceful persecution of Foote is a perplexing speculation.

His political opinions were conscientious enough. He was a true Republican, giving his ardent sympathies to the Americans, to the French, and to his own native country. He was long a constitutional democrat, but became inflamed by the new French doctrines, and used to scoff at Wilkes as " a hackneyed old knave, a demagogue schemer, a blasphemer, whose patriotism was a pretext and whose politics were a trade." He was popular among those who knew him as a stern and sincere Liberal, such as were many others at that time.

He went abroad to France, and got entangled in the doings of the United Irishmen in Paris, by whom he was sent to Ireland to further the conspiracy. He was speedily arrested on a charge of high-treason. His friends had a fanciful scheme of having him exchanged for Sir Sidney Smith, which came to nothing.

The account of his strange death in the dock is highly dramatic. His illness had begun early in the morning, before he left prison. He had been found guilty the day before, and counsel were to move in arrest of judgment. His wife came and dressed his hair for the occasion ; but it was noted that he was pale and full of spasms, pains, contortions, and the like. He was seized with convulsions in the dock, and his last words were, not those that were popularly repeated, " We have deceived the Senate," but, " I wish it was over." In his pocket was found a reply to Paine's " Age of Reason," and a devout but rather ambiguously worded prayer. The verdict, too, given according to medical opinion, was not one of suicide, but " in consequence of some acrid or mortal matter taken into his stomach," though how or by whom administered was unknown.

There were some grim incidents attendant on this closing scene. After the unfortunate man sank down and expired in the dock, the Judge proceeded to adjourn the Court. The Sheriff, who was beside the dock, appealed to the Judge in great agitation : " But the body, my Lord ! What am I to do ?" " You will do, Mr. Sheriff, all that is proper and provided for in such cases," recalling the familiar definition of

" archidiaconal functions." After the dissection by the surgeon, some designing people got possession of it, and exhibited it at a penny a head.

Such was the heroine whom Foote, with her agent, was unlucky enough to propose bringing on his stage. So soon as the gossips began to repeat that Foote intended taking this step, her friends, knowing that she would soon be in a critical position, made exertion to stop the business. It might seem strange that Foote should not have thought it rather unchivalrous to exhibit a falling woman who was presently to be tried on a serious charge, or that his ridicule would not further injure her. But Foote, as we know, had no delicacy of feeling; he merely looked at the matter from a tradesman's view. The Lord Chamberlain, who was Lord Hertford, a friend or patron of Foote's, was appealed to, and most naturally, as a step in the interests of decency, interposed and forbade the performance. The Duchess after this victory sent an envoy of hers—Lord Mountstuart, well known to Bozzy's readers as his patron—to fetch Foote to her house, as though to conciliate him. Previously Lord Mountstuart had gone through this play with him, and was so satisfied with the perusal that he borrowed it for the Duchess's perusal. Later, he declared solemnly that, after reading the play through, she had said she could not recognize anything like herself!

After this interview Foote thought that all was well, and that he might appeal for a reversal of the interdict. He addressed a very spirited appeal to the Chamberlain. By-and-by a curious sort of proclamation let the public into the secret of all that had been going on. It ran:

To the Printer.

" The prophetic effusions of the collocators or makers of paragraphs have for once proved true, Mr. Printer : the ' Trip to Calais ' has been rejected by the Lord Chamberlain. To guess from where these gentleman obtained this intelligence (as this address preceded by many days the delivery of the piece to the Chamberlain) would be a very difficult task ; however, you find that what was only prophecy is *now* become history. Till I have an opportunity of laying before the public those scenes which produced his lordship's interdiction, you will print the following letter sent to Lord Hertford in the hope of softening his censure."

At the end we read : " Mr. Foote intends soon to publish the scenes in his ' Trip to Calais ' objected to by the Lord Chamberlain, as a justification of his own conduct, with a prefatory dedication to the Duchess of Kingston."

Foote to the Lord Chamberlain.

" MY LORD,
        " I did intend troubling your lordship with an earlier address ; but the day after I received your prohibitory mandate I had the honour of a visit from Lord Mountstuart, to whose interposition I find I am indebted for your first commands, relative to the ' Trip to Calais,' by Mr. Chetwynd, and your final rejection of it, by Colonel Keen.
        " Lord Mountstuart has, I presume, told your lordship that he read with me those scenes to which your lordship objected ; that he found them collected from general nature, and applicable to none but those

who, through consciousness, were compelled to a self-application.   To such minds, my lord, ' The Whole Duty of Man,' next to the sacred writings, is the severest satire that ever was written ; and to the same mark, if Comedy directs not her aim, her arrows are shot in the air ; for by what touches no man, no man will be amended.

" Lord Mountstuart desired that I would suffer him to take the play with him, and let him leave it with the Duchess of Kingston.   He had my consent, my lord, and at the same time an assurance that I was willing to make any alteration that Her Grace would suggest.   Her Grace saw the play, and in consequence I had an interview with Her Grace.   With the result of that interview I shall not at this time trouble your lordship.   It may, perhaps, be necessary to observe that Her Grace could not discern (which your lordship, I dare say, will readily believe) a single trait in the character of Lady Kitty Crocodile that resembled herself.

" After this representation, your lordship will, I doubt not, permit me to enjoy the fruits of my labour ; nor will you think it reasonable that, because a capricious individual has taken it into her head that I have pinned her ruffle awry, I should be punished by a poniard struck deep in my heart.   Your lordship has too much candour and justice to be the means of giving so violent and ill-directed a blow.

" Your lordship's determination is not only of the greatest importance to me now, but must inevitably decide my fate for the future, as, after this defeat, it will be impossible for me to muster up courage enough to face Folly again.   Between the Muse and the Magistrate there is a natural confederacy.   What the last cannot punish, the first often corrects; but when she not only finds herself deserted by her ancient ally, but sees him armed in the defence of her foe, she has nothing left but a speedy retreat.

"In that case, adieu, my lord, to the stage! *Valeat res ludicra!*—to which I hope I may with justice add, *Plaudite!*—as, during my continuance in the service of the public, I never profited by flattering their passions or falling in with their humours. Upon all occasions I have exerted my little powers (as, indeed, I thought it my duty) in exposing follies, how much soever the favourites of the day; and pernicious prejudices, however protected and popular. This, my lord, has been done (if those may be believed who have the best right to know) sometimes with success. Let me add, too, that in doing this I never lost my credit with the public, because they knew I proceeded upon principle; that I disdained either being the echo or the instrument of any man, however exalted his station; and that I never received reward or protection from any other hands than their own."

We may admire this admirable letter, not merely for its eloquence and sincerity, but for the composition and its high *literary* tone. It shows Foote as a writer of power and *culture*. Still, the cynic may be amused to find its author in the attitude of an aggrieved person, aggrieved because he was stayed in his long course of exhibiting living persons on his stage. Of course, he was still contending that in this case there was no such purpose in view; but even in the absence of any likeness, the character would be considered to be intended for the Duchess.

The appeal, however, was fruitless, probably for the reason just suggested, and Foote, still indignant,

determined on the fatal step of appealing to the
public.   It was strange that he did not at once "scrap"
the piece, as it is called, and write another, for his
pathetic burst that his career was closed, and he himself ruined, was a rhetorical exaggeration.   He accordingly announced that he would print his play, on
which the storm broke out afresh, and finally overwhelmed him.

The Duchess, who behaved with some modera-
tion all through, determined for the second time to
negotiate.   But she chose for her envoys or instruments quite a different class of person from the respectable Lord Mountstuart.   These were the two
rather shady clerics first described.

Lord Hertford, the Chamberlain, was to prove less
pliant to Foote than his predecessors.   He was more
independent, and certainly no officer of the Crown
could have tolerated an attack on a woman who was
presently to stand her trial.   The play was really an
affront to the tribunal which was to try her.*

The general rumour, as voiced by Walpole,
Garrick, and others, was that the Duchess had offered
to buy Foote off, but that he had refused.   Walpole
seemed to know all the details, and heard that he
had offered to read the piece with her, and strike out
what she thought applicable, but "she was too
cunning to bite at this."

The two emissaries, in an affidavit before Sir John
Fielding, now swore that "the mimic had demanded
£2,000 as the price of the suppression."   That there

---

* Asked why his piece was interdicted, Foote said the reason was
that he had refused a place of box-keeper to one of the official's
sons—a stupid, unintelligible jest, though Mr. Forster says there
was a hidden meaning.

was a suggestion of a money payment is likely enough,
from the character of the men. They had attempted to
secure something for themselves—a probable surmise.

" Baffled thus in his hopes, and finding that the
threat of publication could not intimidate the Duchess
into compliance, Mr. Foote had recourse to his levée
of scribblers for the purpose of furnishing newspaper
defamation. The following letter was received only
on the Saturday afternoon, and in the *St. James's
Chronicle* on Saturday evening a most scurrilous
invective against Her Grace of Kingston was dated
from Mr. Foote's theatre in the Haymarket."

Jackson, that licensed blackmailer, later published
this account of the matter : " Mr. Foote, interdicted
by the Lord Chamberlain from representing the
libellous piece called ' A Trip to Calais,' threatened
to publish the scenes and dedicate them to the
Duchess of Kingston. It was in vain that the
malignity as well as the injustice of such a procedure
were represented to Mr. Foote. The mimic would
not yield." A new form of pressure was employed.

Now libellous paragraphs began to appear in the
newspapers, insinuating dark and mysterious charges.
He found his character blackened every day. People
wondered what it all meant. Then the unfortunate
Foote began to waken up to his position. The
celebrated letters that followed tell of the next stage
of the story :

" *To Her Grace the Duchess of Kingston.*

" NORTH END,
" *Sunday, August* 13, 1775.

" MADAM,

" A member of the Privy Council and a friend
of your Grace's (he has begged me not to mention

his name, but I suppose your Grace will easily guess
who) has just left me. He has explained to me,
what I did not conceive, that the publication of the
scenes in the 'Trip to Calais' at this juncture, with
the dedication and preface, might be of infinite ill-
consequence to your affairs.

"I really, madam, wish you no ill, and should be
sorry to do you an injury.

"I therefore give up to that consideration what
neither your Grace's offers nor the threats of your
agents could obtain : the scenes shall not be published,
nor shall anything appear at my theatre or from
me that can hurt you, provided the attacks made
on me in the newspapers do not make it necessary
for me to act in defence of myself. Your Grace
will therefore see the necessity of giving proper
directions."

Never did Foote commit a greater blunder than
in the despatching of this unlucky paper. It may
be said to have ruined him. He wished to conciliate
the woman, and affected in a magnanimous tone to
withdraw the whole. With some disingenuousness,
he pretended, though her trial was actually coming
on, not to know that the publication would be
injurious to her. Had he stopped there, it had
been well. Jackson must have been with her when
Foote's letter arrived. We may take it for granted
that he wrote the lady's reply, which was intended to
entrap the actor into some abusive utterance, which
Jackson intended to publish in his and in other
papers. This rather vulgar introduction, which had
many strokes of her own, such as " Foote is said to be
descended in the female line from one Harnass (or

Harness), a merry-andrew who exhibited at Totnes in Devonshire, and afterwards figured in the character of a mountebank at Plymouth," was despatched at once.

"SIR,

"I was at dinner when I received your ill-judged letter ; as there is little consideration required, I shall sacrifice a few moments to answer it.

"A member of *your* privy council can never hope to be of a Lady's cabinet. I know too well what is due to my own dignity, to enter into a compromise with an extortionable assassin of private reputation. If I before abhorred you for your slander, I now despise you for your concessions. It is a proof of the illiberality of your satire, when you can publish or suppress it as best suits the needy convenience of your purse. You first had the cowardly baseness to draw the sword ; and if I sheathe it until I make you crouch like the subservient vassal as you are, then is there not spirit in an injured woman, nor meanness in a slanderous buffoon.

"To a man, my sex alone would have screened me from attack ; but I am writing to the descendant of a merry-andrew, and prostitute the term of manhood by applying it to Mr. Foote.

"Clothed in my innocence as in a coat of mail, I am proof against a host of foes ; and, conscious of never having intentionally offended a single individual, I doubt not that a brave and generous public will protect me from the malevolence of a theatrical assassin. You shall have cause to remember that, though I would have given liberally for the relief of

23

your necessities, I scorn to be bullied into a purchase of your silence.

"There is something, however, in your *pity* at which my nature revolts. To make an offer of pity at once betrays your insolence and your vanity. I will keep the *pity* you send until the morning before you are turned off, when I will return it by a Cupid, with a box of lip-salve; and a choir of choristers shall chant a stave to your requiem.

"E. KINGSTON.

"KINGSTON HOUSE,
    "*Sunday, August* 13."

Stung to fury by this reply, Foote could not resist sending a bitter, taunting answer, which made a prodigious sensation. The notoriety was, however, dearly purchased. The two venomous clerics whom he had so offensively spoken of were determined on revenge, and speedily made him feel their power.

"MADAM,
    "Though I have neither time nor inclination to answer the illiberal attacks of your agents, yet a public correspondence with your Grace is too great an honour for me to decline.

"I cannot help thinking that it would have been prudent in your Grace to have answered my letter *before dinner*, or at least postponed it to the cool hour of the morning; you would then have found that I had voluntarily granted the request which you had endeavoured by so many different ways to obtain.

"Lord Mountstuart (for whose amiable qualities I have the highest respect, and whose name your agents very unnecessarily produced to the public) must recol-

lect that, when I had the honour to meet him at
Kingston House by your Grace's appointment, instead
of begging relief from your charity, *I rejected your
splendid offers* to suppress the 'Trip to Calais,' with
the contempt they deserved. Indeed, madam, the
humanity of my royal and benevolent master, and the
public protection, have placed me much above the
reach of your bounty.

"But why, madam, put on your *coat of mail*
against me? I have no hostile intentions. Folly,
not vice, is the game I pursue. In those scenes
which you so unaccountably apply to yourself, you
must observe there is not the slightest hint at the little
incidents of your life which have excited the *curiosity*
of the grand inquest for the county of Middlesex. I
am happy, however, madam, to hear that your robe of
innocence is in such perfect repair; I was afraid it
might be a little the worse for wearing. May it
hold out to keep your Grace warm the next
winter!

"The progenitors your Grace has done me the
honour to give me are, I presume, merely metaphorical
persons, and to be considered as the authors of my
muse, and not of my manhood. A merry-andrew
and a prostitute are no bad poetical parents, especially
for a writer of plays—the first, to give the humour
and mirth; the last, to furnish the graces and powers
of attraction. Prostitutes and players too must live
by pleasing the public; not but your Grace may
have heard of ladies who by *private practice* have
accumulated great fortunes.

"If you mean that I really owe my birth to that
pleasant connection, your Grace is grossly deceived.
My father was, in truth, a very useful magistrate and

23—2

respectable country gentleman, as the whole county
of Cornwall will tell you ; my mother, the daughter
of Sir Edward Goodere, Baronet, who represented the
county of Hereford.   Her fortune was large, and her
morals irreproachable till your Grace condescended to
stain them.   She was upwards of fourscore years old
when she died, and, what will surprise your Grace,
was never married but once in her life.

"I am obliged to your Grace for your intended
presence ' on the day' (as you *politely* express it)
'when I am to be turned off.'   But where will your
Grace get the *Cupid* to bring me the lip-salve ?
That family, I am afraid, has long quitted *your*
service.

"Pray, madam, is not J——n the name of your
female confidential secretary ? and is not *she* generally
clothed in black petticoats made of your weeds ?

> " ' So mourn'd the dame of Ephesus her love !'

I fancy your Grace took the hint when you last
resided at Rome.   You heard then, I suppose, of a
certain Pope, and in humble imitation have converted
a *pious parson* into a *chambermaid*.   The scheme is
new in this country, and has, doubtless, its particular
pleasures.   That you may *never want the benefit of
the clergy* in every emergence is the sincere wish of
"Your Grace's most devoted,
"Most obliged humble servant,
"SAM. FOOTE."

The text of these letters, from being often copied,
varies in places.   Thus the Duchess's letter began, "A
servant was directed to return the following answer,"
and the P.S. adds that "the servant has been a

long time writing it." This we may presume was
meant for insolent contempt, and conveyed that the
Duchess did not write or compose the letter, but gave
the servant some "heads" or directions. In the note
it should run : Mr. Foote "is descended," not "is
said to be."

Foote's bitter and elaborate rejoinder has been
extravagantly admired, not only by Walpole and
others of that generation, but by critics of our time,
such as John Forster. I must confess, while willing
and eager to admire, I cannot see very much in the
production. There is little, for instance, in his point
that her letter *must* have been written *after dinner*
—that is, when she had drunk too much. And he
completely "gave himself away," as the phrase runs,
when he retorted on her as to his birth. He fancied
that she had said he was the "offspring of a mountebank and a prostitute"; she had merely said that he
had prostituted his gifts, etc.—an odd mistake ; and
though he might repudiate the mountebank for his
parent, still, was he not himself one, or a mountebank
of a sort ?

As I have said, it is clear that the whole of this
unfortunate quarrel was not between the Duchess
and Foote, but between Foote and her clerical agents.
This pair—Foster and Jackson—saw in the business
an opportunity for trafficking, for "a deal." They
purposed to extract a large sum from Foote, as the
price of his being allowed to perform his play. Foote
was not disposed to be thus blackmailed, as the
sum in question would nullify all his chances of
profits from the theatre. At the same time, it is
likely enough that Foote was not indisposed to
receive such a sum as would fairly compensate him

for his great sacrifice in suppressing his play. Hence, most naturally, the recriminations as to who offered the money. Who can refute or believe these stories? Foote, who was a man of business, and a shrewd one too, saw that there was no profit to be had in dealing with these rascals. He declined, therefore, to treat with them. There can be little doubt that this is what occurred.*

* It may be mentioned in this place that Foote's expressive and most striking features were limned by Sir Joshua in one of his finest portraits, which has a place in the Duke of Newcastle's gallery at Clumber. The attitude and figure are as dramatic and " telling " as the face. A replica, executed by another great artist, is at Knole, and from this the portrait which forms the frontispiece to the present memoir has been taken. Charles Mathews had another copy made for his collection, which copy is now in the Garrick Club ; but it is a rather " poorish " performance. Zoffany also painted a couple of dramatic scenes, one from " The Mayor of Garratt," which seems to give spirited likenesses. Finally, Cooke supplies a small portrait, with a thoughtful expression, by a French artist, which he considered to be the most faithful likeness of all. In two portraits, that of Sterne and that of Foote, Sir Joshua may be held to have excelled all his efforts.

CHAPTER XXIII

FINALE

EVERYTHING now seemed to hurry the luckless Foote to his own destruction, and, with a fatal insensibility, he seemed to think of nothing but punishing those who had injured him. The mysterious allusions to dark criminal acts were still appearing in Jackson's paper, and the actor, blinded or careless, was now busy altering his unlucky "Trip to Calais" into a new piece, which he called "The Capucin." Breathing revenge and fury, he threw all his power into the conception of two revolting characters—both clerics—and intended not so much to ridicule as to make odious his two enemies. Jackson was there as Dr. Viper, an exact portrait of a subservient, unscrupulous scoundrel; while Father Dominic, intended, we may presume, for Foster, was shown as a repulsive Irish monk. This was portrayed by Foote himself.

It is a mystery how the Lord Chamberlain, who had interdicted the "Trip to Calais," could have tolerated this fresh attempt. But Jackson and Foster had no friends at Court, as the Duchess had.

Here is the terribly envenomed portrait of his enemy Jackson, breathing hatred and fury in every stroke:

"*Viper*. Do you know, sirrah, to whom you are speaking? *O'Donnovan*. Oh, you may say that, my dear honey; from the top to the bottom, every inch and cranny of you. *Viper.* Pay the proper respect to my cloth. *O'Donnovan.* What is it you mane? Is it a priest that you are? *Viper.* Without doubt. *O'Donnovan.* Then, upon my shoul, it must be of your own ordination, like Mr. Melchisedeck. A priest! I'll wager you my frock against the price of a Mass that you can't tell how many the Thirty-nine Articles are. *Viper.* An impudent, audacious—— *O'Donnovan.* What! because you was parish clerk to the Moravian meeting-house in the Old Jewry, and used to snuffle out their indecent hymns to the tune of filthy ballads and jigs; and from thence you got expelled for robbing the poor-box. *Viper.* What, me? *O'Donnovan.* Then you became advertisement-sticker to lottery offices, auctioneers, stage-coaches, and mountebank doctors; but being detected in selling the bills for waste paper to grocers, you got your dismissal, you know. *Viper.* Rascal! I know! *O'Donnovan.* After that you turned swindler, and got out of gaol by an Act for the relief of insolvent debtors. *Viper.* Many honest men have been in the same situation. *O'Donnovan.* Oh, yea! lave honesty out of the case, if you plase. Then you became *doer* of the *Scandalous Chronicle,* mowed down reputations like muck, pushed yourself into the pay of Lady Deborah Dripping, produced anonymous paragraphs against her of your own composition, and got paid by her for not putting them into your paper. *Viper* (*aside*). Where the devil could the fellow collect all this story? *O'Donnovan.* Now, from here I suppose you will soon return home a fugitive, and pay your old debts by a new Act of Parliament."

After this, it was scarcely surprising that Jackson

should have struck back, and with a vigour that
was to destroy Foote. But what an infatuation,
and what blindness to consequences! It was the
last and most painful of all Foote's histrionic efforts,
and was also to be the most fatal in its result to
himself. He had the satisfaction of "gibbeting"
his enemy, but it proved his ruin.

It was astonishing that Foote did not see his
danger, and that he had not taken warning by the
dark, scarcely veiled insinuations as to his own
moral character, which now appeared regularly and
mysteriously in the holes and corners of the Press.
But he had not reckoned with the desperate animosity
of his foe. More astonishing still was it that he
should thus put himself on trial on his own stage,
knowing how easy it was for his enemies to send in
hired disturbers to interrupt the piece. It seems
incredible that Foote should have appeared as a
performer, addressing Jackson, who was disguised as
Viper.

At the close of May 1776, Foote opened his season
with "The Bankrupt." It was a sensational night, and
he required much courage to face the ordeal. The
house was packed with an audience of men of rank
and men of letters in all parts. Foote was greeted
with riotous disturbance, yells, etc. The ladies fled
from the boxes. The actor, with great courage, came
forward and pleaded for himself. He told them how
that very day he had brought his libeller before the
Court, and had convicted him. He appealed for
indulgence, and the play was allowed to go on.

But now a sad closing act was to follow. A
report began to be circulated that it was proposed
to bring a serious charge—most serious and degrading

of all known charges—against the manager of the
Haymarket, and that the promoters were merely
waiting till the matter was ripe. The unfortunate
Foote hardly knew what to do, but, after consulting
his friends, determined that boldness was the best
course to take. So he continued to perform for a few
nights, but under such a cloud he was not likely to
have much success. On July 8 the town learned that
a coachman whom Foote had discharged for repeated
irregularities had appeared before the grand jury at
Hicks's Hall on a bill of indictment against Foote for
an offence which need not be named. The bill appears
to have been found—we may presume, on the prose-
cutor's evidence—and motion was made and granted
that the accused should at once be arrested. Officers
were despatched for the purpose. It was remarked
that this worthy coachman was attended by the Rev.
Dr. Jackson as a sort of sponsor ! Foote escaped the
degradation of arrest by a mere chance. He had
heard of the legal proceedings, and, going to Hicks's
Hall with some of his friends, obtained bail, while the
officers were seeking him at his own house. The
object, of course, was, by securing his person, to cause
him to close his theatre. Such was the plot. A few
days later his assailants appeared again at Hicks's Hall
with a fresh charge of the same character, and again
the grand jury returned a true bill, but Foote's
counsel succeeded in removing the whole case to the
Court of King's Bench.

It must have been a sad and painful thing for him
to have to appear on the same night at his theatre,
as, of course, his persecutors attended. Many ladies
were present, strangely enough, who were received
with some indecorous expressions, which obliged

them immediately to retire—a conduct for which they were much applauded by the whole house.

" When the curtain drew up, Foote came forward, and was received with prodigious shouts of applause, a few hisses from the corners of the galleries excepted; however, these being soon silenced, and order restored, he addressed the audience :

" ' Gentlemen,—It was not my intention, after the charge that has been made against me, to appear before the public till I had an opportunity of proving my innocence ; but as this charge was made at the critical point of time when I usually opened my theatre, and having engaged as good a set of performers for your amusement as I could procure, it was the unanimous advice of my friends that I should open my house, in confidence that the public were too noble and too just to discard an old servant for a mere accusation.

" ' I am ready to answer every charge which can be brought against me, and have pursued such legal steps to clear my reputation from the virulent attacks of a public paper as will speedily bring the writer to an issue in the Court of King's Bench, which has this day made the rule absolute against the publisher.

" ' I beg leave to return my thanks for the marks you have now given me of your humanity and justice ; permit me to promise you that I will never disgrace your protection.'

" His situation called forth his sensibilities very powerfully, and a great majority of the audience honoured him both at that moment and throughout the whole course of the comedy with the most unbounded applause."

Of all the chequered incidents and adventures in
the record of our men of letters, this seems the most
tragic and painful, especially when we think of its
arriving at the close of a long and animated career,
when his attraction was beginning to fail, and when
he might naturally be looking for repose. Whether
innocent or guilty, it was impossible to recover from
such a stroke and hide his head in retirement. The
actor is before his public every night, and thus was
Foote constantly recalling the nauseous story to
audiences. And, alas! the verdict of the jury in such
cases is not always convincing for the crowd. There
were many who shook their heads solemnly. No one,
however, who has followed the account of Jackson's
share in the matter, could have the slightest hesitation
in acquitting Foote.

In due course Samuel Foote, the English Aristophanes, had to stand his trial. Here was the terrible
judge, who had put so many in the dock, forced to
appear in that humiliating place. Happily, he was
altogether cleared of the foul charge and acquitted;
and it was proved that the coachman accuser had
been encouraged, if not suborned, by Jackson to
come forward. If this were the case, why was he
not brought to trial in his turn? However, Foote
felt compelled to bring an action against him for
the libellous paragraphs inserted in the papers.
But before it came to trial, the actor died. Everybody stood by him, and the King "commanded"
performances. The trial was attended by royalties
and persons of the first rank, who were, I fancy,
drawn more by curiosity than by respect or friendship. Garrick, true friend to the last, worked
unceasingly for his friend. "God forever bless you,

my dear, kind friend ; may nothing but halcyon days
and nights crown the rest of your life !" So wrote
the fallen jester.

One of the most terrible trials for a person moving
in society is the first appearance before his acquaintances — say, at some familiar club — after passing
through the ordeal of a public trial on some criminal
charge which has ended in acquittal. The hapless
victim who is innocent is forced to confront his
friends and put on a show of indifference ; if his
courage fail him, he had better retire to foreign lands.
How sick at heart he must be ! how hesitating with
everyone he meets, uncertain as he must be of his
reception ! But what must be the feelings of the
accused and acquitted player who has to present
himself to the crowd of the theatre, where there are
certain to be enemies, with others who have formed
an obstinate opinion on the question, and resent the
" fellow's " coming forward as effrontery. And this
was the hapless Foote's sad position. But at once the
old amazing incompressibility came to his aid. With
his back to the wall, as it were, he fought all comers,
then leaped over their heads.

After all, the most convincing, persuasive evidence
for Foote in this distressing business is that of Garrick.
The unhappy man, crushed, overwhelmed, and suspected, found his best friend, sympathizer, and
adherent, in the one whom he had so often libelled,
threatened, denounced, ridiculed — David Garrick !
This generous man rallied to his side at once ; he
had complete faith in his honour ; he encouraged and
fortified him, and gave valuable assistance. He was
almost tender and affectionate in his offers of aid.
This is the best and substantial proof of his belief in

Foote's innocence.   Anyone of less noble gifts might have coldly stood aloof, and said : " This man has been my unfailing libeller ; he has caused me many anxious moments.   Let him now look after himself." Not so David Garrick.   From the beginning to the end of this disastrous business he was on the side of Foote.

In a letter Garrick gives him encouraging news to cheer him, and good-naturedly tells him what a fine account he had had of Foote's new piece—his best performance, and "he never was better pleased." Foote's answer was equally remarkable :

" MY DEAR SIR,

        " I am exceedingly obliged to you for the kind conclusion of your letter.   I promise I would not have hinted it to you but *in the confidence of your friend-ship, and if at the same time I could not with* the greatest truth say that I am most sincerely and affectionately yours.   I have been most cruelly used, but I have, thank God, got to the bottom of this infernal contrivance.   God for ever bless you !"

He was fatigued to death with a crowd of com-forters—had just rid of a roomful.   Naturally his spirits were better.

And again Foote wrote :

" Ten thousand thanks, my dear sir, for your kind message to me by Mr. Woodfall, nor am I less obliged to you for using your influence where I begged it.   I have directed Sewell to advertise all my performances in the *Morning Post* [Woodfall's paper]; and if the gentleman who is supposed to be the editor [Bate] should again turn his thoughts to the drama, *me and my stage he may ever command.*"

After the verdict he seemed to be completely restored to public favour. He even went to Court, where he was warmly received.* His last appearance "on any stage" was in May 1777, in his character of the Devil on Two Sticks. It was remarked that he was sadly changed, grown wasted, and had lack-lustre eyes.

After a time the broken actor seems to have lost heart, and resolved to fly from the scene of his humiliation. He would give up his theatre and go away to foreign parts. It went round that the little theatre was to be sold, and offers began to come in. The most favourable came from an anonymous candidate, who proved to be one of his own friends.

Foote to Garrick.

"*September* 15, 1776.

" MY DEAR SIR,

" I am sorry I could not see you before quitting this country, and am more concerned at the cause; but, as I found your gouty fit was in form, I flatter myself there will be a long parenthesis between this and the next.

" You have no leisure to be sick in such a jostling time. Your opponents are numerous, and Solomon says, 'In a multitude of counsellors there is safety'; but I should suppose his counsellors are of a different stamp from the congregation at Covent Garden.

---

* A Baronet had his diamond ornaments snatched away, on which the irrepressible joker declared that it was no wonder, as he had noted an immense number of parsons about, and had carefully secured his gold snuff-box. Further, the King actually commanded a special performance, and this while the accusation was pending. The incorrigible Foote, on telling the King that the piece was written by one of his chaplains, added, " And dull enough to be by a Bishop."

" There is more of prudence than of pleasure in my
trip to the Continent: to tell you the truth, I am
tired of racking my brain, toiling like a horse, and
crossing seas and mountains in the most dreary
season, merely to pay servants' wages and tradesmen's bills. I have therefore directed my friend
Jewel to discharge the lazy vermin of my hall, and
let my hall, too (hell, it would seem, is the correct
word), if he can meet with a proper tenant: help me
to one if you can.

" You need not doubt but I shall be happy to hear
from you ; my epistolary debts will be always in my
power to pay: is it in man to do more ?   With
anything that France produces I shall be proud to
supply you.

" I kiss Mrs. Garrick's hands, and am,

" Most truly and sincerely yours,

"S. F."

Here was a genuine, almost touching letter. The
careless tone of " a trip " to France could not take in
his friend ; Garrick must have read between the
lines, and seen that he was flying from England for
good. There was more prudence than pleasure in
the step.

Cleverness, unluckily, does not always secure—or
at least rarely secures — remuneration. The two
Colmans, father and son, had really to live by their
wits. The father had no money ; he had debts, which
he satisfied by living almost permanently in the Rules
of the King's Bench. He was a wit of singular
buoyancy, and the best of company for supper, as
Byron said, though he was glad to have " Sherry " as
a dinner companion. There was something piquant

in the notion of this poor debtor—actually managing his theatre from the Rules—arranging pieces which he dared not venture to go and see, controlling his actors whom he could not rehearse. This awkward duress must have been well known to all ; it was impossible to respect a management carried on under such conditions.* Foote was once or twice in the Fleet, but he was too adroit to suffer permanent imprisonment. Impecunious men such as Sheridan gradually learn the art of managing creditors ; such are gifted with a brazen effrontery, and lack shame or delicacy. Colman, who was a worthy, amiable, perhaps honourable man, could not bluster or chicane, and suffered accordingly.

When Foote came to the resolution of disposing of his theatre, he announced that he would receive proposals. The negotiations were going on, but he had no idea that his friend Colman was a candidate. The latter, knowing his Foote well, preferred to employ an agent. The new and old managers used to meet at dinner, and Foote in his rough way would tell how he had seen the agent, who was acting for "some fat-headed blockhead who knew nothing of management, and would ruin himself."

The younger Colman explains the terms of the arrangement. A life annuity of £1,600 was to be paid half-yearly. Foote was also to be paid for his services as an actor, and actually performed three times. He was also to receive £500 for the copyright of his pieces. "With the theatre certain decayed and

---

* Colman recalled Foote's rough treatment of him as a boy, his usual greeting being : "Blow your nose, child." He recalled also the good-natured "Goldy," who, when he was in disgrace and put in a dark room, went in to amuse him with tricks, etc.

moth-eaten articles, which Foote dignified by the collective name of wardrobe, which might have produced
altogether at a sale, if well puffed by a knowing
auctioneer, about £20 at the utmost," were made over
to the new management.   And so his connection
with " the little theatre in the Hay. " ceased for ever.
It was a prodigious bargain for Colman, for Foote
died after the first half-year became due.   The new
manager must have had it almost for nothing.

But now was to come a last warning ; indeed, misfortunes were crowding on him in battalions.   While
playing one night, the poor actor was stricken with
palsy when actually on the stage.   This was to prove
his last appearance.   He was sent down to Brighthelmstone (Brighton), where he seemed to recover.   He
returned to London, and was ordered to go to Paris,
and later to the South of France.   The palsy, however,
was to waylay him at Dover, and he got no farther.

He went away full of gloomy presentiments.   He
wandered through the rooms of his house in Suffolk
Street, which were hung with good portraits, and
stopped before one of Weston.*   After gazing at
it intently for some moments, he said mournfully,
" Poor Weston !"   Then, turning to Jewel, who was
with him : " It will very soon be poor Foote !"

Many of us may recall the old Ship Inn at Dover
where Foote was to play the last scene of his noisy
life.   It was the first stage for the traveller going
abroad, who usually stayed for the night to arrange
for his passage next day in one of the " smacks " or
sloops.   On the other side there was Dessein's old
and familiar house, celebrated by Sterne.   The Ship
lingered on till nigh 1870, when it was closed owing

* Now in the Garrick Club.

to the facilities for making the journey in one day.
I recall it—a stern, fortress-looking building, well
buffeted by the storms of the Channel.   It later did
duty as a warehouse.

In this harbour-side inn it was Foote's fate to utter
the last—the very last—of his thousand and one jests.
And this was addressed, not to the sympathizing,
convivial co-drinkers of the Bedford or of the " nobleman's stable," but to the cook maid and scullions
of the Ship kitchen.   There he gave his last performance—a poor thing, something about the cook being
a traveller as having been in *Grease.**

" Next morning, when sitting at breakfast," says his
friend Cooke, " he was seized with a shivering fit,
which further increasing, he was put to bed.   Another
fit soon succeeded this, which lasted three hours.   He
then seemed composed and inclined to sleep ; but
soon began to breathe low, which continuing for some
little time, he at length, with a deep sigh, expired on
the 21st of October 1777, in the fifty-seventh year of
his age."

Such was the end of this unlucky Yorick.   It

* So soon as Foote was dead, Murphy thought to turn him to
profit by seizing on his good things and fitting them into his own
pieces.   He thought, perhaps, " There is meat on him still."   In
one of his comedies he describes him : " He has wit to ridicule you,
invention to frame a story of you, humour to help it about, and,
when he has set the town a-laughing, he puts on a familiar air and
shakes you by the hand."

After Murphy's death, some notes for a comedy were found
among his papers : " Foote gives a dinner—large company ; each
enters, he glad to see each.   At dinner his wit, affectation, pride ;
his expense, his plate, his jokes.   All laugh ; all go, one by one ;
all abused, one by one.   His toad-eaters stay ; he praises himself—
in a passion against all the world."   How characteristic of the
friendship between wits !

was curious that another bitter satirist — Charles
Churchill—should also have given up the ghost at
Dover fourteen years before. He was seized with
illness, very appropriately, when on his way to visit
Wilkes. He was stopped by a "miliary fever" at
Boulogne, where he made a mock will, and died
shortly after his arrival at Dover. His last words, it
is said, were, "*What a fool I have been !*" Poor
Foote might have made the same despairing ejacu-
lation :

> " And all our yesterdays
> Have lighted fools the way to dusty death."

Foote was but a few years over fifty when he ended
his tumultuous life. The executioner, in the shape of
apoplexy or paralysis, was called in—ever the penalty
for excessive indulgence. This malady, with softening
of the brain, delirium tremens, insanity, etc., usually cuts
short the course of the toper, debauchee, or glutton.
Had he been temperate, Foote might have looked for
a long life, from his unflagging spirits and energy.
And it is sad to think that even Johnson and his
faithful Boswell should both have died prematurely
—the first from over-indulgence in the good things of
the table, the other from a too sottish indulgence in
drink. In the Doctor's case it was rather a deplorable business ; all knew his greedy methods in taking
his food, his gorging it, as it were, till the veins in
his face swelled. He would not speak while he was
thus engrossed. How are we to account for this
weakness in so great a sage and moralist, and one who
so carefully searched his conscience ? The swinging
stroke came in the night, and filled him with dread
and penitence. But after the friendly gratuitous
doctors had brought him round with cantharides, etc.,

our sage could not resist fresh dinner-parties, and " gorged " away as before. According to medical prognostics, it is certain that he would have had another stroke within a few months, which would have despatched him ; but his other diseases—dropsy, asthma, weakness of kidneys and other " internals "— all induced by overeating—brought matters to a final crisis. The hard-working littérateur destroys himself and shortens his life, but in another way. Take the two great stars of the nineteenth century—to wit, Scott and Dickens. There is a strange parallel in the lives of these great men. Both died from overwork, from striving to earn a permanent subsistence for their families. Both loved the country and wished to set up as " squires," and there were many other points of resemblance. But overwork destroyed both. In my own experience, I could name many who have literally thus destroyed themselves by such excesses.

And so it was to be with poor Foote, who to the last fancied himself a power before which all were to tremble, unconscious that the feet were but of clay. A month after Johnson's declaring that Foote would drive Betterton out of the room by his wit and spirit, the Doctor wrote to his friend Mrs. Thrale : " Did you see Foote at Brighthelmstone ? Did you think he would be so soon gone ? ' Life,' says Falstaff, ' is a shuttle.' *He was a fine fellow in his way, and the world is really impoverished by his sinking glories.* Murphy ought to write his life—at least, give to the world a Footeana. Now, will any of his contemporaries bewail him ?"*

Jewel, the treasurer of the theatre, was sent for,

---

* On that suggestion of a " Footeana," a malevolent critic wrote, " One-half had been a string of obscenities."

and brought the body to town. On the Monday following (November 3) he was buried by torchlight in the west cloister of the Abbey. We may wonder who of his friends it was that moved in this matter— probably Garrick. The truth was, at that time "snug lying" in the cloisters was easily obtainable. As it was, no one thought of a monument, though, as a sort of oddity which he himself would have smiled at, a tablet was erected in a Dover church where he did *not* lie:

> " Sacred to the memory of Samuel Foote,
> Who had a tear for every friend,
> And a hand and heart ever ready
> To relieve distress.

" He departed this life Oct. 21, 1777 (on his journey to France), at the Ship Inn, Dover, aged 55 years [*sic*]. This inscription was placed here by his affectionate friend, William Jewel.

This was in St. Martin's, Cannon Street, and the tablet is described as a small one. The strangest thing is to find not far away from it a tablet to his friend Churchill, who also had died elsewhere.

INDEX

ABINGTON, Frances, 37 *n.*; her
  entertainment with Wilkinson,
  172-174
Actors, the training of, 34, 35
Addison, Joseph, 29
Alice in Wonderland, 110
Angelo, the fencing-master, 97, 202,
  204 *n.*
Aprice, an eccentric Welshman,
  145, 146; application to Lord
  Chamberlain to forbid *The
  Author*, 149
Arne, Dr., satirized by Foote, 332
Austen, Jane, 300
Austin, Mr., friend of Tate Wilkin-
  son, 159, 160

Baddeley, Robert, 220
Baker, Mrs., possibly the original of
  Mrs. Crummles, 117, 164
Bannister, Charles, 233; his imita-
  tions of Foote, 272
Barber, a wardrobe-dealer, 242
Barrowby, Dr. William, 29
Barry, Spranger, Wilkinson's imita-
  tion of, 115, 123, 166, 168, 170,
  243, 265
Barsanti, Miss, as Portia, 325
Bedford, The, Coffee House, 29
Beggar's Opera, The, 208
Bentley, Richard, his play *The
  Wishes*, 293
Bernard, John, 124 *n.*
Betterton, Thomas, Johnson's com-
  ment upon, 91
Blake, his acting in *Taste*, 78
Bonfoy, Captain, 118
Boswell, James, 2, 3, 9, 18, 31, 84,
  89, 94, 95, 96, 103, 133, 168;
  Johnson on, 181; his skits on
  Foote and Dodsley, 188, 204;
  and the Robin Hood Debating
  Society, 235; at the Stratford

Jubilee, 303; story of Goldsmith
  and the puppets, 321; repeats to
  Foote a story of Johnson, 322,
  336, 346, 372
Boucicault, Dion, 37, 182
Bourgeois Gentilhomme, Le, 292
Boz Club, The, 31
Bracegirdle, Mrs., 135
Brooke, Gustavus, 37 *n.*
Brough, Lionel, 56
Browne, Sir William, satirized by
  Foote, 297
Brownsmith, under-prompter at
  Drury Lane, 157
Buckstone, J. B., 56
Burney, Fanny, her descriptions
  of Arthur Murphy, 103, 104, 325,
  326
Byron quoted, 368

Callender, an Edinburgh theatrical
  manager, 161
Carlyle on Thomas Moore, 315 *n.*
Censorship, the Dramatic, 50, 51,
  267
Chaigneau, Mr. and Mrs., 121
Chesterfield, Lord, 91, 236, 293,
  331
Chudleigh, Miss, Duchess of Kingston, 337; Foote's play, *A Trip
  to Calais*, written round her,
  341; her champions, 343; the
  play forbidden, 346; her fresh
  negotiations, 350; attacked by
  Foote in the Press, 351; letter
  from Foote, 351; her reply, 353
  his retort, 354
Churchill, Charles: his hatred of
  Murphy, 104; on Foote, 198,
  199, 200, 223, 241; on Shuter,
  259, 372, 374
Cibber, Colley, on Garrick, 135,
  136; on Mrs. Clive, 151

Cider Cellars, The, 45
Clandestine Marriage, The, Murphy's quarrel with Garrick over, 103
Clive, Catherine, 37 *n.*, 151
Clive, Mr. Justice, 205
Clubs, 31
Coal Hole, The, 45
Cock, a fashionable auctioneer, Foote's burlesque of, 60
Cock Lane ghost, the, 229
Cockburn, Lord, 49
Coffee-houses, 29-32
Coleridge, S. T., 31
Colmans, the, 54, 228, 240, 252, 253, 257, 368
Compton, Henry, 56
Cooke, William, biorgapher of Foote, 8, 9, 14, 26, 28, 38, 41, 61, 100, 101, 202, 212, 214, 235, 261, 272, 303; account of Foote's death, 371
Cookes, Sir Thomas, 12, 13
Cooper, Lucy, 241
Coote, Mr., afterwards Earl of Bellamont, 180
Costello, 57, 68, 78, 102
Cradock, Joseph, 94; quoted, 205, 321, 329
Critic, The, 284
Croker, John Wilson, 9, 18; quoted, 49
Cullen, Dr., a famous mimic, 49, 50
Cumberland, Richard, 206, 235, 327, 329
Cumberland, William Augustus, Duke of, leader in riot at Haymarket Theatre, 68, 99, 217
Curran, John, his quotation of Foote's nonsense story, 109

Davies, Thomas, 84; quoted, 85, 88, 96, 208, 306, 308, 321
Delane, Dennis, 37 *n.*; Foote's burlesque of, 59, 265
Delaval, Sir Francis, 201, 207
Diable Boiteux, Le, 296
Dickens, Charles, 31, 46 *n.*, 71, 177, 204 *n.*, 264, 269, 271, 321, 330, 336, 373
Didier, Mrs., 164
Dinely, Sir John, 5, 6
Dinely, Sir John (born Goodere), 8
Doctor Last in his Chariot, 309
Dodd, William, caricatured in *The Minor*, 177, 331, 333

Dominecetti, an Italian quack, 203
Drama, the modern, 268
Dramatic Licensing Act of 1737, the, 37, 50, 153
Dryden, John, 44
Dublin, Foote's appearances in, 118, 166, 263, 308
Dumas, Alexandre, 80, 220

Edgeworth, Maria, 110
Elwin, Whitwell, 192 *n.*
English Stage, Some Account of the, by John Genest, 273

Farmer, Dr. Richard, 205
Farquhar, George, 37
Farrens, the, 37 *n.*
Faulkner, George, 95, 234, 235; takes action against Foote, 238
Fawkener, Alderman, 311; a letter from, 312
Fielding, Henry, his *Tom Thumb*, etc., 50, 252
Fielding, Sir John, 351
FitzHenry, Mrs., 37 *n.*
Fitzherbert, Johnson's anecdote about his servants and Foote, 91, 92
Fletcher, Sir Robert, 206
Foote family, the, 3, 19 *n.*, 97, 98
Foote, Henry, 3
Foote, Mrs., mother of Samuel, 3, 5, 28, 98, 356
Foote, the Rev. G., brother of Samuel, 98, 99
Foote, Mr. Thomas, 19 *n.*
Foote, Samuel:
Christened in 1720, 3; sent to Worcester Grammar School, 9; first efforts in mimicry, 10; goes to Worcester College, Oxford, 12; practical jokes, 14; scholarship declared void, 18; pamphlet on the murder of his uncle, 27; at the Temple, 28; at the coffee-houses, 29; stage-training, 33; first appearances, 40; Dublin journey, 42; mimicry as a profession, 42; a rival in G. A. Stevens, 52; comparison of Foote with Charles Mathews, 52, 53; first performance of *The Diversions of the Morning*, 57; legal stoppage of the performances, and Foote's evasion, 61; first comedy, *The Knights*, 70; flight to

France, 74 ; return and production of *Taste*, 75; relations with Garrick, 80 ; character by Davies, 85 ; comments of Johnson, 89-96 ; as beer-brewer, 91, 92, 94 ; resolves to burlesque Johnson : Johnson's retort, 96 ; meeting with Johnson in Paris, 97 ; imitations before Préville, 97 ; letter to his mother in prison, 98 ; marriage, 99, 100 ; in the Fleet Prison, 101 ; the dismissal and return of his wife, 102; satire on the French, 105 ; quarrel with Murphy, 107 ; persecution of Macklin : nonsense story, 108, 109 ; witness of Wilkinson's imitations, 116 ; engagement of Wilkinson for Irish tour, 117 ; dismissal of Wilkinson and experiment as fortune-teller, 126 ; appearances at Drury Lane in revivals of *Taste* and *Diversions*, 129, 131-133; address to the audience on Wilkinson's withdrawal, 140; production of *The Author*, 146; play banned by the Lord Chamberlain, 150; scheme for playing Shylock falls through, 151; quarrel with Wilkinson, 155-157; burlesqued by Wilkinson, 159 ; lecture at the Haymarket, 160; borrows from Garrick, 162 ; Edinburgh, 163 ; letter to Wilkinson quoted, 165 ; Dublin, 166; scene with Thomas Sheridan, 168 ; threatens Wilkinson, 175 ; caricatures Wilkinson and Whitefield in *The Minor*, 176; on Ireland, 181 ; *The Minor* at the Haymarket, 182 ; reply to critics, 188,189; charged with plagiarism, 189 *n.*; anger at Wilkinson's piracies, 193 ; licence refused, 196; as a humorist, 197, 213-224 ; fear of Churchill, 200; friends, 201 ; practical jokes, 202, 203 ; Foote confused at a dinner, 206 ; encounter with John Henderson, 208; further reconciliation with Wilkinson, 225 ; curious stage methods in *The Orators*, 234; fined for libel on Faulkner, 238; parody of the proceedings, 238 ; snobbishness, 245 ; loses his

leg as result of an accident, 246 ; a theatre manager, 247; licence quoted, 253 ; management, 258; considered as a dramatist, 264-300; best characters compared with those of Goldsmith, 267 ; Goldsmith's indebtedness, 275 ; Sheridan's indebtedness, 279 ; attends Stratford Jubilee to plague Garrick, 301; threat to produce a puppet-show burlesque of Garrick, 304; letter to Garrick, 310 ; letter to Tate Wilkinson, 313 ; *The Maid of Bath* and the Sheridan romance, 316; puppet-shows, 318; plan to satirize Johnson and Goldsmith, 322, 324; a *condottiere*, 337; plans to satirize the Duchess of Kingston, 337; is prevented by the Lord Chamberlain, 346; letter to the Lord Chamberlain, 347; letter to the Duchess of Kingston, 351; her reply, 353; his violent rejoinder, 354; portraits, 358; Jackson's vengeance, 360; Foote charged to appear before a grand jury, 362 ; trial and acquittal, 364 ; action against Jackson, 364; Garrick's admirable friendliness, 364; last appearance, 367 ; Brighthelmstone, 370; at the Ship Inn, Dover, 370 ; death, 371; burial in Westminster Abbey, 374

Foote, Samuel—Parts :
As Bayes, in *The Rehearsal*, 40, 41, 166; Ben Legend, in *Love for Love*, 41; Buck, in *The Englishman in Paris*, 105; Cadwallader, in *The Author*, 146 ; Sir Courtly, 41 ; Demur, in his parody of Dublin action, 239; Fondlewife, in *The Old Bachelor*, 40, 57; Foppington, in *The Relapse*, 40, 41 ; Sir Harry Wildair, in *The Constant Couple*, 41 ; Kitely, in *Every Man in his Humour*, 116; Lecturer and Peter Paragraph, in *The Orators*, 233 ; Sir Luke Limp, in *The Lame Lover*, 289 ; Othello, 38, 40; Sir Paul Pliant, in *The Double Dealer*, 40, 163 ; Sir Penurious Trifle, in *The Knights*, 70 ; Pierre, in *Venice Preserved*,

40; Puzzle, in *Tea*, 121; Shylock, 149, 151, 163; Smirk and Mrs. Cole, in *The Minor*, 227; The Squire, in *The Handsome Housemaid*, 325; Tinsel, in *The Drummer*, 41

Foote, Samuel—Works:
Chronological list, 285; *Author, The*, 146, 285; *Auction, The*, 65, 285; *Bankrupt, The*, 285, 295, 361; *Capucin, The*, 285, 334, quoted, 359; *Cat's Opera, The*, 74; *Commissary, The*, 285, 291; *Cozeners, The*, 264, 285, 330; *Diversions of the Morning, The*, 57, 128, 131, 138, 151, 153, 155, 171, 285; *Devil upon Two Sticks, The*, 263, 285, quoted, 296, 367; *Englishman in Paris, The*, 105, 285; *Englishman Returned from Paris, The*, 285; *Handsome Housemaid, The*, or *Piety in Pattens*, 285, 322, 325; *Knights, The*, 70-74, 146 *n*., 275, quoted 283, 285; *Lame Lover, The*, 250, 278, 285, 289; *Lyar, The*, 285, 292; *Maid of Bath, The*, 285, 314; *Mayor of Garratt, The*, 226, quoted, 230, 231, 260, 285; *Memoirs of Sir John Dinely Goodere, The*, 27 *n*.; *Minor, The*, 176, 183-196, 227, 264, quoted 280, 285; *Nabob, The*, 181, 285, 286, 291; *Orators, The*, 233, 285; *Passions, The*, a treatise, 265 *n*.; *Patron, The*, 285, 293; *Taste*, 75, 130, 171, 285; *Tea*, 61, 62, 64, 65, 121, 124, 157, 171; *Tragedy à la Mode* (part of *Diversions of the Morning*) quoted, 284; *Trip to Calais, A*, 341, 359

Forbes, Lord, 121

Fordyce, Dr., a Quaker physician, satirized by Foote, 299

Forster, John, his article on Foote in the *Quarterly Review*, 2, 18, 27, 58; his intended life of Garrick, 64 *n*., 88; his opinion that Foote was never married, 99, 109; his distrust of Wilkinson's *Memoirs*, 113, 191, 192 *n*.; on *The Mayor of Garratt*, 230, 237, 317; admiration for Foote's rejoinder to the Duchess of Kingston, 357

Foster, Rev. Mr., defender of the Duchess of Kingston, 343, 350, 354, 357; satirized, 359

Fox, Charles, praise of Foote, 198, 331

Garrick, David, 2, 3, 33, 34, 35, 42, 43, 57; Foote's burlesque of, 59, 64 *n*., 65; attitude to Foote over Woodward's skit, 67, 75, 79; Foote's attacks upon, 80; Sir Joshua Reynolds upon, 88; Johnson's comparisons with Foote, 91, 92, 93, 97, 105; prologue to *The Englishman in Paris*, 106, 107; Tate Wilkinson's descriptions, 114, 126; condemned by Foote, 128, 131; his vanity, 133; comparison with Foote by Wilkinson, 135; protest to Wilkinson against burlesques, 137, 138, 140, 141, 145; Foote's indebtedness to and stories of, 162, 167, 192; praised by Churchill, 199, 204, 206; Foote's gibes at, 218, 219, 222, 241; concern for Foote after the latter's accident, 248, 253; as an " actor-manager," 258, 261, 298; the " Jubilee " at Stratford-on-Avon, 301; his " Show " at Drury Lane, and Foote's jealousy, 304, 321, 322; sees *The Handsome Housemaid*, 325, 350; true friendship in Foote's need, 364, 374

Garrick, George, 242, 326

Garrick, Peter, 64

Genest, John, 152 *n*., 257, 264; his *Account of the English Stage*, 273

George II., King, his death, 195

George III., on Foote's costume, 228, 229

George IV. as a mimic, 49

Gibbon, Edward, 77

Glover, Mrs., 37 *n*.

Goldsmith, Oliver, 2, 3, 8, 37 *n*.; his portrait of Croaker in *The Good-Natured Man*, 54, 70, 97; his characters compared with those of Foote, 267; his indebtedness to Foote in *She Stoops to Conquer*, 275; in the *Good-Natured Man*, 278, 298, 302; his jealousy of the puppets, 321, 336; story told by Colman, 369 *n*.

Goodere family, the, 5-8
Goodere murder, the, 20-28
Goodere, Sir Edward, 3, 5, 356
Good-Natured Man, The, compared with *The Lame Lover,* 278
Gower, Dr., Provost of Worcester College, 12, 14, 15
Gower, Lord, Foote dedicates *The Patron* to, 293
Grain, Corney, 34
Grecian, The, Coffee-House, 29
Grossmith, George, 34, 52

Hamilton, Duke of, 338
Hargrave, Francis, 344
Harness, the Rev. Mr., 4 *n.*
Harvey, Mr. Martin, 69
Hayward, Abraham, quoted, 213
Healy, Father, 197
Henderson, John, "the Bath Roscius," 208; as Shylock, 325
Henley, John, "Orator Henley," Foote's ridicule of, 60
Hertford, Lord, forbids production of *A Trip to Calais,* 346
Hervey, Augustus, husband of Miss Chudleigh, 339
Hill, John, 38, 39, 40
Hill's *On Stage Recreation,* 38
Historical Register, The, and the Licensing Act of 1737, 50, 253
Hogarth, William, 169 *n.*
Hook, Theodore, 211
Hunt, Leigh, 271
Hurd, Richard, Bishop of Worcester, 87

Irish actors and playwrights, 36, 37
Irving, Sir Henry, 36, 69, 81, 318 *n.*, 319 *n.*

Jackson, Rev. Dr., defender of the Duchess of Kingston, 343, 350, 351, 352, 354, 357; satirized, 359; retaliation, 360, 362
Jephson, Robert, 310
Jewel, Foote's treasurer, 240, 310, 320, 368, 370, 373
Jewel, Mrs., 164; in *The Handsome Housemaid,* 325
Johnson, Samuel, 3; length of University training, 18, 19; tavern-life, 31; on a lady mimic,

49; on two poets, 67; on Chevalier Taylor, 76, 82, 84; story of Foote and Garrick, 87; admiration for Foote, 89, 91; on Foote's *depeditation,* 90; comment on a report that Foote had been kicked, 90; on Betterton and Foote, 91; anecdote about Fitzherbert's servants and Foote's beer, 92; opinion of Sheridan, 95; Murphy's introduction to, 95; on mimicry, 95; learns of Foote's intention to burlesque him, 96, 103, 108; on Boswell, 181; on Dominecetti, 203; on Foote's truthfulness, 205; enjoyment of Foote's wit, 212, 215, 293, 309; comparison of Foote with a dog, 322; on Foote's satire of the Chesterfield model, 333, 372; letter to Mrs. Thrale on Foote's death, 373
Jones, Mr. H. A., 269 *n.*

Kean, Charles, 37 *n.*, 81
Kellie, Lord, 219
Kelly, Michael, 329
Kemble, John, 38, 81
Kennedy, Dr., a friend of Sterne and Garrick, 204, 225, 298
Kennedy, Mr. Larry, 175
Kenrick, William, 312
King's *Anecdotes,* 12
Kingston, Duke of, 339
Kingston, Duchess of. See Chudleigh, Miss.
Kneller, Sir Godfrey, 77
Knight, Joseph, quoted, 273; his character and his work, 274
Knowles, Sheridan, 37 *n.*

Lacey, Foote's imitation of, 64, 65, 115
Lamb, Charles, 8, 31, 198
Langford, Abraham, caricatured by Foote, 76
Le Fanu, J. S., 233
Leinster, the Duke of, Foote's abuse of his table, 221
Le Sage, his *Le Diable Boiteux,* 296
Linley, Miss, afterwards Mrs. Sheridan, 314
Literary Club, The, 31
Long, Mr., his connection with the Sheridan romance, 314

MacArdell's mezzotint of Garrick as an auctioneer, 76

Macaulay, Mrs. Catherine, 222

Macaulay, T. B., 286

McCulloch, Mr., of Ardwell, 164

Macklin, Charles, 35-38, 39, 40, 47; Foote's imitation of, 63, 105; retirement from the stage, 108; subsequent relations with Foote, 111, 154, 155, 166; fear of being burlesqued by Wilkinson, 169, 170, 252, 265, 310, 312

Macready, William, 36, 37 n., 81

Mahony, an accomplice of Captain Goodere, 22, 23, 24, 26

Mansfield, Lord (Chief Justice), 223, 288

Mathews, Charles, a great mimic, 48, 52, 247, 358

Matthews, Major, satirized in *The Maid of Bath*, 317

Measure for Measure, 130

Melcombe, Lord, satirized in *The Patron*, 293, 294

Mendes, Moses, 241

Merchant of Venice, The, 325

Midas, 230

Miles, Dr., Foote's schoolmaster, 9, 13

Molière, "adapted," in *The Commissary*, 292

Moody, John, 37 n.

Moore, Thomas, 288, 314; Carlyle's remark upon, 315 n.

Moreau, Miss, 57

Morton, Thomas, the comedies of, 54

Mossop, Henry, 36, 37 n., 166; fear of being burlesqued by Wilkinson, 169, 170; in financial difficulties, 171, 265

Mountstuart, Lord, 346, 347, 350, 354

Murphy, Arthur, 36, 37 n., 102, 103; Churchill's verses on, 104; his sequel to *The Englishman in Paris*, 106, 107, 135, 154, 155, 182, 196, 212, 301, 371 n., 373

Murray, Sir J., 109

Names, Foote's fondness for burlesque, 70, 71, 183

Nash, Dr. T. R., 11, 16, 101

Northanger Abbey, 300

Odell, Thomas, 253

Oglethorpe, General, 344

O'Keeffe, John, 37 n.

O'Neill, Eliza, 37 n.

Palmer, his acting in *Taste*, 78, 233

Panjamdrum, earliest use of the word, 109

Paoli, General, 303, 304

Pasquin, 253

Paulet, Lady Harriet, 201

Paulton, Mr., 56

Phelps, Samuel, 37 n.

Phipps, Mrs., 332

Pinero, Sir Arthur, 269 n.

Polwhele, Richard, quoted, 4

Pope, Alexander, 36

Portraits of Foote, 358

Potter, John, builder of the Haymarket Theatre, 251

Préville the French actor, 97

Pulteney, Mr., 338

Puppet-shows, 318

Quick, John, 233

Quin, James, 36, 37 n., 43, 44; Foote's burlesque of, 59; attribution of nonsense story to, 110, 211, 265

Rayner, William, 28

Reddish, Mrs., 224

Rehearsal, The, 48, 58, 123, 166

Rejected Addresses, 53

Reynolds, Frederic, 54

Reynolds, Sir Joshua, upon Garrick, 88, 180; portrait of Foote, 358

Rich, John, 174; threatened by Foote, 193, 194, 253

Richardson's *Pamela*, 326

Rigby, Richard, 262

Rivals, The, 283

Rivarol, the Comte de, 213, 221

Robertson, Principal William, 50 n.

Robin Hood Debating Society, the, 235, 236

Robson, an actor, 164

Rogers, Samuel, 317

Ross, David, 313

Rudd, Mrs., 331

Ruspini, Mr., 242

Ryan, Lacy, Foote's burlesque of, 59

Salutation Tavern, The, 31
Schomberg, Dr. Isaac, 344
School for Scandal, The, compared with *The Minor*, 185, 187, 219, 280
Scott, Sir Walter, 5, 53, 331, 336, 373
Shelley, Percy Bysshe, 18
Sheridan, R. B., 37 *n.* ; portrait of Sir Anthony Absolute, 54 ; indebtedness in *The Critic* to Foote, 58, 70, 77, 78, 284 ; in *The School for Scandal*, 279 ; in *The Rivals*, 283 ; his romance, 314, 368
Sheridan, Thomas, 36, 37 *n.* ; Johnson's opinion of, 94, 116, 117, 121, 126, 166, 168, 227, 228, 232, 233, 265, 313
She Stoops to Conquer compared with *The Knights*, 275
Shuter, Edward, 57, 68, 78, 178, 179, 233, 259, 260, 320
Siddons, Mrs., 81, 304
Smith, General, satirized in *The Nabob*, 288
Smith, Harriet (Madame Berlioz), 37 *n.*
Smith, Sydney, 197, 211, 219
Smith, Sir Sidney, 345
Society of Antiquaries satirized in *The Nabob*, 292
Soupeurs de mon Temps, Les, 32
Sparks, Luke, imitated by Wilkinson, 123 ; indignation at being burlesqued, 136, 137, 193, 194
Sparks, a toper, 180
State protection of theatres, 252
Sterne, Laurence, 204, 263 ; portrait by Reynolds, 358, 370
Stevens, George Alexander, 52
Stewart, Dugald, 49
Strolling players, 38
S t u r g e o n, Major, ridiculed by Foote, 229
Sullivan, Barry, 37 *n.*
Swift, Dean, 235

Talking, the decay of, 31
Tailors, The, a parody, 320
Talleyrand quoted, 84
Taswell, his acting in *Taste*, 78
Taylor, Chevalier, Foote's ridicule of, 66, 76

Taylor, John, 215 ; his recollection of Foote's acting, 271
Terry, Edward, 56
Théâtre Français, the, 128, 252
Thornton, Colonel, 128
Thrale, Mrs., letter from Johnson on Foote's death, 373
Thurtell, John, his murder of William Weare, 20, 118 *n.*
Tooke, Horne, 317, 344
Toole, J. L., 56
Touring, old system of stage, 117
Townshend, Lord, Viceroy of Ireland, 308
Travel in the eighteenth century, 118

Upholsterer, The, 227

Vanbrugh, Sir John, 253
Veil, Sir Thomas de, Foote's burlesque of, 60
Vesey, Agmondesham, 311
Vivian, Johnson, 4
Vivier, the horn-player, 32

Waller, Mr. Lewis, 69
Walpole, Horace, 188, 202, 263 ; on Bentley, 294, 350, 356
Wellington, the first Duke of, 49
Weston, Thomas, 164, 233, 259, 260, 261, 325, 370
White, Charles, an accomplice of Captain Goodere, 23, 24, 26
Whitefield, George, caricatured in *The Minor*, 176, 177, 183, 259
Wilkes, John, conversation with Johnson on Foote, 91, 200, 263, 344
Wilkinson, Tate, 38, 47, 48, 58 ; *Memoirs* and *Wandering Patentee*, 112 ; imitations of Foote, Barry, and Peg Woffington, before Garrick, 114, 115 ; mimicry before Foote, 116 ; first tour with Foote in Ireland, 117 ; description of journey quoted, 118-121 ; first appearance in Dublin, 122 ; further meeting with Foote, 128 ; appearance at Drury Lane, 129 ; comparison of Foote with Garrick, 134-136 ; Sparks's protest against, 137 ; cause of averted riot, 139, 140 ; scene with Aprice, 152 ; benefit and quarrel with Foote, 155-157 ; interview with Garrick, 157 ; burlesques of Foote,

159; letter from Garrick quoted, 164; Foote's rival in Dublin, 167; extraordinary interview with Macklin and Mossop, 169, 170; entertainment with Mrs. Abington, 172-174; threatened by Foote, 175; caricatured as "Shift" in *The Minor*, 177; attends Whitefield's Tabernacle to study and caricature the preacher, 178, 179; reconciliation with Foote, 192; piracies from Foote, 195; on friendly terms with Garrick, 196; Churchill on, 199; opinion of Foote as a wit, 213; further reconciliation, 225; quoted, 226, 229; caricature of Sheridan, 226, 227, 232; account of scene at his benefit, 240, 247, 260; *The Devil upon Two Sticks*, 299; letters from Foote, 313, 320

Windham, his description of Foote's *Diversions*, 64, 65
Woffington, Peg, 37 *n.*, 41; Foote's burlesque of, 59; Wilkinson's imitation, 115, 123, 126, 130, 265
Woodward, Henry, Foote's burlesque of, 58; his retaliation in *Tit for Tat*, 66, 67, 68, 164, 166, 170, 265
Worsdale, James, 76, 77, 78
Wright, Edward, 56
Wright's Coffee-House, a theatrical club, 205

Yates, Richard, 78
Yates, Mrs., 329
York, Duke of, his share in the unfortunate practical joke, 245

Zoffany, his portraits at the Garrick Club, 96, 358

THE END

BILLING AND SONS, LTD., PRINTERS, GUILDFORD

C W